CREATIVITY ANI

Creativity is typically perceived to be a positive, constructive attribute and, yet, highly effective, novel crimes are committed which illustrate that creativity can also be utilised to serve a darker and more destructive end. But how can these 'creative criminals' be stopped?

Adopting a psychological approach, renowned subject experts Cropley and Cropley draw upon concepts such as 'Person', 'Process', 'Press', and 'Product' to explain how existing psychological theories of creativity can be applied to a more subtle subset of ingenuity; that is to say, criminal behaviour and its consequences.

Creativity and Crime does not look at felony involving impulsive, reflexive, or merely deviant behaviour, but rather the novel and resourceful measures employed by certain criminals to more effectively achieve their law-breaking goals. The book transcends the link between crime and creativity and proposes a range of preventive measures for law-enforcers. Scholars and graduates alike will find this an invaluable and illuminating read.

DAVID H. CROPLEY is Associate Professor of Engineering Innovation at the Defence and Systems Institute, University of South Australia.

ARTHUR J. CROPLEY is Emeritus Professor of Psychology at Hamburg University.

CREATIVITY AND CRIME

A Psychological Analysis

DAVID H. CROPLEY

AND

ARTHUR J. CROPLEY

CAMBRIDGE
UNIVERSITY PRESS

CAMBRIDGE
UNIVERSITY PRESS

University Printing House, Cambridge CB2 8BS, United Kingdom

Cambridge University Press is part of the University of Cambridge.

It furthers the University's mission by disseminating knowledge in the pursuit of education, learning and research at the highest international levels of excellence.

www.cambridge.org
Information on this title: www.cambridge.org/9781107562516

First published 2013
First paperback edition 2015

A catalogue record for this publication is available from the British Library

Library of Congress Cataloguing in Publication data
Cropley, David.
Creativity and crime : a psychological analysis / David H. Cropley & Arthur J. Cropley.
pages   cm
Includes bibliographical references and index.
ISBN 978-1-107-02485-4 (hardback)
1. Crime–Sociological aspects.   2. Creative ability.   3. Creative thinking.   I. Cropley, A. J.   II. Title.
HV6025.C855 2013
364.3–dc23
2013009511

ISBN 978-1-107-02485-4 Hardback
ISBN 978-1-107-56251-6 Paperback

Additional resources for this publication at www.cambridge.org/cropley

Contents

Figures

Tables

Introduction

Creativity is almost universally admired. And rightly so. It is a source of growth and renewal at the individual and social level and introduces positive change in spiritual, artistic, scientific, technological, economic, industrial, and other domains. Unfortunately, however, the psychological processes and personal properties that are active in the generation of effective novelty (i.e., in creativity) are capable of being applied not just for positive purposes, but also to achieve negative goals such as gaining unfair advantage, manipulating the system, avoiding responsibilities, or dominating other people. One such negative application of creativity is seen in crime, where perpetrators generate effective novel techniques to achieve statutorily prohibited ends.

Crime now represents 3.6 per cent of the world's gross domestic product and is one of the top twenty global economies. Even if it only occupies twentieth position, this still means that the crime economy is bigger than those of Saudi Arabia, Belgium, Norway, or South Africa, to give a few examples.[1] Most interesting for the present book, however, is not the *quantitative* issue of the sheer size of the crime economy, but its *quality*: according to a speech of Principal Deputy Assistant Secretary Brian Nichols of the US Bureau of International Narcotics and Law-enforcement Affairs, criminals are showing considerable *adaptability*. Nichols linked crime and terrorism directly, and concluded that terrorists are becoming criminal *entrepreneurs*. Thus, crime is not only very big business but commentators are beginning to write about it in terms more usually used in discussions of creativity.[2]

---

[1] These figures are taken from a speech at a meeting of the Commission on Crime Prevention and Criminal Justice (CCPCJ) in Vienna on 23 April 2012, by Yury Fedotov, head of the UN Office on Drugs and Crime (UNODC).

[2] Both these speeches were downloaded from www.huffingtonpost.com/2012/04/23/crime-business-united-nations_n_1445742.html?ref=business on 24 April 2012.

Creativity involves the generation of novelty in order to achieve goals that are in some way relevant and useful for the purposes of the person or persons generating the novelty (see Chapters 3 and 4 for a much more detailed discussion). Crime involves the deliberate commission of statutorily prohibited acts in order to achieve the purposes of the person committing the acts, usually without consideration for the consequences for other people and sometimes with deliberate malice (as in the case of terrorism). Crime and creativity fuse when – to put the matter simply – people generate useful and effective novelty in order to make their statutorily prohibited actions serve their illegal purposes better.[3] This book is not concerned with random violence or destructiveness, reflex aggression, or reckless opportunism, but with deliberate crime for the purpose of acquiring ill-gotten gains, obtaining advantage, or avoiding being apprehended, or of gaining revenge, intimidating opponents, and the like. It is also concerned with a direct link between crime and creativity – in which the creativity is an instrument for improving the benefits obtained by the criminal from the crime.

Mainstream criminology focuses on the study of street crime (murder, rape, assault, robbery, vandalism, drug-trafficking, etc.), crimes that are often impulsive and opportunistic, poorly planned, not infrequently scarcely beneficial to the perpetrator, and sometimes characterised by mindless violence. A simple example involves a teenage boy who was walking down a street in a seedy area in a small Canadian city on his way to a movie he wanted to see. Unfortunately, he had no money, but was hoping to find some way of getting some en route. He then saw a parked pick-up truck with a brand new TV set on the tray. He unloaded the TV and carried it to a nearby bar with a reputation for being a haunt of petty criminals and offered it for sale for $20. He quickly found a buyer and went to the movie.

That evening he was arrested by police, who had had very little difficulty tracking him down. When asked why he had stolen the TV, he said quite simply that he needed the money to go to the movie. When asked why he had asked only $20 for a set worth several hundred dollars, he replied that $20 was what he had needed for a movie ticket, popcorn, etc. When asked what he would do next time he needed money, he replied that he would simply steal something else, whatever offered itself at the time he needed the money. Finally, when asked about the hurt he had inflicted on other

---

[3] There are numerous situations that are difficult to classify, such as breaking of the law for socially approved purposes, and these will be discussed more fully later in the book.

people, he simply shrugged his shoulders, although he did volunteer that he would be 'pissed off' if someone had stolen a TV from him – Cropley and Davis (1976) showed that such inability to empathise with victims was a prominent characteristic of juvenile offenders.

In this book, by contrast, we focus on crimes involving application of cunning and ingenuity, development of new methods or techniques, generation of surprising results, and similar properties. We refer to such crime as *creative* crime or *resourceful* crime (Ekblom and Tilley, 2000) in order to distinguish it from unplanned, impulsive, opportunistic, careless, almost brutish crime, such as in the theft of the TV just mentioned or in thuggish violence, mindless physical destruction, or wild and uncontrolled antisocial behaviour, as in, for instance, risky driving or opportunistic looting. Creative crimes represent *a fusion of crime and creativity*, and are most readily obvious in areas such as fraud, but are also seen in some forms of theft, murder, or terrorism, as well as in cybercrime, organised crime, drug smuggling, people trafficking, exporting of high-tech products to blacklisted buyers, gun running, or illegal migration.

Although writing in a completely different context (police misconduct), Wolfe and Piquero (2011) pointed out that research in the crime area is greatly hampered by the absence of theoretical underpinnings, and is thus forced to look at the phenomena under consideration in terms of individual factors such as age, gender, race, or level of education, that is, bureaucratically. As a result, even where counter-measures are successful, administrators do not know why or how they succeed. Wolfe and Piquero called for application of 'a rigorous theoretical lens' (p. 334) based, in the case of their area of interest, on approaches like organisational theory, control balance theory, social disorganisational theory, or deterrence theory.

Our purpose in this book is to examine the fusion between creativity and crime more closely along the general lines suggested by Wolfe and Piquero (2011), that is, by carrying out an analysis based on theory developed in a completely different area from crime – creativity research. The obvious link is that both creativity and crime involve deviating from the customary ways of doing things. In making this link we hope to generate effective novelty of our own by uniting domains of thought (creativity and crime) that are usually regarded as separate. For instance, there are striking similarities in areas such as personal properties and motivation between creative criminals and people who generate creative products for positive ends.

Making such a link may even arouse resistance, for instance, from those for whom creativity is almost sacred or for whom criminals are helpless victims of social forces in the external world. Nonetheless, we will present a conceptual framework for understanding the various psychological factors involved in creativity (Product, Processes, Personal properties, Personal motives, Personal feelings, social Press) and the various phases of the emergence of a creative product, such as Preparation, Illumination, and Implementation. We will then compare acknowledged creative individuals with criminals in terms of these factors and analyse two case studies of criminal domains in terms of our model. Finally, we will draw attention to some of the practical implications of our analysis and make some suggestions for its application, especially for crime-control strategies, as we do not wish to write a how-to-do-it handbook of creative crime.

CHAPTER ONE

Creativity and crime
Basic principles

Creativity involves generation of novelty that deals effectively with a problem or need of an individual or community. The need may be concrete, abstract, even spiritual. Crime involves deliberate commission of statutorily forbidden acts. The two fuse in the form of purposeful generation and application of effective novelty in order to achieve statutorily prohibited goals, what might be called 'creative crime'. Failure to take the creativity of such criminal behaviour into account limits both understanding of its nature and also thinking about how to counter it. Recognition of the link can be used to go beyond simply demonstrating its existence and analysing its nature by working out some of its implications for practice, such as preventive measures and training of law-enforcers. However, to do this it is necessary to expand the way creativity is conceptualised, since it is customarily thought of as an unquestionably good thing, and to expand the way crime is conceptualised, since it is customarily thought of as an unmitigated bad thing.

Although this book is concerned with what writers over the years have sometimes called the 'dark side' of creativity (e.g., Nebel, 1988; McLaren, 1993; Cropley, Cropley, Kaufman, and Runco, 2010, to name just a few), it does not examine artists, writers, musicians, or similar people, and the way their creativity sometimes leads them to break the law out of impatience with conventional ways, a desire to make an impact by surprising, shocking, or disgusting people, or the uncompromising pursuit of creative freedom in the face of opposition from the uncreative. An example of this might be Andres Serrano's infamous 'Piss Christ' photograph. The 1987 image of a crucifix submerged in a glass of Serrano's urine provoked a variety of strong negative reactions, ranging from accusations of blasphemy and the misuse of government funding through to death threats and hate mail.

The book also leaves unexamined the inner torment or the search for new truths that may bring creative thinkers into conflict not only with others but also with themselves, and possibly lead them to delve into dark shadow-lands of the mind where others fear to go, with possible negative consequences for their physical and psychological health. For instance, there are numerous examples of twentieth-century poets, writers, musicians, and painters who committed suicide, including Sylvia Plath, Anne Sexton, Ernest Hemingway, Virginia Woolf, David Foster Wallace, Jimmy Hendrix, Kurt Cobain, and Janice Joplin. What the book does examine is what James, Clark, and Cropanzano (1999, p. 212) called creativity with 'the intent to harm, hinder, harass, destroy, or achieve unfair or undeserved advantage'. In particular, we are concerned with the variety of ways creativity plays a direct role in crime.

We do not regard creativity, whether with good intentions (benevolent creativity) or bad (malevolent creativity), as a special, possibly unfathomable personal property of a few extraordinary individuals, which sets them aside from other people and gives them the power to create, although sometimes at the price of conflict with the mainstream, possibly even crime. On the contrary, we regard creativity – as defined in Chapters 3 and 4 – as something of which all people are capable, at least as a potential, although admittedly at different levels of profundity (e.g., casual creativity in everyday life vs earth-shaking, paradigm-changing sublime creativity).[1] We do not examine in detail the circumstances such as deprivation or prejudice that some researchers see as more or less forcing some people to turn to crime, or examine the fairness or justice of definitions of crime that proscribe behaviours to which dominant groups in a society object, even though the behaviours may be regarded in some (often less powerful) social subgroups as unobjectionable (e.g., the cultivation and use of marijuana). Such topics are not left undiscussed because we regard them as of no consequence but because they lie outside the scope of the present book.

The main thrust of this book

Although not denying the existence of any of the aspects of creativity and crime just mentioned or denigrating their importance and interest, the book starts with the criminal *products* of creativity, that is, outcomes, actions, behaviours, and/or artefacts that are illegal and thus involve crime. It then examines the processes and personal properties that lead to, or are

[1] We will examine this difference in greater detail in Chapter 3 (p. 56), where we introduce the '4Cs' model of creativity encompassing Big-C creativity, Pro-C creativity, little-c creativity and mini-c creativity.

in some way associated with, such products. Our discussions also give greatest weight to *negative consequences of crime for the rest of society*, not for the criminals. Except in passing, the book has almost nothing to say about *positive* applications of creativity in order to assist perpetrators or potential perpetrators,[2] such as in therapy as a productive and socially approved pastime for incarcerated criminals (e.g., art, theatre, music, or creative writing), or as a pro-social activity for disaffected youth (e.g., participation in rap groups, theatre arts, or music groups), no matter how interesting and important these areas are. This is not because of lack of interest in such activities but because, although admirable, they do not involve the generation of effective novelty (i.e., creativity) as a deliberate means to the end of making crime better serve the purposes of the perpetrator: making a larger haul, getting away with it, achieving a more widespread or lasting effect, or, in the case of terrorists, generating greater devastation.

The con artist who devises a new method for defrauding an organisation or the thief who finds a new way to defeat a security system may develop solutions that exhibit high degrees of novelty and, when they work well, high levels of *effective* novelty. Such solutions solve a problem the criminal has – how to be effective in committing for personal gain acts that are statutorily prohibited and avoiding negative sanctions such as imprisonment. In this sense the perpetrators, the processes and the products display characteristics often associated with creativity. Nonetheless, it seems that the current lexica of creativity and law-enforcement are not fully equipped to describe these situations and specify where they are creative and where they are not. The lack in mainstream thinking about crime of a model for classifying such cases – where the goal of the creative process is to achieve harmful, illegal, or immoral ends – hinders the ability to analyse them and take action against them.

Our purpose in this book is to expand our earlier analyses of negative creativity (e.g., Cropley, Kaufman, and Cropley, 2008; Cropley, Cropley, Kaufman, and Runco, 2010) and apply it directly to crime in order:

- to broaden and deepen understanding of the psychology of creativity by focusing attention on a seldom-discussed aspect – its dark side;
- to broaden and deepen understanding of the dark side by examining the generation of effective novelty for the deliberate purpose of achieving negative ends, especially ends prohibited by law (i.e., crime);

---

[2] As we will show later in Chapter 3 (p. 61), it is customary to discuss creativity in terms of the so-called '4Ps' model: Product, Process, Person, and Press. In discussing crime, however, we will often use 'Perpetrator' as the third P.

- to broaden and deepen understanding of crime by focusing attention on its creative aspects;
- to examine ways in which this knowledge can be used to enhance the response to crime.

To some extent the book represents a cross-disciplinary study, although its main focus is undeniably on the psychological aspects of creativity.

Why study crime and creativity?

Wolfe and Piquero (2011) observed that research on crime is greatly hampered by the absence of theoretical underpinnings. This means that the psychological dynamics of crime – the processes and psychological influences on processes – are only partially understood or are explained in structural terms such as age, gender, race, or level of education. We have already mentioned Wolfe and Piquero's call for a 'rigorous theoretical lens'. Agnew (2011) pointed out that, among other things, a more comprehensive model of crime would offer new insights into understanding it and would suggest new research questions.

Although they were writing in a more general way about the need to study the application (or misapplication) of creativity for many kinds of negative ends and not just crime, James and Taylor (2010) discussed more explicit reasons why more knowledge about the negative application of creativity is needed, which are relevant to this book. The reasons they gave included:

- helping to identify people most likely to generate harmful novelty (when applied to crime this suggests a new dimension for criminological studies, especially forensic psychology);
- identifying the circumstances that promote the generation of negative creativity;
- working out ways of analysing particular situations to assess their 'vulnerability' to negative creativity;
- helping to design counter-measures against negative creativity.

They also mentioned another reason for wanting to recognise and understand negative creativity, which, somewhat adapted for the purposes of this book, involves avoiding the effort and expense wasted in ineffective actions. In other words, they also highlighted the practical importance of improving the efficiency (as distinct from the efficacy) of law-enforcement.

They specifically mentioned the wastefulness of counter-measures aimed at guarding against 'the "wrong" threat' (2010, p. 35).

James and Taylor (2010) also turned specifically to terrorism, quoting Schneier's (2000, p. 238) dictum: 'If you don't know the real threats against the system, how do you know what kind of counter-measures to employ?' They cited the US Committee on Science and Technology for Countering Terrorism (Committee on Science and Technology for Containing Terrorism, 2002, p. 214), which in effect called for more divergent thinking in identifying threats and devising responses capable of frustrating the threats. In other words, the committee called for creativity in law-enforcement. A similar point was made by Wilks and Zimbelman (2004), who called, for instance, for reduction of predictability in audit procedures through the introduction of *surprise* in the form of variations in timing, type, and randomness of checks.

In later chapters (especially Chapters 8–10) we will say more about what this could involve in practice. A simple example of the introduction of effective novelty into policing is to be seen in a measure adopted by the Boston police: officers found it almost impossible to get witnesses to provide information on criminal behaviour because of fear of reprisals if they were seen talking to police. They then set up a dedicated phone number for text messages, which enjoyed considerable success. Following this, they rebuilt an ice-cream truck supplied by a local ice-cream maker to make it into a mixture of ice-cream truck and patrol car. The ice-cream company provided a supply of ice creams in a brand that was well known in the area and very popular with children. On hot summer days the truck drove through the streets of the crime hot spot in the manner of an ice-cream truck, with uniformed officers giving away free ice creams and reminding the children of the text messaging number. The children were enthusiastic, the officers enjoyed the duty, and the number of useable text message tips soared.

An example of a surprising solution for a now familiar crime is the 'auto-immune' airliner in which, in the event of an attempted hijacking, non-lethal dart-pistols would drop from the panels above seats where oxygen masks are usually stored, allowing passengers to outgun hijackers by a wide margin (Hari, 2010). We do not necessarily recommend this solution, but see it as an example of a suggestion for a truly novel counter-measure whose surprisingness may make a contribution to changing the way that people are willing to think about at least some crime, to encouraging novelty in the way that crime is conceptualised, and to approaching its analysis and the design of law-enforcement from a new perspective.

Creativity

The term 'creativity' is in widespread use and is part of everyday vocabulary. Nonetheless, as Chapters 3 and 4 will show in some detail, its meaning is full of connotative nuances. We will argue in greater detail in Chapter 5 that sorting these out and making use of them for purposes other than defining creativity itself (e.g., for understanding some forms of crime better) are hampered by the fact that it is almost universally assumed that creativity is always good. The present section, as well as Chapter 3, in particular, will provide some clarification of what we mean by 'creativity' in this book, and later chapters will examine the problem of the presumption of innocence in the case of creativity.

'Second-generation' creativity

Creativity has been actively discussed over the ages (e.g., Plato in his *Ion*). However, the actual term itself (as against the phenomenon) only appeared in written English less than 150 years ago – in 1875, according to Webster's Dictionary (see: www.merriam-webster.com/dictionary/creativity) – at around the same time as the term 'intelligence' began to be used. Both Lombroso (1889) and Galton (1869), the latter the founder of modern empirical investigation of intelligence, studied elements of what today would be called 'creativity', but used the term 'genius' to refer to it. We will focus in this book on the 'modern creativity era', which can be dated from the ground-breaking presidential address of J. P. Guilford in 1949, when he became president of the American Psychological Association (published as Guilford, 1950).

Guilford called for a more rounded view of human intellectual ability that takes account not just of 'convergent' thinking (in essence, seeking and homing in on the single best answer), but also of 'divergent' thinking (branching out to generate multiple alternative solutions). He also discussed both person and product, but his paper is mostly remembered for its emphasis on cognitive processes. As a result of this focus of interest on relatively recent writers, with the occasional exception of Plato, Lombroso, Francis Bacon and a number of others, we will not discuss the work of pre-Guilfordian thinkers and researchers, except in passing. In addition, our discussion will be very strongly oriented towards psychological considerations, not for instance aesthetics, philosophy, or social sciences other than psychology.

Even though Guilford himself, and subsequently other early psychological thinkers in the modern creativity era, such as Maslow, May, Rogers, Torrance, and many other pioneers, wrote extensively on creativity in ordinary people and as an everyday event, the gold standard for understanding creativity was the work of 'towering historical figures' (McWilliam and Dawson, 2008, p. 634). Ghiselin (1955) for example, focused on figures such as Wolfgang Amadeus Mozart, Vincent van Gogh, Henry James, Henry Moore, Henry Miller, Stephen Spender, and Thomas Wolfe. This is not to suggest that no one writing early in the modern era was interested in anyone apart from such figures. However, a skewing of interest in that direction was apparent, even if far from exclusive.

Research of this kind has not vanished, and indeed we are not suggesting that it should. A fairly recent example would be Csikszentmihalyi's (e.g., 1996) interviews with eminent creators in the course of developing his 'flow' model. However, Kampylis (2010) made the point that acknowledged towering personages sometimes simply repeat public stereotypes of themselves that enhance their special status, such as the idea that they are a kind of conduit for messages from higher powers, that creative ideas come out of the blue, that creative people sacrifice all for creativity, or that they are above conventional standards and norms. Consequently, early first-generation research was dogged by stereotypes tending to mystify or idealise creativity.

Even if they were not confined to such sublime creators, early modern writings tended at least to focus on domains regarded as intrinsically creative or as offering special opportunities for creativity, such as literature, fine art, science, architecture, and similar areas. This continued the approach of pre-Guilfordian studies that focused on sublime or earth-shaking creativity in art (e.g., Cattell, Glascock, and Washburn, 1918; Patrick, 1937), creative writing (e.g., Colvin and Meyer, 1906; Patrick, 1935), science (e.g., Patrick, 1938), mathematics (e.g., Poincaré, 1913; Hadamard, 1945), or invention (e.g., Royce, 1898; Rossman, 1931), to give a few examples. McWilliam and Dawson (2008, p. 634) referred to research focused on towering figures and acknowledged creative fields as involving the 'first generation' of creativity research.

Nichols's (1972) discussion of creativity in the person who will never produce anything acclaimed as creative offered a ground-breaking insight at the time. In more recent years, however, there has been steadily more apparent interest in 'second-generation' (McWilliam and Dawson, 2008) thinking about creativity. This focuses on creativity in the life of people who are not great historical figures and will never become such figures, and who are engaged in activities that are not generally revered as creating sublime beauty, enlarging human understanding, rebuilding society, or transforming human life through, for instance, spiritual, intellectual, or technological advances. Although not ignored earlier, 'ordinary' creativity has been increasingly discussed since the appearance of seminal discussions such as that of Richards, Kinney, Benet, and Merzel (1988), and is now well established as a topic of inquiry (e.g., Cropley, 1990; Kaufman and Beghetto, 2009). In addition to recognising the creativity of a school-child, a homemaker, or an office worker in the course of everyday life, second-generation thinking opens up the creativity discussion to encompass domains such as creative organisation of everyday clerical work or of preparation of family meals and, of central interest in this book, crime. Breaking away from the view of creativity as involving universally acclaimed epoch-making achievements is central to this book.

'Unhooking' creativity from the arts

A second major aspect of recent thinking about creativity is the breaking of the nexus between creativity and the arts: as McWilliam, Dawson, and Tan (2011, p. 113) put it, creativity needed to be 'unhooked'. In a recent review of creativity research in Australia, Cropley (2012) showed that, as is the case in many other countries too, there is a marked tendency to equate creativity with artistic activities. He cited a government review that defined 'creative industries' as involving music; film, television, and entertainment software; performing arts; writing, publishing, and print media; advertising, graphic design, and marketing; architecture, visual arts, and design. McWilliam and Dawson (2008, p. 634) summarised the situation with almost shocking clarity: according to them, creativity has been 'relegated to the borderlands of the visual and performing arts'. Once again, it is clear that although interest in creativity is not and has not been restricted to the arts – the early research on science and engineering cited above is evidence of this – there has, nevertheless, been a pronounced tendency in this direction. Indeed, the assumption that creativity is confined to artistic/aesthetic activities is very plausible: it makes intuitive sense and probably corresponds with everyday understanding of creativity.

However, Woodman, Sawyer, and Griffin (1993) pointed out that creativity is much broader than this. Nowadays it is seen as encompassing a wide range of domains: for instance, there has been research on creativity in architecture (e.g., Williams, Ostwald, and Askland, 2011) and design (e.g., Lewis, 2005), in engineering (e.g., Cropley and Cropley, 2000), in industry, commerce, and business (e.g., Haner, 2005), in occupational therapy (e.g., Schmid, 2012), all the way to sport (e.g., Eisenberg, 2005), domains becoming steadily further removed from fine art. We are extending this discussion even further to include crime.

Further limitations to the understanding of creativity, about which Cropley (2012) complained, were the conflating of creativity with giftedness and the belief that creativity and conventional 'intelligent' behaviour are incompatible with each other. In an overview, McCann (2005) discussed creativity in the context of gifted education, treating it as a factor in giftedness and seeing it as a way of making the education of potential high achievers more effective as well as more interesting for the young people involved. A rather different variant of the confining of creativity to exceptional children is to be found in O'Brien and Donelan's (2008) report, in which the use of creativity for promoting the personal wellbeing and academic achievement of 'disempowered and disenfranchised' students is discussed. What is needed here is an understanding of creativity as a much broader phenomenon that goes beyond artistic achievement and involves far more than a small group of exceptionally clever or otherwise exceptional individuals.

Focus on products

Early modern writers often discussed creativity in terms of *thinking processes* (such as divergent thinking – see above) or *personal characteristics* that facilitate such processes (such as openness, risk taking or tolerance for ambiguity). Even one of the authors of this book (Cropley, 1967) as well as Albert (1990), for instance, went so far as to recommend avoiding study of *products*, because of their belief (at that time) that it is too difficult to establish objective criteria of the creativity of products and any such criteria are too unstable across cultures and across eras. However, Guilford himself (e.g., 1950) referred to the need for creativity to lead to something useful. MacKinnon (1978, p. 187) concluded that analysis of creative products is 'the bedrock of all studies of creativity'. More recently, the emphasis on creative products was put with particular vigour by Bailin (1988, p. 5): 'The only coherent way in which to view creativity is in terms of the production of valuable products.' She urged writers to focus on products, labelling efforts to foster creativity without reference to products 'misleading' and 'dangerous'. As we will show later, the study of products is now well established (e.g., Besemer and O'Quin, 1999; Hennessey and Amabile, 1999; Cropley and Cropley, 2010a).

Runco (2010) turned his attention directly to the dark side of creativity and argued that the mental processes and personal properties underlying creativity are neither good nor bad in themselves and that it is the *products* that arouse approval or condemnation. Although we do not share his position entirely, in the present book creativity is understood in the first instance as involving generation of novel products (see Chapter 3 for a more detailed discussion). Furthermore, we will focus on products that have a *useful application* (whether the product is a physical object, a manufacturing or administrative process, a service, a system, a way of conceptualising some issue, or something else that can be applied to solving a problem or achieving an end). It is important to notice that the end to be achieved need not be socially approved; a murderer may achieve the end of killing someone through the generation of an effectively novel method, just as a police officer may generate a novel and effective method of catching or deterring such a person.

In the case of crime, a 'useful' product involves products that the majority of society disapproves of – including helping a criminal achieve statutorily prohibited goals more effectively. The people to whom the product is useful are criminals, and the products are often novel techniques for acquiring other people's possessions or otherwise doing them harm for personal gain, or for avoiding the consequences of such actions. Thus, the link between crime and creativity involves the generation of effective novelty for the purpose of being a more successful criminal, however success is defined by the particular miscreant.

Malevolent creativity

It is clear that regardless of the fact that processes and personality traits involved in creativity may be value free, as Runco (2010) argued, the *results* of creativity are not. On the contrary, they are value laden: it is repugnant, for instance, to think of admiring the work of a mass murderer who found highly effective novel ways of murdering people, whereas the work of a person who generated effective novelty in order to cure the sick seems to be obviously admirable. The processes and personal properties involved in the two actions may be the same, so that distinguishing between them may seem to be difficult, but the products are very different.

Researchers studying creativity use a variety of terms to attempt to give expression to either 'good' or 'bad' aspects of creativity. These include 'conscientious' creativity (Kampylis and Valtanen, 2010, p. 209), 'cantankerous' creativity (Silvia, Kaufman, Reiter-Palmon, and Wigert, 2011), 'perverse' creativity (Salcedo-Albarán, Kuszewski, de Leon-Beltran, and Garay, 2009, p. 4), and 'unbridled' creativity (Craft, Gardner, and Claxton, 2008, p. 169). It is apparent that all but the first of these terms focus on the negative end of the goodness–badness continuum. This is a reflection of the fact that creativity is frequently regarded as more or less self-evidently good (see Chapter 5), so that terms to express its goodness are scarcely needed, whereas 'bad' creativity is a conceptual problem and requires a variety of terms to try to express its essential nature.

In this section we want to open up discussion of an issue that has been approached in a fragmented, uncoordinated way in the past: not just 'bad' creativity but the application of creativity to achieve *deliberate negative consequences* for other people. We have already referred to this above as 'malevolent' creativity (e.g., Cropley et al., 2008, p. 105). At least two factors contribute to such creativity. The first is the product or outcome of the activity. This is typically the generation of an effective or useful novel solution to a problem. The second is *the intent of the actor* – that is, the individual, or possibly the organisation, generating the effective novelty. Without the intention of causing harm, negative creativity is not malevolent, even though its results may be harmful or undesirable.

McLaren's (1993) seminal work on the dark side of creativity contains many instructive examples of negative products and outcomes that may be differentiated from malevolent creativity through the absence of intent. It seems unlikely that mediaeval clergy, for example, set out to impoverish their congregations by commissioning elaborately decorated, expensive and undoubtedly artistically creative cathedrals. And yet there is no denying that the money and resources lavished on these religious monuments might, as McLaren points out, instead have been used to satisfy more earthly needs. Thus the products of artistic creativity embodied in these structures were merely aesthetic exercises in self-indulgence; but although they constitute an example of negative creativity, since they harmed many people, they cannot be regarded as malevolent.

Malevolent creativity is probably most obvious in the case of high-level, cerebral, white-collar offending that is remote from everyday life, such as financial swindles involving ingenious and complex machinations, sweeping vision, and 'creative accounting'; see, for instance, the case of Enron. Indeed, we will pay particular attention to fraud in Chapter 8, because it is here that the role of ingenuity, making of unexpected associations, the courage to try something novel, and the like in being a better criminal are most obvious. However, malevolent creativity is also seen in offences that touch the day-to-day life of relatively ordinary people, ranging from shop theft, burglary, and robbery to murder and, ultimately, terrorism. Our interest goes beyond 'dramatic' crime and also encompasses the application of creativity to relatively everyday offences.

Introducing the concept of malevolent (actually having harmful intent) and benevolent (beneficial intent) creativity expands the available classifications of creativity, including those representative of the dark side, from two categories (positive–negative) to four (deliberately good, deliberately bad, unintentionally bad and – difficult to imagine in practice, but theoretically possible – unintentionally good). This categorisation serves a purpose that is more than merely technical. In particular, it makes it possible to turn attention from the *output of the creative process or activity alone* to the motivation of the generator of the novelty and the process itself. When a creative process, for example, the development of a novel form of terrorist attack (like the attacks on 9/11), results in an outcome that is undeniably negative, it can now be further examined and an attempt made to understand the intent of the actor(s). Where the intent is deliberately to cause harm to others, as was the case on 9/11, the label 'negative' creativity is replaced with *consciously malevolent creativity*. The terrorists in question set out to create a novel 'solution' to their problem that would, if it were successful, undeniably and without any shadow of doubt, result in the deaths of many innocent people and the widespread destruction of property.

This negative outcome was not the result of an accidental set of circumstances, nor was it an unfortunate by-product of some other activity, both of which might cause us to label it as *failed benevolence* (good intent, bad outcome). Because it was both novel and effective, it was creative, and because of the nature of the intent it was not merely negative creativity, but *consciously malevolent creativity*. Similarly, when benevolent intent results in a positive outcome or product, then the label positive creativity is replaced with *consciously benevolent creativity*, although this phenomenon is of no interest in the present book. However, addition of the factor intent also now acknowledges the possibility that malevolent intent may, serendipitously, result in a positive outcome. In this latter case we would now use the label *failed malevolence*.

There is considerable value to be gained from the more differentiated understanding that results from an analysis of the dark side of creativity. At a primary level, negative creativity recognises that the product of the creative process may be bad. Thus the invention of the internal combustion engine, leading as it has to pollution and many deaths in automobile accidents, is an example of negative creativity. However, it not an example of malevolent creativity: it seems certain that Karl Benz, who designed and built the first four-stroke engine, did not do so with the deliberate intent of polluting the environment or killing people. In fact, he almost certainly had good intentions. In a more differentiated analysis, an appropriate secondary label for this invention, at least with respect to the polluting/safety aspects of the engine, would be *failed benevolence*. The negative aspects of the invention are unintended and unforeseen consequences of solving the primary problem that the device was created to solve and indeed succeeded in doing so.

The dimensions of malevolence

Kampylis and Valtanen (2010) argued that a relatively simple approach to negative creativity that goes no further than distinguishing between its malevolent/destructive and benevolent/constructive aspects is not enough. They called for a multidimensional approach capable of offering a wider and deeper understanding of the dark side of creativity, and argued that holistic approaches can offer effective frameworks for formulating and answering key questions about who should benefit from creativity and how its use for dark purposes can be avoided. They argued that three dimensions need to be considered in assessing the positive/negative nature of creativity, and proposed what they called the 'Creativity Consequences Analytical Framework' (p. 206).

This framework has three dimensions: the intention of the creator (i.e., Motivation), the effects or consequences of Process and Product *for the creator*, and the consequences of Process and Product *for other people*, either individuals, groups, or even the entire society.[3] They use their framework to analyse four examples of creativity: Galileo Galilei's endorsement of the heliocentric theory of the solar system for which he was placed under house arrest for the rest of his life and a few years earlier might well have gone to the stake (positive intention, good outcome for other people, bad outcome for Galileo), Alexander Fleming's discovery of penicillin (good intention, good result for society, good result for Fleming, who won the Nobel Prize), Christopher Columbus's discovery of North America (good intentions, dubious results for Columbus, very bad results for Native

---

[3] Their approach is supported by Sternberg's (2010) distinction between 'intrapersonal', 'interpersonal', and 'extrapersonal' benefits flowing from creativity, which will be discussed in more detail in Chapter 6, p. 117).

Table 1.1 *Possible combinations of motivation and effects*
of generation of novelty

Motivation	Effect for creator	Effect for others	Example[a]
Positive	Positive	Positive	Alexander Fleming
Positive	Positive	Negative	Robert Oppenheimer
Positive	Negative	Positive	Galileo Galilei
Positive	Negative	Negative	Christopher Columbus
Negative	Positive	Negative	Trojan horse
Negative	Negative	Positive	Guy Fawkes
Negative	Positive	Positive	Giuseppe Garibaldi
Negative	Negative	Negative	Bernie Madoff

[a] There is no suggestion here that the people listed in this column should be regarded as criminals, although the creativity of several of them produced bad results for at least some people.

Americans), and the Trojan horse (malevolent intentions, good results for the Greeks, catastrophic results for the Trojans).

In fact, the 2 × 2 × 2 matrix of the Kampylis and Valtanen (2010) model yields eight combinations in all. We extend the Kampylis and Valtanen analysis in Table 1.1 by showing all eight combinations, incorporating their four examples but adding our versions of the cases they did not specifically discuss. Some of the combinations involve what we call 'creative law-breaking'. For instance, negative intention, negative outcome for other people, good outcome for the creative perpetrator would be the archetypal definition of 'successful' malevolent creativity, as in the case of the Trojan horse. Negative intention, negative outcome for the perpetrator and positive outcome for other people could involve unsuccessful creative law-breaking, as in the case of the Gunpowder Plot against King James I in 1605, where negative intention led to disaster for the plotters but no harm for the intended victim. Negative intention, negative result for other people and (ultimately) negative effect for the perpetrators would be represented by Bernie Madoff, who undoubtedly hoped for a Trojan horse effect.

Types of malevolent creativity

If we now add to the classification system the extent to which the environment assists or hinders the generation and implementation of novelty (referred to later in this book as an aspect of 'Press': See Chapter 3), we

Table 1.2 *Product, Person, and Press – types of creativity*

Motivation	Outcome	Environment	Label
Malevolent	Bad	Supportive	Conscious malevolence
Malevolent	Good	Supportive	Failed malevolence
Benevolent	Bad	Supportive	Failed Benevolence
Benevolent	Good	Supportive	Conscious benevolence
Malevolent	Bad	Obstructive	Resilient malevolence
Malevolent	Good	Obstructive	Frustrated malevolence
Benevolent	Bad	Obstructive	Frustrated benevolence
Benevolent	Good	Obstructive	Resilient benevolence

achieve a somewhat different categorisation of the outcomes of creativity from those described by Kampylis and Valtanen. These are shown in Table 1.2. This approach is more productive from the point of view of countering law-breaking because it allows more differentiated consideration of the way the environment facilitates or, more interesting for law-enforcement, inhibits generation of effective negative creativity. For the purpose of differentiating the dark side more precisely, we will treat Process and Press together as representative of those factors that influence what happens between the formation of intent and the realisation of the end product. These will be categorised using two poles, supportive vs obstructive; Process and Press act either to support the activity for which a useful, novel product is the output, or they act to undermine it.

The table thus distinguishes between creative activities that take place in circumstances that are either supportive of the intent, or that attempt to act against the intent. Thus, while intent may be malevolent, and a negative outcome may result, we can conceive of two pathways to this result. One arises from a situation where both the Process and the Press act in concert with the intent, whereas the other arises from a situation where Process and Press act in opposition to the intent. Malevolent intent that achieves a negative outcome in spite of the Process and Press is *resilient malevolence*, in contrast to conscious malevolence that succeeds because of the support of the Process and Press.[4] The terrorist attacks on 9/11 again

[4] The system outlined in Table 1.2 can be applied to the historical examples given in Table 1.1 to attempt a speculative categorisation of their generation of novelty: Alexander Fleming = conscious benevolence; Robert Oppenheimer = (possibly) failed benevolence; Galileo Galilei = resilient benevolence; Christopher Columbus = (from the point of view of Native Americans) failed benevolence; Trojan horse = resilient malevolence; Guy Fawkes = failed malevolence; Bernie Madoff = (for a time) resilient malevolence; 9/11 plotters = resilient malevolence.

assist us in understanding the different forms of the dark side of creativity. It can be argued that the hijackers of the aircraft involved in the Twin Towers attacks and the Pentagon attack succeeded in spite of an obstructive Press. In other words, the normal security measures that were part of the environment in which those attacks were made failed to prevent them. The creativity of the attacks was therefore not only intentionally harmful, but also resilient enough not to be deterred by a non-supportive environment.

Creative law-breaking, as we understand it throughout this book, can now be described somewhat more precisely. It does not involve doing something that is statutorily prohibited by accident (perhaps allowing your speed to creep up without noticing in a speed-restricted area), as an oversight, in ignorance, or under the mistaken impression that what you are doing is legal (i.e., without conscious intention). It also does not involve failed benevolence – trying to do good but achieving a bad outcome. Successful creative law-breaking is an example of malevolent creativity and, since law-breakers have to defeat the efforts of an environment (Press) that does its best to thwart them, of resilient malevolence. In considering combating law-breaking activities (the Product), we can then ask how to alter the effects of the Person (personal properties, motivation) or the Process (perhaps by focusing on a specific phase or phases – see Chapter 3) by changing the Press. There has been little specific research on law-breaking within the creativity framework, although it is a reasonable hypothesis that those elements that either inhibit or foster benevolent creativity also foster or inhibit malevolent creativity. Similarly, the phases through which an individual and/or organisation proceeds as an idea is first conceived and then exploited are probably the same irrespective of the intended purpose of the result – good or bad.

Crime

What is meant by 'crime' is also by no means as clear-cut as might be thought at first glance. For instance, in critical criminology all 'blameworthy' acts (Agnew, 2011, p. 6) may be referred to as involving 'crime', whether they are statutorily proscribed or not. For instance, the use of advertising to persuade children to eat unhealthy food, which is legal but may well be socially injurious by contributing among other things to obesity-related illnesses, is regarded by some critics as criminal. Many blameworthy acts may be committed by corporations or governments (e.g., the provision of unsafe working conditions for employees or the aggressive use of military force for political purposes), so that critical criminologists regard the need to draw such acts to public attention as particularly urgent.

Some theorists go so far as to regard the very idea of crime as being a social construction: Parnell (2003, p. 19), for instance, cited Durkheim that: 'The interests of authority and its needs for self-legitimation determine crime ... not the nature of the acts in question.' Felson (2002, p. 17) put it even more clearly: 'society and its justice system manufacture crime'. The idea that crime is simply a social construction and that what is criminal changes according to the needs of those in power, or that acts not actually proscribed by prevailing law can be crimes, whereas statutorily proscribed acts may not be criminal at all, makes discussion of 'crime' and 'criminality' difficult. In fact, like creativity, crime, too, is in the eye of the beholder. In this book, we will use the term 'crime' as it is understood in mainstream criminology (Agnew, 2011): the commission of transgressions against prevailing law.

The relationship between crime and creativity

The taxonomic relationship between creativity and crime (in the sense of transgressions against prevailing law) needs to be clarified at this point. In simple terms: is creativity a subset of crime? Is crime a subset of creativity? Are the two related at all? Some modern creative individuals have broken laws on, for instance, public indecency or blasphemy, or have used legally proscribed materials such as stolen human body parts for creative effect, so that there really is such a thing as creativity that breaks the law (for an overview, see Brower and Stahl, 2011): the use of crime to enhance creativity. Adopting the second of the two orientations just cited, however, it is also possible to look at crime as a field of action in which creativity can be applied in the service of the evil-doing (i.e., creativity that enhances crime). This makes it possible to apply concepts developed in creativity research to the special case of crime.

The purpose of the book is not to claim that all crime is creative, or that the proportion of creative individuals among criminals is unusually high. Indeed, much crime is mindless, brutal, opportunistic, and thus unplanned, impulsive, almost reflexive, so that there is no obvious link to creativity at all.[5] Nonetheless, even if the proportion of creative criminals is the same as in the general population or in any recognisable minority

---

[5] As we have already noted, our focus here is on 'creative', 'resourceful' crime (Ekblom and Tilley, 2000).

group (such as, let us say, left-handers), ignoring special characteristics of the creative minority and conceptualising their crime in the same terms as that of their less creative colleagues seems to be too undifferentiated. In calling for a more differentiated understanding of crime, Ruggiero (2010) argued that imposing a narrow corset on the way it is conceptualised may actually hinder understanding of crime and hence law-enforcement.

Indeed, Gamman and Raein (2010, p. 171) concluded that behaviour in 'environments that have the potential for more than one kind of behaviour' (some of which are illegal) is governed by an interplay among '*complex* emotions, desires, and needs' (emphasis added), and is not necessarily simply the emission of more or less routine responses. Complex environments even offer the possibility of 'illicit *pleasure*' (emphasis added) (p. 170). Thus, there may be a bright side to crime, for some perpetrators at least. Hollin (1989) complained around twenty-five years ago that psychological treatment approaches to prevention of crime and rehabilitation of criminals such as therapy, educational measures, or programmes of socially acceptable alternative activities suffer from the problem that they are not derived from a sufficiently well-founded and highly differentiated understanding of the psychology of crime. For instance, on the basis of evidence showing that educational attainment in criminals is typically low, it is simply assumed that provision of education will eliminate crime. It is entirely possible, however, that such measures serve simply to help make criminals smarter (and perhaps *better* criminals).

Social sciences and crime

The various social sciences analyse and seek to understand crime largely by looking at questions such as why it occurs in the first place, how to prevent it, what factors result in some people breaking the law, how to classify such acts and assess the damage they cause, how to catch offenders, how to treat them once they have been apprehended, how to assess their culpability, how to determine the likelihood of recidivism, how to ascertain whether they are a danger to the broader community, or whether they can be reformed and what kind of therapy would achieve this. Within these areas of inquiry there are widely differing views, some of which see crime as no more than a social construction that has little to do with inherently wrongful or reprehensible acts at all, but is a mechanism for social control employed by those with power (behaviour they wish to suppress is declared to be deviant or criminal), or as an adaptive way for criminals to cope in certain environments (such as environments where status and affluence are achieved by defying authority, practising violence, or ignoring the law).

The cultural approach

A sociological approach to the question of why people break the law emphasises structural factors of the community *outside* the individual, such as employment, housing, education, family circumstances, or group membership, while a more anthropological approach emphasises community traditions, customs, and practices (culture) and their maintenance through systems of friendship, kinship networks, or shared symbols. Urban design focuses on aspects of the use of space such as the effect of small relatively inaccessible spaces on territoriality and defence against outsiders, or the presence in a neighbourhood of plentiful opportunities for crime. The study of interior design and crime shows, for instance, that some shopfitting concepts deliberately encourage people to defy convention, and by doing so may actually challenge certain individuals to think and act in novel but unlawful ways, thus encouraging crime.

In such approaches, the prevailing circumstances are frequently presented as an immutable given – at least from the point of view of the individual – and each person is seen as having to find a way of getting along as well as possible under these circumstances by learning and applying values, norms, behavioural skills, and the like appropriate to the situation: the environment is the teacher and the individual person is its captive pupil, willing or unwilling. Crime is thought to result from one of two situations. The first is defective social learning (as in the *cultural disorganisation* approach), according to which some people fail to learn how to cope with their environment since there are no systematic or consistent models or mentors, and through ignorance or incompetence they behave in prohibited ways. The second is the *deviant subcultures* approach, according to which people successfully learn norms but these are deviant or antisocial, that is, some people learn how to cope with their environment very well, except that the way they do it is – even if effective from their point of view – against the law.

The individualistic approach

Sampson and Wilson (1995) drew attention to two other approaches to understanding crime, which they dismissively referred to as 'fallacies' (p. 52) and rejected out of hand: the 'materialistic' approach and the 'individualistic' approach. Both of these see the individual as being more actively involved in interactions with the external world. The former can be stated with exaggerated simplicity as arguing that people behave in ways that enhance their material welfare – crime occurs if it is perceived by the law-breaker as bringing greater benefit than loss. This approach echoes the concepts set out in Game Theory, first described by John von Neumann in a paper delivered in 1926. Wilks and Zimbelman (2004), for example, writing about fraudulent financial reporting, use the principles of strategic decision making and non-cooperative games to suggest approaches to preventing and detecting fraud. The individual not only judges the relative magnitude of profit and loss (the quantitative aspect) but also identifies what is a profit and what a loss (the qualitative aspect).

The individualistic approach, which is epitomised by psychological ways of looking at crime, gives even greater emphasis to the role of the individual. Once again reduced to the barest essentials (see Chapter 2 for a more detailed discussion), psychology looks for answers to the questions posed above (for example: why do particular people break the law?) by focusing mainly on factors *inside* the individual, such as personality, intelligence, motives, or attitudes, although it cannot be denied that the external world plays a role in the development of all the personal characteristics just mentioned, even though the extent of its effects (as against, for instance, the effects of biological factors) may be debated.

The discussion of creativity and crime in this book falls into the individualistic category in its broadest sense. This includes materialistic motivation insofar as it reflects the primacy of the role of the individual. The book examines the special case of the deliberate generation of effective novelty (creativity) by criminals for the specific purpose of being better at crime – regardless of whether 'being better at crime' is manifested by killing innocent people to further a political aim or embezzling large sums of money for personal gain. The extent and effectiveness of the materialistic goals of this creativity are seen as depending on properties of the individual, such as special cognitive processes (for instance divergent thinking) and appropriate personal properties and motivation (such as willingness to take risks or tolerance of uncertainty), and the interaction of these properties and processes with environmental Press.

Of course, this does not mean that the kinds of factor emphasised by sociologists, anthropologists, ethnologists, or designers are irrelevant – even the most creative criminal may have turned to crime or may eventually turn away from it because of the factors these disciplines focus on. However, application of the individualistic approach is capable of adding to understanding of crime. In the present book, the individualistic approach will be followed in order to show that there is a link between crime and creativity, and to develop some ideas on what this means for practice, especially the practice of law-enforcement.

Despite its focus on the individual perpetrator, a number of possible crime–creativity links are not the focus of discussion here, including:

- Proscribed behaviour resulting from personal traits such as reckless-ness or unconventionality or subclinical patterns of disturbed personal adjustment such as uncontrolled impulsivity, which encourage breaking rules and promote generation of novelty but sometimes lead to socially deviant behaviour that crosses the line into criminality. Habitual reck-less high-speed driving out of contempt for petty bureaucratic road rules by a creative artist or scientist that eventually led to a car crash with fatal consequences for a passer-by would be an example.
- Crimes committed by creative people in the course of their everyday lives. A murder committed by a creative individual in a fit of jealousy would be an example.
- Violations of statutorily proscribed social taboos for artistic purposes. An example is artists who make use of legally forbidden behaviour such as public obscenity, blasphemy, or creating a public nuisance to add to the impact of their work.

The negative catalogue also includes creativity that is not directly involved in the actual commission of a crime, such as:

- Creative work done by people who also commit criminal acts. An exam-ple would be the creativity of a burglar who painted or wrote poems as a hobby when not engaged in burgling.
- Creative work done by apprehended persons such as prisoners or people in rehabilitation programmes. Examples would be art therapy or drama groups in prisons or in programmes for at-risk youths.

A difficult group for our purposes in this section (defining creative crime) consists of people who break the law to achieve ends that are now regarded as worthy and, indeed, may have been regarded as wor-thy by many people even at the time the crime occurred, even though the behaviour was officially prohibited in the perpetrators' society at the time it occurred. Examples include people like Galileo, Gandhi, or resist-ers against Nazism or Communism, who stood up for what they believed to be right and true – and are now accepted as having been right to do so – even though it meant breaking prevailing law in their society and often led to imprisonment or even execution. Gandhi's tactic of civil disobedience and passive resistance, for example, involved generation of considerable novelty, which proved to be not only *effective* but also *elegant* (it achieved its goals without destruction or widespread chaos and was somehow appealing) and *generic* (it was capable of being applied in other settings with equal effectiveness, even after it lost its novelty). These concepts (elegance and genesis in creativity) are important aspects of functional creativity (see Chapter 3, pp. 52–54). Whether these are regarded as 'crimes' or not, they still serve to illustrate the intersection of creativity and proscribed behaviours and actions, and therefore have some value for the present discussion.

The rationale of this book

The rationale of this book can be summarised as follows:

- The social sciences offer insights for conceptualising crime as well as methods and techniques for studying it. Examples include fairly obvious disciplines such as sociology and anthropology, but also others like geography and design.
- Psychology has the potential to make a particularly strong contribution, although not all possibilities in this field have been exploited. The link between crime and *creativity* is one example of a novel approach that has remained largely unexplored. This is probably because of the almost universal tendency to equate creativity only with good things.
- Discussion of creativity and crime also deepens understanding of the dark side of creativity.
- Understanding the creativity involved in some crime opens up new ways of looking at prevention and counter-measures, especially in connection with areas of crime (such as scams or terrorism) that depend heavily on surprise for their effectiveness.

The approach in this book is psychological rather than criminological, and is largely focused on understanding creativity. The application of ideas from psychology to the study of crime is not novel. It is part of a now well-established approach in the study of criminology aimed at understanding criminogenic factors in the physical, personal, social and institutional environment, such as ability, personality, motivation, attitudes, age, gender, family background, group membership and group interactions, socio-economic status, education and employment history, or effects of the built environment. Social sciences such as sociology or anthropology provide valuable insights into factors like these, and thus support a more proactive reaction to crime, but – without denigrating the value of these or other related disciplines – it can be argued that psychology has the potential to offer special perspectives, one of these being the application of creativity theory to crime. This point will be developed more fully in later chapters.

However, the book will go beyond merely demonstrating the existence of a link between crime and creativity and analysing its nature, and will work out some of the implications of this link for practice, such as preventive measures and training of law-enforcers. Hilton (2010, p. 142) emphasised the potential practical usefulness of attempts to look at crime from an unusual angle, and argued that 'knowledge of deviant rule breakers and criminals should be acquired to inform *the development of preventative change*' (emphasis added). The following chapters will begin development of some of the requisite knowledge.

CHAPTER TWO

The social science approach to crime

Crime takes place in an ecology involving interactions among the Perpetrators, the Processes, and the communities and physical environment (Press) in which it occurs. The various social sciences focus on different aspects of these interactions: sociology and anthropology, for instance, tend to have a 'reactive' image of crime, the core idea of which is that crime is caused by forces outside the individual to which perpetrators merely react. A more 'proactive' view – typical of psychology – gives greater weight to personal properties of the individual such as intelligence, motivation, or personality, which the perpetrator imposes on his or her environment. Knowledge of the individual properties of the processes and the characteristics of the perpetrator underlying proactive crime offers prospects for disrupting the processes and limiting the effects of the personal properties, i.e., for law-enforcement.

What has social science got to do with crime? We introduced the important role that the social sciences play in relation to research in crime in Chapter 1. We will now explore the social sciences in more detail in order to establish a framework that underpins the fundamental purpose of this book – namely investigation of the link between creativity and crime. A concept from criminology, 'proactive policing', provides a helpful starting point for this discussion. Proactive policing or preventive law-enforcement emphasises the physical, personal, and social environment in which crime occurs, to be sure, but – especially important for this book – it also examines the active contribution of characteristics and behaviour of offenders themselves. Licate (2010, p. 15) refers to this approach as involving 'environmental' criminology. For the purposes of this book it seems better to speak of an 'ecological' approach (see also Formosa, 2010; Marzbali et al., 2011), thus emphasising that the 'environment' being referred to includes not only physical features but also human actors, the *social* environment, and dynamic interactions among all the elements involved (i.e., to the 'ecology' of crime or, in terms of creativity theory, 'Press').

The purpose of an ecological approach goes beyond recording offences, their date and time, the extent of losses or injuries involved, the victims' details and similar information and includes actions such as targeting active criminals, identifying at-risk individuals, managing crime hotspots, understanding the relationship between factors such as urban design and crime, drawing conclusions about linked series of crimes, and – from the point of view of the general public probably the most important of all – devising effective preventive measures (i.e., *preventing* or avoiding crime rather than administering it).

A proactive approach is attractive because, among other things, it is thought to be more effective in combating crime. Ratcliffe (2008) argued that measures that are vague and diffuse in their conceptualisation of crime and of preventive or rehabilitation measures are significantly less effective than conceptually clear, goal-directed approaches: he specifically mentioned several well-known programmes whose effectiveness is reduced by lack of clear focus. Licate (2010) reviewed the relevant literature and also concluded that understanding of the causes and contributing factors underlying crime adds considerably to the effectiveness of law-enforcement. Manning (2001) stated the problem succinctly: law-enforcers lack a generalised conception of *the nature of crime*, its causes, dynamics, and meaning. Peterson (2005) made a similar point by arguing that, from the point of view of proactive policing, many law-enforcers lack concepts for understanding what to look for or for understanding the significance of what they observe, of what constitutes 'intelligence' in the sense of intelligence-led policing. We will review some contributions of social science to working out the necessary concepts.

The contribution of social sciences

As Coleman (2008, p. 307) put it, law-enforcers need 'systems to generate useful knowledge' or, in the words of Gottschalk and Gudmundsen (2009, p. 55), a suitable 'knowledge organisation structure'. Among other things, the social sciences contribute to this by providing:

- *concepts for specifying what to look for* when focusing on proactive handling of offenders (e.g., criminogenic factors such as personality, attitudes, values, beliefs and cognition, family structure, social status, roles and bonds, social learning, subgroup membership and associated traditions and rituals, economic status, place of residence, educational level, gender and age);

- *data collection and analysis methods and techniques* for obtaining information that goes beyond anecdotes and general impressions in collecting and making sense of such information (e.g., collecting and analysing police report narratives, using survey methods for evaluating the effectiveness of proactive programmes, constructing topographical maps of the distribution of crimes, special techniques for recording and analysing interviews);
- *concepts for interpreting what has been observed* (e.g., anticipation of particular kinds of crime and specifying locations and dates, identification of potential offenders, identification of at-risk individuals, establishment of culpability, estimation of likelihood of re-offending, determination of fitness to plead, recognition of mitigating factors, assessment of prospects for rehabilitation);
- ways of conceptualising *how to handle criminals* (e.g., therapy, rehabilitation, prevention/deterrence).

Social science approaches to crime can be contrasted with structural, organisational and administrative analyses, which focus on factors like allocation of resources, ensuring availability of up-to-date technology, logging response times, calculating clear-up rates, or measuring density of police presence, absenteeism, and the like. Social sciences such as sociology or anthropology, as well as economics, geography, even design, are in a position to deliver much of the insight into the nature, causes, and contributing factors required for the necessary generalised conception of crime. Licate (2010) made this explicit by referring to the usefulness of social sciences for 'informing' the analysis of crime.

The various social sciences make a contribution to crime analysis each in its own way. A number of these will be presented below. The purpose of this presentation is not to deliver a comprehensive overview of theory in the social sciences in question, but to emphasise a small number of central ideas from each discipline in order to give an idea of the general nature of its approach to crime. The purpose of this, in turn, is to provide a context into which to place the psychological approach, and especially the creativity analysis that is found in later chapters. Andrews and Bonta (2010) argued that psychology has a particular potential for offering special insights, and in this book a number of these insights will be developed. In particular, it will become apparent that psychology involves an intense focus on perpetrators' *intentions*, *personal properties*, and *thinking processes*. Extending the psychological discussion to encompass the creativity of the *products* of crime broadens the analysis by, among other things, considering the factors that lead to – from the point of view of the criminal – 'good' products. Law-enforcement can then be seen as aimed at (a) negating the 'good' aspects of the products and (b) disrupting the processes that lead to them.

Geography

One law-enforcement function in which social sciences can play a major role is *crime analysis*. This involves systematic analysis of crime data for the purpose of identifying and analysing patterns and trends. Information on such patterns can help law-enforcement agencies deploy resources in a more effective manner, and assist in identifying and apprehending suspects, but crime analysis also plays a role in devising solutions to crimes and formulating prevention strategies. Probably the most obvious application of geography to this kind of analysis of crime is to be seen in the process of 'spatial crime analysis' as it is applied with the help of geography (Ratcliffe, 2008). This is based on what Tobler (1970, p. 236) called the 'First law of geography': similar things tend to cluster together; the more similar the more closely they cluster. In this case, the similar things are infringements of the law and criminals. Special techniques of geography, such as geocoding, and related tools, such as specialised IT software, support geospatial information processing which shows that infringements of the law, especially similar kinds of infringement, tend to cluster together, while criminals also often cluster in close geographic proximity to their offences. This phenomenon offer insights into the physical ecology of crime, for instance, through crime mapping and geographic profiling (see below).

In the case of *crime mapping* (e.g., Boba, 2005; Wolff and Asche, 2009), geographical locations at which crimes occur and related concrete details such as time of day or day of the week are recorded and then used to construct topographical maps of the incidence of crime or of particular kinds of offence, from which factors such as locations in which there is an accumulation of crimes or of crimes of a particular type, time of day at which crimes occur with greater or lesser frequency, fluctuations in the incidence of crime over weeks or months, and similar patterns of crime can be worked out with a high level of precision. For instance, Breetzke (2006) pointed out that in South Africa more than 50 per cent of all crimes are committed within a relatively small number of distinct geographical areas. Katyal (2002) concluded that in Minneapolis, and by inference other cities in the USA, 50 per cent of call-outs to which police respond involve only 3 per cent of locations in the city in question. Licate (2010) drew attention to the fact that repeat offenders often break the law at the same time of day or on the same day of the week.

Crime mapping is of obvious value in making decisions on issues such as deployment of resources. However, spatial crime analysis can go further, especially through the application of Tobler's First Law. It can also be used for *geographic profiling*, which focuses on spatial aspects of the behaviour of criminals. For instance, on the basis of crime mapping of a series of related crimes it is sometimes possible to calculate where the criminals committing them probably live. Cooper et al. (2000) showed that geographic profiling is highly accurate in locating offenders, and is thus of considerable value in detection and apprehension, with spin-off benefits for prevention (at least during incarceration) and (possibly) deterrence.

Sociology

Very broadly stated, the goal of sociological research on crime is to identify the properties of communities that lead to crime. Such properties are thought to promote crime more or less *independently of the individual characteristics of the people involved*. The approach focuses on two central issues: (a) 'proximate *structural* characteristics' (emphasis added), on the one hand, and (b) '*mediating processes* of community social organisation' (emphasis added), on the other (Sampson and Wilson, 1995, p. 45). Some communities are classified as 'high crime' communities (e.g., Agnew, 1999, p. 124). In the case of structural characteristics, these communities display structural properties such as economic deprivation (poverty, unemployment, welfare dependency), low education, poor housing, high population density (overcrowding, high mobility), and family disruption.

Mediating processes – through which structural characteristics such as those just cited lead to crime – are traditionally understood in two broad ways: the subcultural deviance approach and the social disorganisation approach. The fundamental idea of both these explanations of the mediating processes connecting structural characteristics to criminal activity – spelled out by Shepard (2006) – is the notion of 'consensus': this argues that there is usually a high level of agreement (consensus) within a community on what a worthwhile person is like and what obligations people have to other people, as well as of appropriate behaviour for social activities such as getting what you want, getting ahead, dealing with slights or insults, or interacting with authority, to mention a few examples. Such consensus leads to stability of the community; people can interact with each other in an orderly fashion because they know pretty well what others expect of them and what they can expect of others, what they have to do to be accepted, and so on.

Subcultural deviance

The theory of subcultural deviance, usually regarded as initially developed by Merton (1938/1993) and further developed by Cohen (1955), argues that some communities, or potent subgroups within them such as gangs, succeed in transmitting to the young deviant information on norms and values, as well as on specific patterns of behaviour that make it possible for developing individuals to get along in the particular community. There is consensus to be sure (in principle a good thing), but the values, norms, and behaviours differ from what is acceptable in the society at large, and are thus regarded by the majority as deviant. When the deviant norms involve helping yourself to what you want, regardless of legal ownership, or intimidating people into giving it to you, reacting with violence in conflicts, vandalising property for fun, intimidating and exploiting those weaker than yourself, defying authority, refusing to go to school, or deliberately disrupting classroom procedures, and similar behaviours, they are regarded as criminal. Thus, the origin of crime is seen not as resulting from absence of norms, values, and the like, but from adoption of norms related to membership of a deviant community – subcultural deviance, in fact.

Cultural disorganisation

By contrast, this model argues that the problem lies not in the content of norms but in the fact that the process of their transmission is disrupted. Structural characteristics such as economic deprivation (poverty, unemployment, welfare dependency), low education, poor housing, high population density (overcrowding, high mobility), and family disruption lead to anonymity, instability, and mutual distrust. Communication among people is poor, and there is little reflection on shared values or active concern about the needs of others, little modelling of helpful or considerate behaviour, and little social control, either formal (e.g., by parents, community agencies, or clubs, teachers, and the like) or informal (by neighbours, shopkeepers, after-school employers, and similar people). As a result, the community is not able to transmit its norms and socially desired behaviours; that is, there is a low level of consensus. This situation is exacerbated if the community in question is physically isolated from the mainstream of society, for instance, because it is a slum, a ghetto, or an isolated housing estate. This approach sees criminals not as successful learners of norms and behaviours that are, unfortunately, unacceptable to most members of the society, as in the deviant subculture approach, but as members of a socially disorganised community in which consensus on norms cannot be achieved.

Anthropology

Forensic anthropology

Anthropology is divided into numerous sub-areas, such as biological anthropology or economic anthropology. Probably the most obviously connected with crime is forensic anthropology, which involves assisting in the investigation of offences or suspected offences, particularly homicides, through the examination of bodies or skeletons or body parts such as hair, anatomical peculiarities, or past injuries/medical treatment, and the like, in order to ascertain whether remains are human, how old they are, how long they have been at the site where they were discovered, probable cause of death, age, race, gender, and similar information. Byers (2007) gives a more comprehensive overview of this sub-discipline. Despite its obvious fascination, it is more closely related to the reactive than the proactive approach, and is thus of limited interest in the present context.

Cultural anthropology

Of greatest interest here is cultural anthropology. In a nutshell, this studies the enduring, repetitive structure of the mental life of the members of a community, what can be called its 'culture': the knowledge, beliefs, myths, symbols, morals, customs, games, rules of etiquette, and similar factors that are shared by the people in the community (e.g., Harris, 2006). These cultural characteristics promote social organisation and order. They are acquired through, among other things, child-rearing practices, and are transmitted by communication between people, both verbal and non-verbal, as well as by example. People exposed to different environments acquire different knowledge, beliefs, customs, and the like, so that cultures in the sense just sketched out are local in nature.

Crime results from the fact that different groups in a community have different cultures. They understand what is right and what is wrong differently, and this produces *dis*order and social disorganisation. Of particular interest are the ways powerful authorities, the media, and the citizenry define certain groups and practices as criminal and try to maintain social order by dealing with these groups and practices through social controls and sanctions, as well as the forms of neighbourhood control (enforcement of cultural characteristics) through application of authority and power. In doing this, anthropology looks at the ability of *culture, tradition,* and *ritual* to reinforce orderly and socially organised norms in processes such as, for instance, conflict resolution. What constitutes crime is specified by those with power, for instance through the media, the courts, or formal law-making bodies.

Crime can be a culture-making force – people develop a sense of belonging through adhering to beliefs, myths, symbols, or customs they share with other people, even though these are regarded by other communities as crime. 'Reframing' (e.g., Hilton, 2010, p. 138) crime as, for instance, part of the way 'we' cope with unjust treatment by 'them', or as a symbol of 'our' strength and courage may eliminate guilt feelings, transfer the guilt to the victims of the crime, or make mistreatment of others seem reasonable. From the opposite perspective, labelling subgroups as criminals can make it easier for the majority to deal with differences between 'our' beliefs, myths, morals, etc. and 'theirs': labelling them 'criminal' can legitimise the use of compulsion to deal with uncomfortable others.

Design

Urban design

One area in which design concepts are applied to the study of crime is urban design, the area in which 'physical and social worlds meet' (Formosa, 2010, p. 150). The basic idea here is that there is a link between behaviour and space, especially land use and structural and zoning parameters. The link to crime is thought to arise from one or more of:

(a) a correlation between crime, social issues, and land use;
(b) the fact that aspects of design offer enhanced or reduced opportunities for crime; or
(c) the phenomenon that criminal and victim follow pathways that are controlled by the space they operate in, so that who commits what offence against whom is partly determined by design factors (Formosa, 2010).

Katyal (2002) argued that crime can be prevented or at least reduced by changing the design and placement of many common and relatively simple items, such as doors, bus stops, and park benches. He gave the example of toilet entrances in public places, where replacing entrance doors with right-angle entrance passageways permits the sounds of crime to be heard outside and thus reduces victims' isolation and increases the likelihood of assistance coming to their aid, which makes the toilets a less attractive site for muggings and similar offences. According to Katyal, many countries such as Australia, Canada, Great Britain, Japan, and the Netherlands have used architectural design techniques to prevent crime. He gave the example of the 2000 Sydney Olympics, where architecture was purposefully employed to reduce crime by restricting access to sites, changing parking patterns, and creating visibility around stadiums.

The design discipline has shown, among other things (e.g., Marzbali et al., 2011), that appropriate design of buildings and the arrangement of streets and outdoor spaces in mass housing projects can reduce crime and fear of crime. This may seem at first to be a platitude. However, design research has provided a set of concepts that can be applied to data (obtained, for instance, using geographical methods such as crime mapping) to work out the dynamics of the relationships between design and crime – the mechanisms through which design affects crime. Such concepts include 'social cohesiveness' and 'neighbourliness' at a fairly high level of abstraction and generality, although these two notions do not contain much surprise value; who would not expect that members of a socially cohesive community who place great value on neighbourliness would be likely to refrain from burgling each other's residences or mugging each other in the street?

However, the application of concepts such as 'territoriality', 'defensible space', and 'surveillance' (e.g., Roberts and Erickson, 2010) yields findings that sometimes run counter to received wisdom or are strongly counter-intuitive. For instance, open spaces and clearly defined play spaces, car parks, and the like encourage 'natural surveillance', while nooks and crannies such as spaces under stairs, blind alleys, or small intimate spaces between buildings encourage gangs to exert territorial claims and defend their territory. This means that large open spaces with well-defined 'official' pathways providing the only access between them are unfavourable for crime and therefore favourable for prevention, even though they restrict movement across estates, regiment people, and reduce intimacy. Permeability (the possibility of movement from one part of the estate to another via gaps between buildings, private informal pathways, short cuts across properties, and the like) and the intimacy of small semi-private spaces and gathering places – although they seem cosy, welcoming, and intimate and likely to work against loneliness and alienation – promote appropriation and defence of territories by, for instance, disaffected youth, and thus favour disorderliness, petty theft, criminal damage, intimidation, and minor assaults, or burglary. Recent research (e.g., Kitchen, 2007) has shown that encouraging *natural surveillance* (i.e., making what is happening readily visible because it occurs in open view and not in concealed spaces) and reducing territoriality leads to large reductions in crime.

Natural surveillance also suggests design-based solutions to vandalism and crime on public transport. The concept of making what is happening readily visible takes the form, in this case, of the proliferation of closed-circuit television (CCTV) on buses and trains in many developed countries. Somewhat curiously, however, authorities seem to have neglected the obvious, and much cheaper, solution of simply encouraging more people to use public transport. The natural surveillance provided by a large number of fellow passengers is a strong deterrent to criminal behaviour, both as an aspect of design and as a means for rectifying cultural disorganisation and subcultural deviance. In the authors' home town, this certainly seems to have been overlooked as a solution. During peak times, the trains are too full of commuters to make any deviant behaviour feasible and CCTV cameras are redundant. At night time, on the infrequent services, the CCTV cameras simply document the fact that the trains are empty! If the system were designed to make it attractive to users at *all* times, by providing fast, frequent services, there would be no need for CCTV cameras, security guards, or other expensive sticking plasters. The point here is that the issue is fundamentally one of design.

Shop design

Focusing on design in the narrower sense of interior design or shopfitting makes it obvious that the open access to goods offered by many in-store promotions almost invites shop stealing by making goods easily available, making it easy to steal without being seen, providing an easy getaway, and making stolen goods readily saleable by the thief after they have been stolen (for instance, through their attractiveness). However, as Gamman and Raein (2010) pointed out, the design of in-store promotions goes further than simply providing easy access to goods. Its purpose is to excite shoppers and motivate them to buy. The design of environments appropriate to this goal arouses 'complex emotions, desires and needs', not just the ones intended by the designers (Gamman and Raein, 2010, p. 171): Gamman and Raein cite an extreme example given by Dunne and Raby (2001) of a man who married his television set.

In order to arouse fascinated interest on the part of customers, retail environments seek to activate the imagination of the customer through a degree of openness and ambiguity. However, desirable as it may be from the point of view of the retailer, 'engagement with objects and environments that have the potential for more than one type of behaviour' may provoke, in addition to the desired buying behaviour, covetousness (in principle what the retailer wants) and visions of acquisition through alternative avenues such as shop stealing. It may also arouse competitiveness, curiosity, and the like, such as a feeling of challenge to subvert security systems through novel and unexpected behaviour (i.e., through creativity). Thus, the very properties of design in shopfitting that give it its potency in provoking purchasing behaviour may also activate creative behaviour aimed at successfully outwitting the system.

The model just outlined shows how design can go beyond simply offering easy and safe opportunities for crime to which people such as shop thieves react when they spot an opportunity. It can also act upon the psyche of shop thieves in such a way as to incite or provoke crime. Such crime results from an interaction between the individual criminal's psychological make-up (referred to in creativity theory as 'Person', by us as 'Perpetrator'), and provocative properties of the designed environment such as openness, ambiguity, and flexibility (referred to in creativity theory as 'Press'). For some people, such properties provide a challenge to generate effective novelty. The counter (anti-crime) function of design is to 'block' the antisocial actions of 'abusers of products, systems and services' (Gamman and Raein, 2010, p. 168), or to design out, reduce, or redirect their behaviour. A purely external approach to prevention would seek physical solutions to the issues here (e.g., improved screening devices), but Gamman and Raein emphasised (2010, p. 168) what they called 'user- and abuser-centered design', which emphasises focusing on properties of individual criminals, an important one of which, as we will show, is creativity.

Ethnography

Ethnography provides a link or bridge between the disciplines already reviewed and psychology. It gives great emphasis to the individual person in understanding and interpreting the environment. The basic idea is that people's actions are 'the result of individuals *drawing on* the structure of their "culture"' (emphasis added) (Crang and Cook, 2007, p. 5), not just responding to what the environment chances to offer. Although still giving considerable weight to the external world, attention is paid to what that world 'means' to people experiencing it – to the way in which the individual interprets the world and applies this interpretation in behaviour. This may differ sharply from person to person even within a single social setting. This approach can be contrasted with the idea of the individual being more or less passively shaped by the environment through, for instance, social learning, maintenance of tradition, or the practice of rituals.

To a considerable extent, ethnography is more a method for collecting data than a distinct sub-discipline. The fundamental task of researchers is to 'understand parts of the world as they are *experienced and understood in the everyday lives* of the people who actually "live them out"' (emphasis added) (Crang and Cook, 2007, p. 4). Ethnographers typically focus on a specific community at a particular place and time – they examine a specific setting in great detail. Ethnographic information is collected in the form of 'contextually detailed' accounts given by the people involved in the community being investigated, and requires the application of data-collection methods that are 'capable of recovering the *lived detail* of the landscape' (emphasis added) (Scheppele, 2004, p. 401). The data are essentially records of what people say and do and, because of the emphasis on *lived* detail, what they say and do in real life. The most common methods for collecting such data are interviews, observational techniques such as participant observation, and study of archives/records. As Scheppele (2004, p. 397) put it, this means examining a 'whole specimen' of life, which encompasses the community or persons being investigated and their interactions with the world, in order to determine 'routine practice' – the way things are routinely done in the community or by the persons in question.

From our point of view, the major contribution of ethnography to the study of crime is to be found in the intimate, highly focused (on an individual person) information about crime and criminals that it yields. This is depicted in striking manner by Hayward and Young (2004). They especially criticised the contribution of mainstream sociology, which, according to them, involves two ways of looking at crime: rational choice theory and positivism. These resemble what we earlier called 'subcultural deviance' and 'cultural disorganisation'. In their view, these approaches assume that structural factors such as inequality, unemployment, poverty, living in a slum, lack of education, or family breakdown lead more or less inevitably to crime. Hayward and Young (2004, p. 263) see these approaches as conceptualising criminals as '*pallid* ... individuals' (emphasis added). What such approaches overlook is the 'adrenaline rush' of crime (Hayward and Young, 2004, p. 263): the *vivid* feelings of pleasure, panic, anger, humiliation, excitement, or fear that accompany it. In capturing these aspects as they are experienced by the individual criminal, ethnography reveals that crime is not always an almost mechanical reaction to circumstances, but something which has special charms of its own – the adrenaline rush, for instance. This approach thus gives great emphasis to 'the existential psychodynamics of the actor' (p. 265), a topic that is of great importance for our discussion of creativity in crime.

Psychological approaches

Andrews, Bonta, and Wormith (2006) summarised the practical contribution of the 'fourth generation' of psychological approaches to crime as involving:

(a) assessment of risks, strengths, needs, and responsiveness of criminals (i.e., Perpetrator); and
(b) development of service plans, service delivery, and assessment of intermediate outcomes in working with perpetrators (i.e., Press).

As far as the question of how people get to be criminals is concerned, Andrews et al. saw the psychology of crime as largely a matter of understanding the role of personality factors such as weak self-control or high antagonism, on the one hand, and aspects of social learning such as antisocial cognition, self-referential ideation, or risky thinking, on the other. The practical application of this approach involves three main areas:

(a) Assessing fitness to plead, level of culpability, existence of mitigating factors, prospects of rehabilitation/recidivism, and similar issues (Bartol and Bartol, 2010; Pirelli, Gottdiener, and Zapf, 2011). This is the main focus of *forensic psychology.*
(b) Designing and delivering therapeutic (rehabilitative) or preventive treatment of convicted criminals and therapy/prevention with people thought likely to become hardened offenders (such as at-risk juveniles). This area is predominantly *clinical* in orientation.
(c) Identifying psychological criminogenic risk factors in order to understand why people become criminals in the first place, with the hope of preventing that happening, a more criminological approach.

The three domains are interconnected. For instance, in an overview, Andrews et al. (2006, p. 11) made the link between criminogenic factors and treatment quite explicit by working out the eight main risk factors and mapping appropriate clinical approaches onto them. To take two examples, they recommended training in problem-solving and anger management for people displaying an antisocial personality pattern (number two in the four most important risk factors – the big four), or training in recognising risky thinking and feelings for people displaying antisocial cognition (number three). Striking by contrast with sociology or anthropology is the belief that there is a direct link between the personal make-up of the criminal and the extent and kind of crime that is displayed, so that preventive measures focus on targeted therapy aimed at the particular psychological element involved in different kinds of crime, not on diffuse structural measures such as better housing or regular employment.

Forensic psychology

A very broad definition of forensic psychology is that it involves the study of the behaviour of people within the legal system, including offenders, witnesses, victims, police, judges and magistrates, prisoners and prison staff. For the purposes of this book we will treat it more narrowly as concerned with the detection of crime and treatment of criminals. Forensic psychologists may play a role in the investigative phase of law-enforcement, for instance, by profiling the perpetrator or by advising on interrogation. When a case comes to trial they may advise on jury selection or on how to present evidence. They frequently advise courts on matters such as fitness of an accused person to stand trial, culpability, mitigating factors, risk of re-offending, or appropriate sentencing. This not infrequently involves the use of psychological tests, such as an IQ test to establish whether a criminal was mentally capable of forming the intention to commit an offence or of understanding the consequences of the actions involved, or a personality test to determine whether a criminal is suffering from a psychiatric disturbance or is mentally ill. They may also advise the court on credibility of witnesses or deliberate deceit.

Clinical approaches to crime

Clinically oriented forensic psychologists or specialists in clinical psychology focus on mental disorder and crime or on the mental health care of offenders and inmates, especially design and delivery of therapy or counselling to perpetrators or victims, with a focus on issues such as interpersonal disturbances (aggression, anger management), crisis management, anxiety, depression, or disturbances of self-image. Research suggests that cognitive behaviour therapy is the best approach to preventing recidivism in convicted criminals (e.g., Landenberger and Lipsey, 2005).

This approach addresses problems in areas such as immature thinking, poor decision making, poor problem-solving skills, inability to recognise wrongdoing, inability to delay gratification of needs, or lack of understanding of other people's rights or needs. Since people are – at least in principle – able to regulate their own emotions through conscious effort, cognitive therapies can also help with anger management, control of impulses, or avoidance of violence as a problem-solving technique. Of particular interest in the present context is that the self-help element of cognitive behaviour therapy – in which people learn how to reflect upon and take responsibility for their own behaviour – seems to be a major determinant of its effectiveness in preventing crime. In other words, treating criminals as self-determining actors in their own crime and not as helpless victims of structural factors such as low income or poor housing seems to help them stop offending.

Criminogenic factors

Criminogenic factors are the forces that lead people to break the law. Andrews and Bonta (2010) concluded that study of these is now the dominant psychological approach to crime. They identified temperament, personality, intelligence, and self-image, as well as criminogenic cognition (e.g., antisocial attitudes, values, and beliefs) as disposing people to crime. Krohn, Lizotte, and Hall (2009) reviewed relevant psychological risk factors and came to a similar conclusion: in addition to unfavourable external social factors such as negative labelling, social disorganisation, or institutional anomie, risk factors include inappropriate social learning or self-referential ideation (i.e., ego-centrism), defective coping skills, such as inability to deal with stress, weaknesses in aspects of personality, such as impulse control, and risky motivation, such as foolhardy thrill seeking or retaliatory aggression.

In this book, however, interest is not directly focused on any of these three domains (i.e., we are not asking how to judge culpability, how and why people come to be criminals in the first place, or how to help them avoid crime or stop once they do). All of these involve the person of the criminal or the process of becoming a criminal and the factors involved in this process, that is, they give greatest weight to causal factors and treatment. By contrast, we are primarily interested here in the quality of the crime itself (i.e., the *product* of crime), and especially *creative* crime. Nonetheless, person and process cast some light on our main interest, and we will briefly outline some of the key ideas below.

Special features of the psychological approach

There is a substantial difference between the approaches of geography, sociology, and anthropology sketched out above and the fundamental orientation of psychology. These differences can be regarded as forming a continuum based on the degree of emphasis given to the 'existential psychodynamics of the actor'. Geography, sociology, and anthropology are nearer the end of the continuum giving *low* priority to the psychodynamics of the perpetrator; psychology lies towards the other pole, which gives the psychodynamics a high priority. Design and ethnography lie in the middle, design closer to the low end, ethnography closer to psychology.

This characterisation of the way social sciences approach crime is depicted schematically in Figure 2.1 below. The axis in the figure represents the continuum ranging from low emphasis on the existential psychodynamics of the perpetrator (*reactive* view of crime) to high emphasis (*proactive* view). The positions of the various social sciences along the continuum are purely intuitive: they are not based on any strict quantitative analysis of the disciplines according to set criteria. In addition, they are not drawn to scale and thus do not express exact distances between social sciences. Nonetheless, they are meant to give an idea of their relationship to each other and to the poles of the continuum, so that larger and smaller distances between points on the continuum are meant to express larger/smaller, although not exactly quantified, differences between disciplines. For instance, we see geography, sociology, and anthropology as closer to each other than they are to design, ethnography, and psychology, while the individual disciplines in the geography, sociology, and anthropology cluster at the reactive end of the continuum are closer to each other than the disciplines in the design, ethnography, and psychology cluster at the proactive end.

The differences depicted in Figure 2.1 are crucial to a discussion of crime and creativity for several reasons.

1. Whereas other social sciences see structural properties of the physical environment or the community as decisive in activating crime, with the individual reacting to whatever circumstances offer and almost seeming to be regarded as a passive pawn, psychology, and especially our approach via creativity theory, as will become clearer in Chapter 6, assigns a much more active role to the individual. Criminals are seen as imposing their own psychological make-up on the environment, rather than vice versa (for instance, they attend selectively to the external

Geography   Anthropology   Design   Psychology

Sociology   Ethnography

Low emphasis on existential   **High emphasis on existential**
psychodynamics   **psychodynamics**
(Reactive)   **(Proactive)**

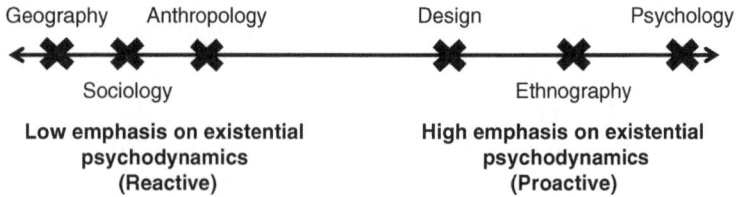

Figure 2.1 Relationship among social sciences regarding emphasis on the individual

world, interpret what they observe in terms of their own experience, store information in mental categories they themselves have developed, and recover stored information selectively in terms of their own priorities). All of this is affected by intelligence, as well as motivation and emotion: the external world acts not upon a *tabula rasa* but on a functioning individual system of knowledge, values, beliefs, attitudes, aspirations, and motives. Ethnography offers special insights into this aspect of crime.

2. Other approaches say why crime occurs in a community as a general phenomenon, but say little about which specific individuals in the community will become active criminals (for instance, not everybody who experiences unfavourable structural conditions becomes a criminal), what specific kind of crime they will specialise in, or what specific individual treatment (as against general actions like redesigning the built environment, helping communities to negotiate and transmit shared pro-social norms, or eliminating stigmatisation of out-groups) will discourage crime. As was pointed out using the example of Andrews et al. (2006), psychologists are often in a position to make specific treatment recommendations for specific patterns of disturbance.

3. Other approaches do not show why some people's crime is marked by ingenuity and novelty whereas other people's is routine and repetitive, how to recognise and assess the personal properties involved, or how to negate their effects. They do not, for instance, take account of the fact that crime seems to be regarded by some criminals as fun rather that an agonised reaction to unbearable injustice that is forced upon people who have limited personal resources.

These remarks are not meant to imply that the structural approaches to understanding crime briefly outlined above do not accurately represent the situation of some criminals. However, we focus here on *resourceful criminals*, such as Shirley Pitts, Bernie Madoff, Jeffrey Skilling, or Osama bin Laden: vigorous, enterprising, self-determining actors, not simple opportunists reacting robotically to circumstances, hapless victims of social disorganisation, or unwitting players of a social role thrust on them by the structural features of the community in which they grew up. Indeed, Ruggiero (2010) argued that the deficit approach just summarised may actually hinder understanding of crime by imposing a narrow corset on thinking in the area. Our purpose here is to *broaden* the way crime is looked at, not to convince readers that there is only one true path.

Structuralist vs individualist approaches

There is, in fact, a spectrum of approaches that differ principally by virtue of the fact that different approaches give greater emphasis to certain aspects of the ecology of crime than to others. The differences among them have just been depicted schematically in Figure 2.1 – at the cost, of course, of loss of detail – by distinguishing between degree of emphasis on existential 'psychodynamics'. We will now add some flesh to the bare bones of Figure 2.1 by giving some detail of two stereotypical ways of looking at perpetrators: the 'structuralist' view at one pole, the 'individualist' at the other. The structuralist approach emphasises the structural properties of the person's community (e.g., average educational level, employment levels, housing conditions, family structures). The individualist approach, by contrast, emphasises individual psychological properties of the perpetrator.

Table 2.1 presents such a schematic. It is important to bear in mind that the discussion here is focused on developing a framework for *conceptualising* perpetrators. The structuralist approach, for instance, is not seen as a literal description of criminals but as a list of the kinds of variable that are given greatest emphasis in structuralist analyses of crime, while the same is true for the properties listed as individualist; they are the kinds of variable most emphasised in individualist discussions. The 'domains' around which the table is constructed are based on the 6Ps of creativity (Product, Perpetrator's psychological properties, Perpetrator's motivation, Perpetrator's feelings, Process, Press), which are presented more fully in Chapter 3. The characterisations of the two approaches in Table 2.1 are dialectic in nature (e.g., each dimension, such as, let us say, Motivation, is presented as a dichotomy, in this case 'reactive' versus 'proactive' motivation).

These are undoubtedly false dichotomies in two ways: (a) a particular approach may take account of the Perpetrator's psychological characteristics, environmental Press or properties of Products in ways listed in Table 2.1 as actually typical for the other approach (e.g., both

Table 2.1 *Structuralist vs individualist stereotypes of criminals*

	Approach	
Domain	Structuralist	Individualist
Motivation	**Reactive**	**Proactive**
	Reflexive reaction to momentary opportunity	Calculating/opportunistic
	Derived from whatever the environment offers	Goal oriented
	Opportunistic	Rises to a challenge
	Takes foolish risks	Open to calculated risks
	Thoughtlessly thrill seeking	Seeks excitement
Personality	**Pallid**	**Vivid**
	Apathetic, hostile, resentful	Challenging
	Ego-centric	Calculating
	Impulsive	Self-confident
	Passive	Resourceful
Attitudes	**Diffuse**	**Specific**
	Diffusely aggressive	Actively antisocial
	Generalised hostility	Targeted hostility
	Anti-authority	Attitudes, values, and beliefs play a key role in crime
	Angry	
Thinking (Process)	**Undifferentiated/Concrete**	**Differentiated/Abstract**
	Stereotyped	Individualised
	Conventional	Insightful
	Self-referential	Understands cause and effect
	Poor planning skill	Possesses planning skills
	Few coping strategies	Has acquired coping strategies
Environment (Press)	**Compelling**	**Facilitating**
	Offers irresistible immediate opportunities	Offers opportunities that can be exploited with planning
	Provokes impulsive reactions	Can be dealt with systematically
	Directly triggers behaviour	Has an indirect effect mediated by motives, personality, attitudes, and ideas
Nature of crime (Product)	**Routine**	**Resourceful**
	Unplanned	Calculated
	Opportunist	Personalised
	Stereotyped, predictable	Less predictable
	Shaped by the immediate environment	Shaped by criminal's motivation, personality, attitudes, and ideation

models acknowledge the effects of thrill seeking in motivation for crime). However, the discussion of thrill seeking is far more typical of the individualist approach and is therefore placed under that heading in Table 2.1; (b) an individual perpetrator may be affected by both structuralist and individualist factors, rather than representing a 'pure' type. Thus, to some extent, the structuralist vs individualist dichotomy spelled out in Table 2.1 may be more a stereotype than a description of facts. Nonetheless, there is a strong tendency for much criminological research in sociology and anthropology to be predominantly structuralist in nature and in psychology to be most clearly individualist in orientation, with geography and planning giving some prominence to individualist aspects and ethnology being closer to the individualist end of the spectrum.

This schematic of the range of ways of looking at crime makes plain how a psychological approach can broaden research in the area, and also suggests a direction in which thinking can be expanded. The structuralist stereotype is of an *unresourceful* criminal: angry and resentful, unable to control impulses, pre-programmed, more or less controlled by chance environmental events, unable to calculate risk – in short, what Hayward and Young (2004, p. 263) called (see above) 'pallid' – lacking in the thrill of planning, the build-up of anticipatory excitement, or the self-congratulation and the feeling of having outsmarted law-enforcers.

Although a great deal of emotion was obviously involved, the offending of Jason Downie outlined below is a good example of unresourceful crime conducted without planning or purpose, almost without personal involvement, despite its horrifying consequences. Downie, a nineteen-year-old youth, had an unwanted and unreturned sexual infatuation for Chantelle Rowe, a sixteen-year-old girl. Late at night, Downie went to her home with the intention of persuading her to have sex with him. He entered the house and apparently disturbed Chantelle's father, Andrew Rowe, who was either still awake or was awakened by the noise of Downie's entry. On being confronted in the kitchen by Mr Rowe, Downie seized a kitchen knife and stabbed him ten to fifteen times, then once more in the back as the victim turned away. By this time, Chantelle's mother, Rose Rowe, had also been disturbed and entered the kitchen, only to be confronted by the murder scene. Jason then attacked her, too, stabbing her fifty times, apparently simply because she had seen him.

Finally, he went into Chantelle's room, where the girl was hiding under her bed. He pulled her out and stabbed her, too, two or three times. Thinking she was dead, Jason removed her clothes, but she regained consciousness and struggled. He ran to the kitchen to get another knife, then resumed stabbing her, and when she began to lose consciousness raped her. Following the attack, he removed her damaged clothing and re-dressed her in clean clothes. Following this, he left the house and simply resumed living his normal life. On being arrested, Downie told an obviously fabricated absurd tale about an unknown man who had been at the murders, then pleaded guilty when this story was rejected out of hand, and was sentenced to thirty-five years in prison.

Downie was apparently motivated to enter the Rowe residence by anger and resentment at being rejected, but probably had only vague intentions, so that the actual murders were unplanned. He may have panicked on being detected by Mr Rowe, and seems to have gone into a frenzy in which he scarcely knew what he was doing: he stabbed his three victims over a hundred times in all and broke off at least one knife in a victim's body. He killed Mrs Rowe simply because she was there. He left substantial evidence such as DNA at the scene, and even wrote about the crime on Facebook. Downie's letters to his mother expressed regret, but do not seem to reveal any genuine remorse or empathy for his victims or the family of the victims.

The individual approach, by contrast, looks more at deliberate purposeful acts of crime in the commission of which criminals are in command of their faculties, work according to a plan or system, and are oriented towards achieving some concrete goal, namely, *resourceful* crime. It thus seems sensible to turn to the area of focus in psychology that gives particular emphasis to resourceful acts involving coming up with surprising solutions, doing things in new and unexpected ways, developing novel products that may bring great reward but may lead to disaster, having the courage to take a chance, tolerating the ensuing uncertainty, or living as a social outsider. One area in which such issues have been examined in detail involves research on creativity, and we will apply this approach in the remainder of this book. Of particular importance is the fact that, as Chapter 3 will show, the psychological characteristics that are listed in Table 2.1 as typical of the individualistic, resourceful approach to crime are strikingly reminiscent of the personal properties that are emphasised in the study of the 6Ps of creativity.

CHAPTER THREE

Basic creativity concepts

Most discussions of creativity focus on two key components. First, creativity must involve something new or different. Second, creativity must also be relevant to the task at hand and must effectively achieve what it set out to achieve. These two components immediately draw attention to the outcome, or result, of creativity, that is, to Product. However, despite the importance of the public manifestation of creativity in the form of Product, all creative outcomes (including the criminal ones) result from a production Process and interactions among a number of psychological dimensions of the Person (or in the case of criminals, the Perpetrator) – Personal properties, Personal motivation, Personal feelings/moods – and environmental Press. Together these dimensions represent a framework of 6Ps that can be used to structure understanding of creativity. Creativity in the sense just outlined is not confined to the arts, but occurs in a wide range of fields, including engineering, business, mental health, and sport. Crime, too, can be looked at in terms of this framework of dimensions of creativity.

As we pointed out in Chapter 1, creativity has been unhooked from the arts – where it seems intuitively to belong. It is now understood that generation of effective novelty occurs in a much wider range of fields. However, using creativity concepts to analyse areas such as management practice, health care, sport, or crime – to which the link is less obvious than to the arts – requires establishing a conceptual framework for understanding the various factors involved, and doing this is the purpose of the present chapter.

Creative Products

Novel, relevant, and effective products

Although discussions of creativity – especially artistic or aesthetic creativity – often treat it as either a process or a set of personal properties, at least since Morgan (1953), modern thinking in Western European/North American societies has accepted that the essential core of creativity – its *sine qua non* – is *novel products*. This is particularly true in the case of crime: merely thinking about breaking the law or wanting to do it are not usually subject to legal sanctions. Consequently, our discussion of the nature of creativity will start with products. Novelty in a product is not confined to form (what the product looks like or how it is constructed), but may also be manifested in function (what the product does) or system (in what organisational arrangement it does it). The novelty may also apply not to concrete characteristics of products at all but to the way they are conceptualised (how an issue is thought about – the 'paradigm' for understanding it) or to the processes through which products – even non-novel ones – are produced. A broad definition of Product is therefore any artefact, system, process, or service.

For instance, the introduction by the Ford Motor Company in 1908 of the assembly line to build automobiles involved the generation of novelty not in the form of a new product (the automobile already existed, although it was admittedly a recent invention) but rather in a new way of conceptualising the task of assembling a piece of machinery (instead of a single worker building the whole machine, specialists built specific pieces of it), a novel way of organising the work (the work came to the worker) and a new procedure for implementing these two novelties (the assembly line). The new method of mass production led to a huge surge in sales of the existing product by reducing its price and, as a result, making it available to a vastly wider range of buyers, thus also providing an example of how creativity can benefit a firm (the Ford Motor Company) and – in the eyes of car lovers, at least – the society. After introducing the production line, Ford also paid the workers far more than had been the standard (the '$5 day', or about double the rates prevailing at that time). This was necessary partly to offset the boredom of the new process. So, taken together, the overall 'outcome' was not just the production-line idea, but also extended to the change in how the workers were paid; that is, the outcome was a new *system*.

Novelty was defined by Bruner (1962) in a more psychological way as the achievement of 'surprise' in a beholder. However, surprisingness alone is not sufficient for a product to be creative. Surprise on its own may involve mere 'pseudo-creativity', which is novel only in the sense of non-conformity, lack of discipline, blind rejection of what already exists or simply letting oneself go. These properties may be observed in many genuinely creative people, and thus be confused with creativity, but they are not actually an inherent part of it. It is also possible to distinguish what can be called 'quasi-creativity'. This has many of the elements of genuine creativity – such as a high level of fantasy – but its connection with reality is tenuous. An example would be the 'creativity' of daydreams.

Consequently, there is widespread, almost universal agreement that a creative product must not just display novelty, but must also be helpful in some way and appropriate to the task at hand. These two definitive elements of novelty and usefulness were stated from very early in the modern era: Stein (1953, p. 311) defined creativity as involving 'a *novel* work that is accepted as … *useful*' (emphasis added), and Barron (1955) stated that a creative product must display 'uncommonness' (p. 478), to be sure, but also be 'adaptive to reality' (p. 479). Using Bruner's (1962) terminology, creative products must be *effective* and *relevant*. In the more recent literature this view is stated by many writers (e.g., Sternberg, Kaufman, and Pretz, 2002; Kozbelt, Beghetto, and Runco, 2010). Effective and relevant outcomes may include tangible objects such as *objets d'art* or machines, but also ideas, processes, procedures, services, or systems (Woodman, Sawyer, and Griffin, 1993). Thus, 'genuine' creativity requires at least two further elements over and above mere novelty. A product or response must deal with the issue at stake (relevance) and must offer some kind of genuine solution (effectiveness). Otherwise, every far-fetched, outrageous, or preposterous idea or every act of non-conformity would, by virtue of being surprising, be creative.

Of course, what is meant by an 'effective' product may differ from, let us say, fine art to engineering to business to crime. In the former case criteria such as beauty may play a decisive role (i.e., form predominates). By contrast, an engineering product – let us say a bridge built to conduct traffic across a river – must be capable of doing its job (i.e., function is paramount). No matter how aesthetically pleasing they were, the Tacoma Narrows Bridge in Washington or the Westgate Bridge in Melbourne would be acclaimed by few people as triumphs of engineering creativity, even though the former was beautiful to look at (form was novel and pleasing), and the latter was novel in some aspects of building technology (process was novel). Despite this, both fell down, causing enormous expense and major disruption to traffic, and in the case of the Westgate Bridge substantial loss of life (thus, the products were ineffective). Nonetheless, the criteria of novelty, relevance, and effectiveness prevail, *mutatis mutandis*. In crime, successful acquisition of ill-gotten gains or avoidance of apprehension are two indicators of effectiveness to which law-breakers would probably give high priority, whereas they might be of little or no significance in other areas.

Functional creative products

We have distinguished elsewhere (e.g., Cropley and Cropley, 2010b) between products that are effective and relevant in an artistic or aesthetic sense (e.g., generation of beauty, achievement of truth or authenticity in understanding the world, or similar purposes) and those that are useful for some practical purpose such as building cars more cheaply, selling more of some product, curing a disease, solving a mathematical equation or, in the case of crime, acquiring other people's property, intimidating people, behaving in an antisocial manner and getting away with it, and the like. We called this latter kind of creativity 'functional' creativity. It has already been pointed out that relevant and effective novelty is indispensable for creativity. However, we regard this as defining the minimum profile of a creative product; a product that does not go beyond this reaches the lowest level of creativity, which we call 'originality' (e.g., Cropley and Cropley, 2005; Cropley and Cropley, 2009).

However, a functional product can go beyond 'mere' relevant and effective novelty. For instance, in addition to being novel, relevant, and effective it can look the part, fit together well, make an impression of being complete, be obviously what is needed, or make sense. In other words, it can be 'elegant'. Grudin (1990) referred to 'the *grace* of great things' (emphasis added). Such grace, or elegance, as we call it, is often readily recognisable simply by looking at the product: as Rechtin and Maier (2000) put it, citing Wernher von Braun, 'The eye is a fine architect. Believe it!' Not infrequently, elegance is associated with simplicity or parsimony (as opposed to unnecessary 'overkill'). Elegance adds value to an original product, and this increases its creativity. In the real world, elegance may mean that a product is recognised for what it is, is accepted, applauded, and adopted, while it may also mean that a particular product defeats a rival, for instance, in the marketplace or in the competition between criminals and law-enforcers.

Finally comes 'genesis': the property of a relevant, effective, and novel product that makes it transferable to different (quite possibly unanticipated) situations (transferability), opens up new ways of looking at known problems (seminality), or draws attention to the existence of previously unnoticed problems (germinality). These four dimensions of a creative product are shown in Table 3.1. We take the view that the

Table 3.1 *The hierarchical organisation of functional Products*

Criterion	Kind of Product				
	Routine	Original	Elegant	Generic	Pseudo- or quasi-creativity
Effectiveness	+	+	+	+	-
Novelty	-	+	+	+	+
Elegance	-	-	+	+	?
Genesis	-	-	-	+	?

progression from routine, to original, then elegant and finally generic products represents not only an increase in amount of creativity (quantitative difference in creativity), but also a change in *kind* of creativity (qualitative difference). A generic solution is thus not only more creative than a routine one, but is also a different kind of solution: it affects the field into which it is introduced not just to a greater extent than a routine one, but also in a different way, for instance, by changing the prevailing paradigm.

The idea of functional creativity is of particular importance in discussing creativity in crime. As we have defined creative crime, it involves deliberate application of relevant and effective novelty for concrete gain – more or less a definition of functional creativity. It is also apparent, however, that some creative crime goes beyond 'mere' relevant and effective novelty and is almost admirable in its elegance. An example is the criminal gang recently arrested and charged in Venice for a long series of art thefts. One member, who was an expert in the value of Old Masters such as works by Canaletto or Gaudi, identified relevant paintings in grand salons in Venice. A second member, who worked in a photography studio, located visual images of the paintings and transferred them electronically onto canvas in the exact proportions of the originals. A third member touched up the electronic prints with oil paint so that they looked real, and a fourth, who had access to the grand houses as an honoured guest, cut out the originals from their frames and replaced them with the forgeries. In a ten-year period the gang succeeded in stealing more than forty Old Masters and making a good living for themselves, while none of the owners ever noticed the difference.

Finally, while it is true that some creative crime may involve one-off relevant and effective novelty that can only be applied a single time in a specific setting, other variants may either be applicable repeatedly or transferable to new settings (i.e., they may be generic). An example of the latter would be the use of massive email campaigns for approaching possibly millions of potential victims for scams. This general approach is now reappearing in constantly changing variants that are, it seems, not losing their potency. Paradoxically, the generic effect of creativity in crime may ultimately cause it to be less helpful to the perpetrators who generated it than to law-enforcers: novel crime may reveal previously unnoticed vulnerabilities (germinality) or show law-enforcers how to close off already known ones (seminality), thus generating effectively novel behaviour in what for perpetrators is the opposition. The generic effects may even have the advantage of being longer lasting as a defensive measure than as a criminal tactic.

The 11 September 2001 attacks and subsequent incidents such as Richard Reid's attempted use of a shoe bomb offer examples: law-enforcers have introduced effective new counter-measures such as securing cockpit doors, reducing the volume of liquids that passengers are permitted to take on board with them, and more comprehensive scanning of passengers prior to boarding, which close off some methods of attack, but may, of course, provoke further creativity on the part of the criminals in an example of the 'arms race' (see p. 204) between law-enforcers and law-breakers. In a similar way, the Great Train Robbery revealed previously unnoticed problems in the transportation of very large sums of money by train, and provoked defensive measures.

Kinds of creative product

In short, then, creativity involves an idea, a process, a service, a conceptual model, or a tangible object that is at least new, different, and effective, and may also be elegant and generic. However, this raises the question for whom a product, process, or idea should be new: for all human beings throughout history, for the society or the era of the creator, or for the creator alone? Requiring that products be new in all human history would mean that a person would not be regarded as creative if someone else somewhere else had had the same idea at some time or other, even though the first person knew nothing of this. On the other hand, defining creativity in terms of the point of view of the person in question only would mean that total ignorance would guarantee creativity, since every idea would be new for someone who knew nothing!

According to Florida (2002, p. 8), creativity involves the production of 'meaningful new forms'. He went on to point out that such forms include:

- music, plays, and the like that can be performed again and again;
- theorems or strategies that can be applied in many situations;
- systems for understanding the world;
- physical objects that can be made, sold and used.

Important in this approach to creativity are, firstly, the emphasis on products and, secondly, the idea that such products must be, so to speak, *public* (other people get to know about them and find them good in some way) and also *enduring* (their application or use persists for some time – in some cases for a very long time). The emphasis on meaningful new forms in discussing what constitutes a creative product is useful in practical settings (such as crime): a creative product has to be good for something and someone must be able to see that this is the case.

Florida's (2002) approach means that the creativity of a clever remark or a bright idea that achieved momentary recognition in, let us say, dinner-table conversation, but led to nothing and was soon forgotten is of limited interest because it does not become *public* (see previous paragraph) and has no *enduring* effect. Even in the case of the September 11 attacks, where the effectiveness of the novelty was very short-lived and diminished even while the attacks were still in progress (the passengers on UA93 were able to thwart the attack on the Capitol once they became aware of what was happening), and counter-measures that have prevented a repetition have been put in place, the terrorists' creativity has had wide and enduring public effects and may eventually spawn new (and from the point of terrorists improved) variants. Thus, rapid loss of effectiveness of novelty does not mean that the novelty is not creative: what is important is that the novelty provokes enduring after-effects, and that these become operative in a broader setting than simply a single situation. The clever remark in the example given above would become the object of our attention if it set off a chain of events that went beyond the dinner table at which it was made and provoked changes in some product, process, or system.

In fact, however, the word 'creativity' is used to refer to products ranging from being novel only in the sense that they have recently come into existence, regardless of relevance and effectiveness – such as is the case with a wisecrack or even a child's drawing on what was until a few minutes before a blank piece of paper – all the way to great works that are widely hailed as enlarging human perspectives in some way not previously seen in all history. The former involves 'mundane' creativity (e.g., Cohen and Ambrose, 1999), the latter 'sublime' creativity. Boden (2004, p. 1) made a distinction between 'P-creativity' (creativity involving generating something that is novel for the person who generates it) and 'H-creativity' (creativity involving novelty that no-one has ever thought of before in all human history).

Differentiating between two extremes involving, on the one hand, the creativity of, say, a Leonardo da Vinci or a Johann Sebastian Bach, which not only yielded enduring products but also changed the paradigm in an area and inspired other people to follow new pathways, and, on the other, that of, let us say, a home cook, who varied the ingredients of a well-known dish and produced an effectively novel one-off taste effect that, however, never became known outside the family and was soon forgotten even there, restricts the study of creativity to the dichotomy of sublime vs ordinary creativity. However, Kaufman and Beghetto (2009) extended the discussion to encompass four levels of creativity, referred to in a picturesque way as involving 'Big-C', 'Pro-C', 'little-c', or 'mini-c' creativity, thus generating in addition to the 4Ps model a 4Cs model for expanding understanding of one of the Ps, namely Product.

Big-C can be compared with what we called 'sublime' creativity above and Boden called 'H-creativity'. It involves 'towering historical figures' (McWilliam and Dawson, 2008, p. 634): it transforms society, for instance by physically changing the world we live in through, among other things, new technologies and methods of production or by changing the way individual people experience or understand the world they live in. Examples of little-c and mini-c, by contrast, would include the invention by a secretary of a novel filing system that made her work more efficient but remained unknown and was soon forgotten by the person in question on changing jobs, or the creativity of the cook mentioned above. Pro-C involves systematic and purposeful generation of useful and effective novelty that goes beyond a private one-off experience such as the one just outlined, for instance by becoming public and even exciting admiration, but does not achieve the transformative status of Big-C.

Even in the case of Big-C, it is possible to distinguish between two ways of producing effective and relevant surprise: by means of new applications of existing principles or by development of new principles. Some writers have contrasted 'secondary' (a different application of the already known) and 'primary' creativity (development of new principles). Other authors have distinguished between 'minor' creativity (simply extending the known) and 'major' creativity (going beyond the known – changing the paradigm). This distinction is similar to Kirton's (1989) distinction between adaptors and innovators, Christensen's (1997) distinction between sustaining and disruptive innovation, or Bodankin and Tziner's (2009, p. 549) between 'destructive' and 'constructive' deviance, and offers a useful concept for considering creative crime, as will be discussed in more detail in later chapters.

A more differentiated approach in this connection is the distinction among 'levels' of creativity made by Taylor (1975): 'expressive spontaneity' requires only the free production of ideas, without regard to their effectiveness or relevance. This seems to be related to mini-c creativity and clearly has a role in some creativity-training procedures such as brainstorming, and may well be helpful in the generation of novelty, but may often lead to pseudo- or quasi-creativity and is not sufficient by itself for sublime creativity. 'Technical creativity' requires mastery of special skills or techniques, for instance, with words or paints or a musical instrument or other tools. It seems to be related to Pro-C creativity but, despite its importance in some creative activities (such as painting or playing music or designing your own computer games), technical skill is not sufficient as a universal definition of creativity. 'Inventive creativity' involves applying the already known in new ways, 'innovative creativity' requires expanding known principles, while 'emergent creativity' encompasses the development of new principles. The latter is clearly related to Big-C creativity. As a general but not universal rule, children often show expressive spontaneity, but lack knowledge of a field or skill with tools or special techniques. In this sense, they can be said to display creativity, but in the usual run of events only in a limited sense. Our discussions of crime and creativity focus mostly on 'inventive creativity', 'innovative creativity', and 'emergent creativity'.

Everyday creativity

About forty years ago the idea of creativity in the person who will never achieve anything creative was introduced into the discussion by Nichols (1972). More recently, there has been a considerable amount of research on 'everyday' creativity (e.g., Richards et al., 1988). Although they may not produce innovative or emergent creativity, a high proportion of adults engage in the production of (at least for them) new ideas or products, for instance, in the course of 'creative' hobbies, or simply in everyday life, as in the example of the cook given above (mini-c creativity). Thus, it is certainly possible, in the sense of everyday, minor, humble, little-c, or mini-c creativity, to speak of creativity as a widely distributed characteristic seen in large numbers of people, not just the socially acclaimed, or even, in the case of crime, not even the socially approved of.

McWilliam and Dawson (2008, p. 634) pointed out that 'second-generation creativity', which focuses on the creativity of relatively ordinary people, is becoming more widely recognised. (The 'first generation' of creativity studies basically saw it as defined by Big-C, with 'ordinary' creativity being regarded as a praiseworthy step down from the real thing.) This insight may prove to be particularly helpful in understanding creative crime, where creativity does not normally draw universal applause, but is somehow creative, all the same. What is needed is a way of conceptualising creativity that can distinguish systematically between its expression in sublime and more or less automatically admirable forms and in day-to-day – possibly reprehensible – forms such as crime.

Generality vs specificity of creativity

In recent writings, authors have disagreed about whether creativity can be defined in a general way or only in specific areas such as fine arts or science, or even more specifically within fields such as performing arts vs literary arts (for a very recent compact summary, see Baer, 2011). There is no doubt that specific processes or particular personal qualifications are important for creativity in specific fields. For instance, discrimination among tones might be important for musical creativity but not for sculpture, relevant specialised knowledge might be extremely important for creativity in physics but less important in poetry, and the particular skills that are needed for sculpture may be quite different from those needed for creative cooking. Abilities, knowledge, skills, and techniques play a role in all fields of creativity, to be sure, but the particular factors for one domain may be different from those needed for creativity in another – knowledge is perhaps relatively more important in science, technique in music, to take an example. The specific contents of an element such as knowledge may also vary according to the particular field or activity in question: the specific knowledge required for designing and building bridges may not be very relevant for creative research in, let us say, botany, but both require a knowledge base. Both mathematical creativity and creative writing require mastery of a set of abstract symbols for representing ideas, although the two symbol systems may be quite different. Thus, there is specificity in creativity, but generality too.

At the scholarly level, there has been disagreement among researchers for many years about whether a unified model of creativity can be developed. Baer (1998) and Plucker (1998) reviewed much of the discussion, coming to contradictory conclusions: creativity is domain specific (Baer) vs creativity is general (Plucker). Ludwig (1998) analysed creativity in different fields and concluded that there are differences between fields based on the demands of the field, but that a general approach is also possible. Simonton (2009) described a hierarchy of domains with hard science at the top, social science in the middle, and arts/humanities at the bottom. One aspect of this is that domains that have a high level of consensus about what constitutes the body of knowledge (like engineering or maths) seem to deal with creativity somewhat differently from domains which lack a strong consensus. In the former case, creativity has to occur within a set of constraints, whereas in the latter, creativity can occur in a more unfettered way. In engineering, for instance, a bridge can be as creative as you like, *as long as it is effective*. In creative writing, by contrast, there is probably far more scope for creativity to be unfettered by rules, conventions, etc. Later in this chapter we present a schema for recognising products that we believe can be applied to all kinds of creativity, from what we call 'functional' creativity to 'aesthetic' creativity, while at the same time allowing for differences across domains. Eisenman (2010) concluded that incarcerated criminals do not display creativity as a general characteristic, but that they do display it in their area of specialisation (i.e., crime).

An outstanding example of the combination of novelty, relevance, and effectiveness to produce effective novelty (creativity) in a field lying far outside artistic/aesthetic creativity is to be seen in the invention in the 1940s by a major league baseball pitcher named Rip Sewell of the 'eephus pitch', which deviated from all the conventions (i.e., it was novel), lay within the rules of baseball (i.e., it was relevant), and proved almost impossible for batters to hit (i.e., it was effective). For those interested in baseball, the eephus pitch involves throwing the ball in a long slow high loop whose trajectory is judged so well by the pitcher that it drops below shoulder height (necessary for a legal delivery in baseball) just as it reaches the batter. In over 300 major league games Sewell never had a single eephus pitch hit for a home run in a pennant game. Nonetheless, this pitch is unknown to most baseball followers and is scorned as a 'junk ball' among aficionados who have heard of it.

The eephus pitch is reminiscent of the underarm 'grubber' bowled at the Melbourne Cricket Ground by Trevor Chappell in February 1981 as the last delivery of an international cricket match between Australia and New Zealand. Chappell rolled the ball along the ground with a delivery action similar to lawn bowls. This delivery, too, was within the existing rules, novel (previously unknown), relevant (it addressed Australia's problem of preventing New Zealand from scoring a six) and effective (it really did make it impossible for New Zealand to score the runs they needed). Like the eephus pitch, this delivery was regarded as junk (against the spirit of the game) and was subsequently banned. As we will argue later (see Chapter 5), societies regard creativity as in principle good, but only if it remains within tolerable limits.

For the purposes of the present chapter, we take the position that, although it cannot be denied that there are differences among domains in which creativity occurs, such as engineering, advertising, finance, commerce, warfare, fine arts, literature, dance, business, sport, and so on, these do not mean that there are fundamental differences in what is meant by 'creativity'. The basic principle of deliberate introduction of relevant and effective novelty always applies, whether the domain is baseball/cricket or high art. As we will show in the following section, this process also always involves cognitive, personal, motivational, and social aspects, although the precise details of what is meant by 'novelty' and 'usefulness', as well as the details of cognition, personality, motivation, and social aspects may differ across fields; in crime the social field seems to be the world of criminals. As a result, we believe that a broad discussion of creativity based on a parsimonious, relatively unified set of concepts is possible. These are spelled out in following sections.

Where do creative products come from?

Creativity as a system

Treffinger, Sortore, and Cross (1993, p. 556) emphasised the importance of what they called the 'full "ecological system" of creativity'. This involves recognition of interactions among psychological properties of the individual, aspects of the creative process, effects of the situation, characteristics of the task itself and the nature of the desired product. Creativity involves:

- thinking, personality, and motivation (*intra*personal factors);
- interactions with other people (*inter*personal factors);
- supportive or inhibitory aspects of the social and physical environment.

These factors interact to form a system encompassing characteristics of the field in which effective novelty is to be generated, the person, and the environment. Some of these are psychological, others social, some even physical, while they sometimes include aspects of the setting or of the historical age. They even include lucky breaks or other aspects of opportunity. Creativity thus results from this system of interacting factors, some of them located within the individual person, some in the knowledge and skills of the field, and some in the social setting.

Csikszentmihalyi (1999) gave great emphasis to the latter. He described 'acceptance by a particular field of judges' (p. 316) as absolutely essential for a product to count as creative, thus arguing that creativity is essentially a positive category of judgement in the minds of observers, a term they use to praise products that they find exceptionally good. When a number of observers agree that a product is creative, then it is. Csikszentmihalyi called this social definition of effectiveness 'socio-cultural validation'. However, for our purposes it is important to note that socio-cultural validation does not require *universal* approval: if it did, crime would only be creative if everybody approved of it – something which is difficult to imagine. The crucial idea is that only *a particular field of judges* need approve. In the case of crime, this field would presumably consist of criminals and accomplices.

The 6Ps of creativity

In a semantic sense, the term 'creativity' is used in three ways: it refers to (a) a *result* or *output* – for instance, we might say that a person designed some clothing that was very creative; the creativity lies in what came out at the end, the clothing; (b) a *cause* (a cluster of personal characteristics that encourage or enable or even compel people to generate relevant and effective novelty – the designer's personal characteristic of creativity led her to design clothing that people found new and attractive; the creativity resides in the person and causes the creative behaviour); or (c) a *process* through which relevant and effective novelty in the sense discussed above comes into existence (the clothing designer used creative thinking as the mechanism for generating the new ideas for her product range; the creativity lay in the process). Indeed, from early in the modern era psychological researchers have looked at creativity from the point of view of the 'three Ps' (e.g., Barron, 1955): Person, Product, and Process. Rhodes (1961, p. 305) added a fourth 'P' (Press; i.e., the pressure exerted by the environment).

Because it is the visible manifestations of creativity (i.e., Product) that are most obvious to observers, we have already discussed this aspect in some detail. We turn now to the remaining Ps (Process, Person, Press). However, following Cropley and Cropley (2009), we differentiate several aspects of the *Person* to create a framework of 6Ps of creativity: in addition to Product, Process, and Press, Personal *properties*, Personal *motivation*, and Personal *feelings/mood*. This finer distinction among factors relating to the psychology of the individual actor (Person) is necessary because research has shown that the psychological dimensions of the person just listed (personal properties, motivation, feelings/mood) are not freely inter-changeable, but are separate dimensions. They do not relate to creativity in a unitary way, and even affect each other or interact with each other in such a way that different combinations of personal properties, motiv-ation, and feelings/mood have differing consequences for creativity. For instance, Helson (1999) showed that personal properties such as openness and flexibility are only favourable to creativity when they are accompan-ied by motivational states such as tolerance for ambiguity and optimism. When they are accompanied by motivational states such as risk avoid-ance or anxiety the same personal properties (openness, flexibility) hinder creativity.

Because the relationship of Product to what already exists is the key issue in creativity – especially the way in which it deviates from the usual – we will turn first to the environmental factors involved (Press). Subsequently we will examine Process and the three dimensions of Person.

Press (environmental and social factors)
The original discussion of Press by Rhodes (1961) focused on education, and Press was seen as involving the level of support (or lack thereof) for creativity in the classroom provided by the teacher or the facilitatory or inhibitory influence of the classroom climate or atmosphere on creative activities. However, we understand the term somewhat more generally as also referring to both (a) the facilitatory or inhibitory influence of climate or atmosphere on any creative activity, and (b) the reaction of the environ-ment, especially the social environment, to a creative product, that is, not just whether the environment provides helpful conditions or not, but also the nature of the reaction (positive or negative, accepting or rejecting).

The essence of creativity has already been described as involving genera-tion of novelty. This involves doing things differently from the way they are usually done – otherwise there would be no novelty. Looked at from the point of view of the external world, this means that creativity could be seen as *living your own life your own way* (Moustakis, 1977). According to Barron (1969), living your life your own way involves resisting the efforts of the society to impose conformity or, as Burkhardt (1985) put it, fighting against the society's pathological desire for sameness, what Sternberg and Lubart (1995) called 'defying the crowd'.

The idea of creativity as involving deviation from the usual can be looked at in terms of 'norms'. For present purposes, Press can be thought of as involving rules about the behaviour and ways of treating other people that are acceptable in a particular social setting. Norms also specify what kinds of ideas are tolerable and what constitutes a 'good' person. They provide 'filters' (Fromm, 1990) through which behaviours and ideas must pass and carry out constant 'surveillance' (Amabile, Goldfarb, and Brackfield, 1990) in order to detect and deter deviance. Societies are prepared to tolerate breaking the rules to a certain degree, although which rules can be broken or how large a deviation is accepted varies from society to society and from time to time, as well as according to the age, social position, occupation, and other characteristics of the individual doing the rule-breaking. For instance, at a wedding, British or North American societies would tolerate behaviour by a twenty-one-year-old art student that would not be tolerated from the local bank manager, such as dancing naked during the speeches.

It is possible, in fact, to distinguish between socially 'orthodox' effective novelty and socially 'radical' deviation: 'orthodox creativity' involves generating effective novelty while remaining within socially prescribed limits, whereas 'radical creativity' involves venturing into the area of socially frowned-upon ideas or actions. This distinction is similar to Millward and Freeman's (2002) distinction between novelty that stays *within the existing social system* and novelty that *challenges the system*. Radical creativity may be socially unacceptable and even labelled 'cheating', 'mental illness' or, most interesting for the present book, 'crime'. In fact, for practical purposes social acceptability is possibly the core difference between novelty that is lauded as 'creative' and novelty that is condemned as crime. This issue is discussed in more detail in Chapter 6.

Norm-breaking is not identical with crime: to be condemned a product need not break any formal laws, but needs only to depart too sharply from what people are used to. In a study with schoolboy soccer players in Hamburg, Germany, Herrmann (1987) taught his team to make totally unexpected moves, such as passing the ball straight to an opponent with the words, 'Here. Have it if you want it!' Apparently following an intuitive principle along the lines: 'He passed it to me so I should pass it back

to him when he calls', the astonished opponents would then often pass it
back to Herrmann's player once he had moved unchallenged into a highly
favourable position right in front of goal, frequently with a disastrous
result for their own goalie! Although perfectly legal, this novel behaviour caused consternation among opposing players and outbursts of rage
among their coaches, who found it so surprising that they denounced it
as cheating and tried to get it banned. In 1997, after losing a chess match
to the computer program 'Deep Blue', Garry Kasparov complained in the
press that the program had cheated, despite adhering to the formal rules
of chess. Although legal and highly effective (after all, Deep Blue won), in
Kasparov's view, the computer's moves lay outside the boundaries of what
could be expected from a machine (i.e., they were too surprising), and he
claimed that a human being was actually making them.

Process
Numbers of psychologically oriented authors have discussed the creative
process, usually from the point of view of *thinking* that yields creative
products. It was often argued in the past that creativity is mysterious and
unknowable, a divine spark that is beyond human analysis. However,
Guilford (1950) laid the groundwork for a relatively down-to-earth and
systematic way of conceptualising it that has continued to dominate
thinking about creative thinking. He argued that schoolchildren, students, employees, even managers, are one-sidedly trained in the application of their intelligence in a way that leads to maintenance of the status
quo or achievement of change mainly through polishing what already
exists. He called this 'convergent' thinking. Guilford then pointed out
that people are capable of applying their intellect in a different way, which
involves branching out from the given to envisage previously unknown
possibilities and arrive at unexpected or even surprising answers: 'divergent' thinking.

According to Boden (2004), surprise can be achieved through three
basic processes:

- by making unfamiliar combinations of familiar ideas;
- through exploration of ideas;
- through transformation of ideas.

In order to explore, combine, or transform ideas, a person must first of
all be familiar with them, that is, know that they exist – this implies a
link between knowledge and creativity, since the more a person knows the
richer the store of ideas that can be drawn on.

The essence of divergent thinking is cognitive processes like:

- building broad categories;
- crossing boundaries;
- uniting disparate ideas;
- imagining almost anything;
- building unusual chains of associations;
- synthesising apparently unrelated elements of information;
- transforming information in unlikely ways;
- shifting perspective so as to see things in a new light;
- constructing unexpected analogies.

Such processes can be contrasted with sticking to the tried and trusted, playing it safe, looking at the new in terms of the old, putting everything in its proper place and using everything as it was intended to be used, always being right, and so on; these latter processes have already been referred to as involving 'convergent thinking'.[1]

One of the most familiar techniques for promoting appropriate Process in creativity is brainstorming. This is one of many techniques that have been devised over the last half-century to address what is often referred to as *creative problem-solving*. Other techniques that may be familiar include the use of analogies and metaphors, mind-mapping, slip-writing, morphological analysis, and the Delphi technique. While it is tempting to associate only divergent thinking with such methods, it is, in fact, quite normal for them to include both an idea generating (divergent) phase, followed by an evaluative (convergent) phase. This reflects the fact that in moving from creativity as an abstract construct (generation of effective novelty) to creativity as a practical tool for problem-solving, it is necessary both to generate the effective novelty and to *implement* it. Basically, in the wider problem-solving process, convergent thinking is vital! It is a matter of the right process at the right time, as we highlight in the extended phase model outlined below (pp. 83ff.).

Personal properties

Eysenck (1997) speculated that creativity may have little to do with cognitive processes at all, and may be the result of a special *personality* constellation. However, Helson (1996) concluded that there is no single, unitary,

---

[1] We are not suggesting that convergent processes are bad. However, a one-sided insistence on convergent thinking to the exclusion of divergent thinking restricts generation of relevant and effective novelty and thus inhibits creativity, which is disadvantageous in situations where creativity would be helpful.

differentiated personality profile that is typical of all highly creative people and also distinguishes them as a group from the less creative. Nonetheless, this does not negate the idea that certain traits are related to production of effective novelty, either in a positive way (i.e., they facilitate its appearance), or in a negative way (i.e., they inhibit it). Indeed, most writers in the area agree that personality is at least involved in creativity, and various authors have published reviews of the personal characteristics that are of importance. Cropley (2001) listed a number of personal characteristics that earlier research suggests are related to creativity. These include:

- inner-directedness;
- ego strength;
- flexibility;
- tolerance of complexity;
- self-confidence.

Batey and Furnham (2006) reviewed more recent research relating creativity to personality by studying the relationship between creativity and the Big Five components of personality. The relevant literature has been summarised and reviewed recently by Martinsen (2011). However, in a comprehensive review Silvia et al. (2011) showed that the only one of the Big Five dimensions on which there is unanimity about the existence of a link to creativity is openness. Indeed, Cropley (2001) concluded that openness is the core of the creative personality: some people like to go beyond the conventional and enjoy (are open to) the unexpected, whereas others consistently display caution, preferring to stick to the tried and trusted. Personality properties just mentioned such as inner-directedness, flexibility, or self-confidence lead to openness and thus foster creativity.

In keeping with the tendency to regard creativity as always good, the personality traits mentioned to this point all involve admirable characteristics. In fact, some studies have reported that there are also undesirable traits associated with creativity, such as self-centredness, self-justification, lack of concern about others, arrogance, dishonesty, willingness to lie and greater skill at lying, hostility, and even destructiveness (e.g., Nebel, 1988; Silvia et al., 2011; Gino and Ariely, 2012). However, there is some disagreement about these characteristics: for instance, Silvia et al. carried out a highly differentiated analysis in which they were at pains to avoid conflating disagreeableness and hostility, and concluded that low agreeableness has often been mistaken for hostility. They argued that creative people are often not even disagreeable but simply pretentious. Some of these personal characteristics will be examined more closely in Chapter 7 (e.g., Table 7.1, p. 150), because they resemble traits known to be prominent in criminals.

Personal motivation
Studies of famous creative people from the past have confirmed that motivation plays an important role in their achievements (for an overview, see Cropley, 2001). According to Perkins (1981), creativity is the result of, among other things:

- the drive to create order out of chaos;
- willingness to take risks;
- willingness to ask unexpected questions;
- the feeling of being challenged by an area.

For instance, Newton, Copernicus, Galileo, Keppler, and Darwin were marked by tenacity and perseverance. Facaoaru (1985) showed that creative engineers were characterised not only by special intellectual characteristics but also by motivational factors such as determination. Sir Harold Kroto, winner of the Nobel Prize for Chemistry in 1996 for the discovery of the Fullerenes (one example is the spherical fullerene or 'Buckyball', a stable carbon sphere consisting of as many as sixty individual atoms and resembling a soccer ball in shape; another is the cylindrical fullerene, or 'Buckytube', known more commonly as the carbon nanotube), strongly emphasised intrinsic motivation in discussing his own work, while William Phillips, winner of the 1997 Nobel Prize for Physics for development of techniques for cooling and trapping atoms with laser light, was repeatedly described as possessing 'insatiable curiosity'.

Mumford and Moertl (2003) described two case studies of innovation in social systems (management practice and student selection for admission to university) and concluded that both were driven by 'intense dissatisfaction' (p. 262) with the status quo. Einstein's (Miller, 1992) description of how his recognition that existing theories of thermodynamics were inadequate motivated him to develop the special theory of relativity and then the general theory is an example of this phenomenon. Einstein continued to be dissatisfied with his own theory, and worked on it for much of the rest of his life. Gabora and Holmes (2010, p. 280) put this view in a much more striking way by concluding that: 'The painting, novel or technological feat is the tangible evidence left behind of a mind's struggle to resolve a feeling of tension or imbalance.'

Personal feelings/mood

In an overview of research on mood and creativity, Kaufman (2003) showed that mood is a precursor to creativity, accompanies it, and results from it. Akinola and Mendes (2008) examined evidence that negative emotions promote creativity – they mentioned Emily Dickinson and Robert Schumann as famous historical examples. On the basis of a laboratory study (i.e., not the anecdotal evidence of case studies of luminaries from the past), they concluded that at least in artistic domains, when people who are biologically prone to negative affect (such as depression) are exposed to situations that cause extreme negative affect they are most creative. They attribute this to an increase in 'self-reflective thought' (p. 1677) and an increase in perseverance (i.e., to both cognitive and motivational effects of affect). These authors argued that there is a biological link between creativity and depression involving adrenaline metabolism. However, Baas, De Dreu, and Nijstad's (2008) meta-analytic findings showed that mood (feelings) affects creative output in complex ways, and that both negative and positive mood/feelings can enhance or detract from it: for example, hedonically negative moods such as anger or fear can enhance creativity by increasing perseverance, whereas hedonically positive moods encourage flexibility and daring in thinking. Baas et al. (2008) also showed that feelings affect creativity differently according to the way a particular task is conceived of, what they called the 'cognitive framing' of the task. Negative mood enhances performance on tasks that are presented as deadly serious and highly demanding by encouraging concentration, precision, and highly systematic divergent thinking, whereas performance on tasks requiring speculation, taking a chance, and the like is facilitated by positive mood.

The special aspects of process, personal properties, personal motivation, and personal feelings/mood that promote creativity are summarised in Table 3.2. The entries in the right-hand column are not meant to be exhaustive, but merely to give an idea of what is meant by the reference to creativity-facilitating processes, personal properties, personal motives, and personal feelings.

Thus, the stereotypically creative Person is seen as possessing special personal properties such as independence, openness and flexibility, being motivated by curiosity, willingness to take risks or pleasure in uncertainty, and experiencing positive feelings/moods such as optimism in the face of a challenge, satisfaction in doing something differently. Such a person is in a good position to acquire and apply skills such as coming up with the unexpected, seeing things differently from most

Table 3.2 *Creativity-facilitating aspects of Process and Person*

Aspect of creativity	Examples of aspects favourable for creativity
Process	Seeing previously unnoticed problems
	Combining previously unlinked ideas
	Drawing apparently irrational conclusions
	Making broad associations
	Recognising surprising links
	Making unusual suggestions
Personal properties	High ego strength
	Openness
	Acceptance of fantasy
	Independence
	Flexibility
Personal motivation	Curiosity
	Willingness to take risks
	Tolerance of ambiguity
	Being excited by conflicts/contradictions
	Being spurred on by risk/uncertainty
	Having the courage of one's convictions
Personal feelings/mood	Atypical values
	High self-esteem
	Positive feelings in contact with uncertainty
	Feeling of satisfaction upon doing something differently
	Enjoying being challenged

people, or linking ideas not usually regarded as belonging together (Process).

A simple dichotomisation of each of these four areas (personal properties, motivation, feelings/mood, thinking skills) into favourable/unfavourable for creativity (+/-) would yield $2^4 = 16$ possible combinations. These theoretical possibilities are shown in Table 3.3. A plus sign indicates a favourable state for creativity, a minus sign an unfavourable one. This table shows that there are many combinations of circumstances in which people might possess some (or even most) of the characteristics necessary for creativity (although some combinations are harder to imagine than others in practice).

Column 1 depicts a person in whom all four elements are favourably developed, and represents 'fully realised' creativity, Column 2 describes a person in whom the personal properties, thinking skills, and motivation

Table 3.3 *Possible combinations of psychological prerequisites for creativity*

	Possible combinations															
	1	2	3	4	5	6	7	8	9	10	11	12	13	14	15	16
Personal properties	+	+	+	+	–	–	–	–	+	+	+	+	–	–	–	–
Motivation	+	+	+	–	+	+	–	–	–	–	–	+	+	+	–	–
Thinking	+	+	–	+	+	–	+	–	–	+	–	–	+	–	+	–
Feelings	+	–	+	+	+	+	+	+	–	–	+	–	–	–	–	–

are favourable, but the feelings are unfavourable ('stifled' creativity, blocked by negative feelings or mood). In Column 3 the person lacks the ability to get unusual ideas, make atypical links, or explore ideas, despite the desire to be creative, a good feeling about being exposed to novelty, and openness, flexibility, and the like ('frustrated' creativity). The person depicted in Column 4 could be creative but the motivation is missing ('abandoned' creativity). The various incomplete combinations could all be given similar labels. Gabora (2002, p. 170) gave the amusing example of the 'beer-can theory': a person who is good at divergent thinking but lacks the cognitive capacity to organise and control it (i.e., convergent thinking) is like the cans of beer in a six-pack, where all the elements of a whole are present but 'the plastic thingy holding them all together is missing'.

The link between the 6Ps and crime

The link between crime and environmental Press is particularly obvious when Press is looked at in terms of social pressure to conform. In fact, it could be said that creativity and crime are both *based on law-breaking*. The fundamental thing about creativity that makes it creative is the breaking of social laws, norms, or conventions, and the fundamental thing about crime that makes it crime is also the breaking of laws: the difference lies, as we will argue elsewhere (Chapter 7), in the kind of laws that are broken, in the consequences for both the perpetrator and other people, and in the intentions of the perpetrator. It is not our intention to suggest here that crime is simply a matter of being too creative for the majority of the society to accept. However, it is apparent that the social deviation element of generation of novelty (defying the crowd) provides an interface between creativity and crime. It is even sometimes argued (e.g., Brower and Stahl, 2011) that all creativity involves crime or that all creative individuals are criminals, except that some of them are fortunate enough to have their deviant behaviour hailed as creative, whereas with others the behaviour is condemned and sanctioned. The soccer coach mentioned above represents an example of the generation of effective (and perfectly legal novelty) that came close to getting him banned as antisocial.

However, although the reaction of the surrounding environment to deviant behaviour (an aspect of Press) is undoubtedly important, we are arguing in this book that the link between creativity and crime goes well beyond this. The best way to understand creativity overall is to look at it from the point of view of the 6Ps. These help us to understand the role played by various elements in a creative *ecology* involving Product, Person, and Press. As we move into a specific discussion of creativity and resourceful crime, it will become apparent that there are aspects of each of these Ps that are particular to the intersection of creativity and crime. An especially important aspect of this, foreshadowed in Chapter 2, is that there appears to be a particular kind of Person – the resourceful criminal or Perpetrator – who shares many similarities with the creative Person. For this reason we have concluded this chapter by highlighting those creativity-facilitating aspects of Person (or in the case of crime, Perpetrator) and Process which will later (see Chapter 7) form the basis of a comparison of the individualist profile of law-breakers identified in Chapter 2 with that of creatives.

CHAPTER FOUR

The paradoxes of creativity

Creativity is marked by paradoxes: apparently contradictory sets of circumstances that are nonetheless simultaneously true. These include the Process paradox, the Person paradox, the Product paradox and the Press paradox. However, a phase model of creativity helps reconcile the paradoxes: contradictory phenomena are both true, to be sure, but at different points or phases in the generation of effective novelty. They may also apply to different Ps. There are seven phases: Preparation, Activation, Generation, Illumination, Verification, Implementation, and Validation. The generation of relevant and effective novelty can be looked at in terms of forty-two nodes, each node involving a particular P (such as Personal properties or Personal motivation) and a specific phase (examples: Personal properties in the phase of Generation; Personal motivation in the phase of Verification). These nodes require different psychological properties and make different contributions to generating effective novelty. Disruption of only one or two nodes or failure to switch from one node to another when it becomes necessary (oscillation) may be sufficient to block generation of effective novelty. This has implications for the practice of law-enforcement and the training of law-enforcers.

In Chapters 2 and 3 we stressed the importance of psychology in understanding creativity. We drew particular attention to the importance of aspects of the creative Person (or in the context of crime, the criminal Perpetrator) and will develop this analysis further in a later chapter. At this stage, however, it is important to return, for a brief while, to the full set of 6Ps: three aspects of Person, Process, Product, and Press. In particular, we will show in this chapter how Person, Process, and Press influence creativity and the creative Product changes at different points in the generation of effective novelty. If creativity and crime are linked, as we suggest, then understanding what factors are active and how they interact in the generation of a creative product will provide insights into crime and into how to disrupt it.

Bundles of paradoxes

Psychological research (e.g., Csikszentmihalyi, 2006) has shown that conditions like those listed in Table 4.1 (p. 80) are not necessarily universally favourable or unfavourable for the production of creativity – something that is facilitatory under some circumstances may be inhibitory under others. In fact, discussions of creativity are marked by contradictory findings that are nonetheless *simultaneously true*. This led Cropley (1997, p. 8) to label the whole area 'a bundle of paradoxes'. The paradoxes can be examined in terms of the 6Ps outlined in Chapter 3.

Paradoxical processes

Creativity was initially, that is, immediately following Guilford's (1950) seminal paper, regarded as being primarily a matter of divergent thinking. Despite the fact that Guilford did not himself argue for the formula creativity = divergent thinking, this position was widely accepted in the early years. Indeed, some writers implied that the main way of achieving effective novelty is to engage in unfettered thinking and stumble upon something effectively novel more or less by accident (for instance, this interpretation is sometimes made of the flow approach of Csikszentmihalyi, 1996). Sternberg and Davidson (1999, p. 68) referred to the role of 'haphazard recombinations' in creative thinking.

Quite early in the modern era, however, various authors, including Facaoaru (1985) in Europe and Sternberg (1985) in North America, argued that creativity also requires *convergent* thinking such as mastery of the facts, accuracy, strict logic, correct technique, or recognising a good result. In practical settings there are well-known cases of famous producers of Big-C creativity who had to learn standard technical skill before their work was accepted (e.g., Vincent van Gogh). Other authors who emphasised the importance in creativity of convergent thinking include Brophy (1998) and Rickards (1993). Ward and Kolomyts (2010) drew the research findings together and showed that creativity depends upon the interaction of a variety of cognitive factors including not only associative thinking or combining of concepts and images (aspects of divergent thinking) but also processes such as accurate representation and recall of information, or evaluation of candidate solutions and selection of the best (convergent thinking).

Rickards (1999), among others, related this to *metacognition*, which includes monitoring or control of one's own divergent thinking in terms of convergent issues such as practicability, common sense, and the like. Kuszewski (2009) gave particular emphasis to *control*, and used the beer-can analogy mentioned in the previous chapter to illustrate the problem of processing numerous individual elements or pieces of information (as in divergent thinking) without being able to make the necessary structuring linkages, possessing criteria for recognising a good combination or solution, or the ability to comprehend and implement suggestions for change (as in convergent thinking). Without such control, novelty that is generated may be restricted to pseudo-creativity or quasi-creativity.

The situation is similar with regard to knowledge and creativity. Some writers (e.g., Hausman, 1984) have argued that creativity is so novel that it is *unprecedented*, and thus has no connection to anything that went before. However, others such as Bailin (1988) have concluded that creative products are always conceived by both the creative person and external observers in terms of *existing knowledge*. In fact, the Canadian Intellectual Property Office reported (2007) that 90 per cent of new patents are *improvements of existing knowledge*. Scott (1999) listed a number of creativity researchers who all give a prominent place to existing knowledge in creativity (e.g., Albert, Amabile, Campbell, Chi, Feldhusen, Gardner, Gruber, Mednick, Simonton, Wallas, and Weisberg).

We have already mentioned Boden (2004), who made the point that it is impossible to generate effective surprise out of knowledge you do not possess. As Louis Pasteur, the celebrated father of vaccination, put it in a frequently cited aphorism he uttered in a lecture in 1854 (Peterson, 1954, p. 473): 'Chance favours only *the prepared mind*' [italics added]. Despite this, in some ways knowledge is the enemy of creativity: as Jasper (2004, p. 13) put it: 'Too much … may leave you unable to respond flexibly … [but] too little leaves you without routines and resources to deploy.' The contrasting case studies which follow show that while knowledge is indispensable for creativity it can also be a threat to it.

The veterinary pathologist Eugen Semmer (1870) discovered penicillin many years before Alexander Fleming, but did not realise that he had done so. Two horses that were apparently dying from what we would now call 'infections' were admitted to Semmer's clinic in Riga, and he left work in the evening expecting to carry out pathological examinations of the dead horses upon his return next day. However, when he arrived in the morning he discovered that the animals had unexpectedly and inexplicably recovered. Semmer applied his scientific knowledge and mastery of exploratory methods and demonstrated that their recovery was linked to the unintended presence of spores of the fungus *penicillium notatum* in his laboratory. He also confirmed the effects of penicillin by injecting spores into the blood of other animals suffering from infections, and these animals, too, recovered. However, apparently blinded by the narrow nature of his special knowledge (he was a pathologist and was waiting for the horses to die, which meant that their recovery was a nuisance), he did not recognise that he had stumbled on an important life-saver (what we now call 'antibiotics'), and instead went to considerable lengths to eradicate the spores from his laboratory.

This left Alexander Fleming to win the Nobel Prize, seventy years later, for discovering penicillin. It is interesting to note that Fleming also discovered penicillin accidentally when he left infected material in a Petri dish for two weeks in 1928 while he went on holiday, and returned to find that the dish had been invaded by mould, and that the mould had killed the bacteria. As in Semmer's case, the mould consisted of spores of *penicillium notatum*. Fleming also published his results but realised that there might be a possible practical application of his observations and suggested that this be explored, although he did not fully recognise the significance of the mould, and it was left to Howard Florey and colleagues to develop a practical version of what we now call 'penicillin'.

The other side of this paradox is neatly illustrated by events in 1896 (see Nobel Foundation, 1967), when the French physicist, Antoine Henri Becquerel, while studying properties of minerals that had been exposed to the recently discovered X-rays, happened to leave a photographic plate and a container with uranium compounds in it in a drawer of his desk. On opening the drawer some time later, he noticed to his surprise that the photographic plate had fogged, and this unexpected event piqued his curiosity. Instead of throwing the 'ruined' plate away, he began to study it intensively. He eventually concluded that the uranium compounds had emitted some kind of rays similar to X-rays, apparently without any source of energy, and that these unknown rays were responsible for the fogging. He was able to confirm that the mystery rays emanated from the uranium compounds, and that they differed qualitatively from X-rays. After initially being called 'Becquerel rays', the newly discovered phenomenon subsequently became known as 'radioactivity', and earned Becquerel the 1904 Nobel Prize (together with Marie and Pierre Curie).

Had Becquerel not possessed the general knowledge that permitted him to realise that the fogging of the photographic plate was unusual and important, the specific knowledge that told him that some kind of radiation had caused the phenomenon, and the research skills that enabled him to clarify the whole situation, he would not have discovered radioactivity.

In fact, had Becquerel not already been engaged in relevant research, the uranium compounds and the photographic plate would not have found themselves in the drawer together in the first place: thus, Becquerel's knowledge and skills made it possible for him to achieve a creative breakthrough, whereas Semmer's blocked a breakthrough.

The tension between divergent and convergent thinking, and an illustration of how each is an important aspect of the wider process of creativity, is found in engineering design. Modern systems-design processes first attempt to capture the 'requirements' of the system through a set of statements that seek to spell out both *what is needed* (the capability) and *what is not allowed* (constraints) (see, for example, Martin, 1997, p. 44). Together, these statements define the problem space, for which there is always more than one possible design. Divergent thinking then generates possible design solutions that are capable of meeting the need, and convergent thinking rules out those that are not permitted by the constraints. These two forms of requirement statement capture the paradox of engineering design. Successful design requires the ability both to think creatively, and to think analytically. Without the limitations imposed by the constraints, it would be impossible to sift through the broad range of novel solutions to settle on a single, effective design.

The paradoxical personality

Helson (1983) drew attention to the fact that the 'creative' personality seems to be simultaneously stereotypically *masculine* (autonomous, self-confident, tough) and yet also stereotypically *feminine* (sensitive, intuitive, responsible). McMullan (1978) showed that creativity requires possession of a *paradoxical* personality characterised by seven polarities: openness vs drive to close incomplete gestalts; acceptance of unconscious material into consciousness vs maintenance of a strong sense of reality; critical and destructive attitude vs constructive problem-solving; cool neutrality vs passionate engagement; self-centredness vs altruism; self-criticism and self-doubt vs self-confidence; tension and concentration vs relaxedness. Most recently, Csikszentmihalyi (1996) has referred to the importance of a 'complex' personality that combines contradictions such as sensitivity occurring together with toughness, or high intelligence with naivety.

A further paradox arises in the area of motivation: as Kasof, Chen, Himsel, and Greenberger (2007) put it, the discussion involves: 'some researchers claiming negative effects of extrinsic motivation … other researchers claiming positive effects ... and still others reporting mixed effects' (p. 105). According to Amabile (e.g., 1983), creativity is based on intrinsic motivation, the wish to carry out an activity for the sake of the activity itself, and is inhibited by the hope of obtaining external rewards. This latter form of motivation (represented, for instance, by marks on tests) is referred to as 'extrinsic'. She voiced the view that in educational settings extrinsic motivation may be fatal for creativity: it is extremely seductive, and once schoolchildren have been exposed to it they are in danger of shaping their behaviour, and even their thinking, into forms that lead to external rewards such as personal recognition by teachers, praise from parents, or good grades, prizes, and other concrete rewards. More recently, however, researchers, including Amabile herself (e.g., Collins and Amabile, 1998), have accepted that extrinsic motivation is not necessarily fatal to creativity. Indeed, there is evidence that extrinsic motivation, if appropriately applied, can foster creativity (for a review of research, see Eisenberger and Rhoades, 2001). We will also suggest in Chapter 8 that extrinsic motivation may play an important role in some creative crime, especially fraud.

In fact, Unsworth (2001) distinguished four patterns of motivation in creativity. The person can be driven by external pressure to solve problems defined by other people (she called this 'responsive' creativity – the most clearly externally motivated creativity), the person may be motivated by external pressure to solve self-discovered problems ('expected' creativity – a mixed kind of motivation), the person may be self-motivated but the problem may be defined externally ('contributory' creativity – a second pattern of mixed motivation) and, finally, the person may be self-motivated to solve self-defined problems ('proactive' creativity – the most clearly internally motivated form). The crucial point for our purposes here is that all four of these constellations can lead to creativity. Reducing this to a bipolar dimension, we distinguish between 'proactive' motivation at one pole (internal motivation and self-discovered problems) and 'reactive' motivation at the other (external motivation and imposed problems), with various 'mixed' constellations between the poles. Both of these can lead to creativity, and, thus, a further paradox arises.

In his 'triad' model Necka (1986) distinguished five classes of creativity motive: instrumental motives, playful motives, intrinsic motives, control motives, and expressive motives. In contrast to Amabile, he argued that creativity can, for instance, be a means to an end at one point – for example, a person might write a book in the hope of making money (instrumental or extrinsic motivation) – but in the course of writing the person might become aware of the feeling of having an important message that must be expressed, regardless of the consequences (expressive or intrinsic motivation). The idea of a dynamically changing structure of creativity motivation is supported by Gruber and Davis (1988) in their 'evolving systems' approach.

The Press paradox

Press is understood here as involving the social environment into which relevant and effective novelty is introduced. It has already been pointed out that creativity requires doing things differently from the way they are usually done, or even defying the norms of society. Sternberg and Lubart (1995, p. 41) referred to this as 'contrarianism' (although they were writing about giftedness in general and not specifically creativity): in a certain sense, creative people have to be defiant of social norms, even those who do not call attention to themselves through antisocial behaviour. However, as Simonton (1988) and Csikszentmihalyi (1988, 1996) emphasised, a creative product requires 'sociocultural validation'. It must not only be brought into existence, but must also be accepted by other people. As Besemer (2006, p. 171) put it in a down-to-earth way: 'consumers don't like too many surprises'. Thus, creativity must surprise beholders, but not too much.

The paradoxes of creativity are summarised in Table 4.1 (see p. 80). The properties in the left-hand column are those typically associated in popular opinion and also in much of the literature with the idealised image of creativity to be discussed in Chapter 5. By contrast, the properties listed in the right-hand column are not traditionally associated with creativity, but are nonetheless a necessary part of the wider process of generating effective novelty. It is here that the essential nature of the paradoxes becomes apparent. Characteristics in both the left- and right-hand columns of the table are necessary for creativity or at least facilitative of it, despite the fact that they appear contradictory. For instance, conceptualising a situation broadly but also conceptualising it precisely are helpful for creativity. The entries in the table are meant as examples only; they do not constitute an all-inclusive list.

The phases of creativity

How are we to understand these paradoxes? Csikszentmihalyi (2006) argued that contradictory findings result from the fact that the creative

Table 4.1 Examples of paradoxical aspects of the 6Ps of creativity

P	Paradox	
Process	**Divergent thinking** Creativity involves: conceptualising a situation broadly asking unexpected questions making remote associations seeing unexpected links finding problems restructuring problems generating solution criteria communicating a situation to others in a loose and general way	**Convergent thinking** Creativity involves: conceptualising a situation precisely accepting the way a situation is presented reapplying the already known recognising familiar patterns in material working on the problem as presented accepting existing problem definitions working according to existing criteria communicating a situation to others clearly and precisely
Personal properties	**Innovative personality** A creative person is: tolerant of ambiguity flexible independent non-conforming inner-directed open-minded	**Adaptive personality** A creative person is: eager to eliminate ambiguity inclined to do things in known ways eager to win the agreement of others accepting of prevailing norms inclined to go along with others closed-minded
Motivation	**Proactive motivation** A creative person is driven by: the urge to push ahead risk taking low drive for closure drive to seek the new/surprising the urge to generate variety	**Reactive motivation** A creative person is driven by: the urge to cooperate with others risk avoidance drive for rapid closure drive to avoid the new/surprising the urge to get it right

	Generative feelings	Conserving feelings
Feelings	A creative person feels: pleasure in finding a novel solution excitement in the face of uncertainty/a delayed solution optimism when problems arise the desire to do more when successful enjoyment of challenge when unsuccessful	A creative person feels: pleasure in already having an easy solution anxiety in the face of uncertainty/a delayed solution pessimism if problems arise relief and feeling of closure when successful disappointment and discouragement when unsuccessful
	Radical product	**Routine product**
Product	A creative product is: novel elegant seminal germinal	A creative product is: relevant (matches task specification) correct effective
	Radical novelty	**Orthodox novelty**
Social	Creativity: threatens existing social structures shocks or horrifies people	Creativity: remains within existing social structures pleases people

process may include distinct *phases* or different *forms* that draw on *different psychological resources*. The idea of phases is well established in creativity research. In introspective studies in which they reflected upon their own creativity, among others Alexander Bain, Hermann Helmholtz, and Henri Poincaré identified and named stages (see Sawyer et al., 2003). Hadamard (1945), also reflecting on his own creativity in mathematics, identified four phases: preparation, incubation, illumination, and précising. The father of brainstorming, Osborn (1953), also argued for a seven-step creativity process involving orientation (identifying the problem), preparation (gathering relevant data), analysis (breaking it all down into its constituent elements), ideation (collecting a large number of alternative solution possibilities), incubation (letting it all churn), synthesis (putting it all together), and evaluation (judging the value of the result).

An early empirical investigation along these lines was that of Prindle (1906). He studied inventors and concluded that every invention is the result of *a series of small steps*, each step advancing the development of the invention by a small amount by adding something on to what has already been achieved. The gain in one step creates a new jumping-off point for the next step, and so on. Another early empirical study was that of Rossman (1931). He also studied inventors and identified seven steps or phases in the emergence of a workable new idea: problem awareness, problem analysis, survey of information, formulation of solutions, analysis of solutions, invention of a new solution, and testing of new ideas.

The classical phase model, first introduced into creativity research about ninety years ago by Wallas (1926), is more general than a small-step, incremental approach. Of central importance for the present discussion is that it sees the differences between phases in the production of a creative product as not simply *quantitative* (for instance, step-by-step increases in *amount* of knowledge), but as *qualitative* (involving different *kinds* of operation). Initially, Wallas (1926) suggested that there were seven phases: Encounter (a problem or challenge is identified), Preparation (information is gathered), Concentration (an effort is made to solve the problem), Incubation (ideas churn in the person's head), Illumination (what seems to be a solution becomes apparent), Verification (the individual checks out the apparent solution), and Persuasion (the individual attempts to convince others that the product really does solve the problem).

The extended phase model

In modern discussions it has become customary to reduce the Wallas model to four phases: Preparation, Incubation, Illumination, and Verification. Indeed, it would be possible to reduce creativity to one step, but this would lose the detail of how the paradoxes can facilitate or inhibit the process. Four stages, while simpler and more compact than the seven identified by people like Osborn, risks masking the effects of some of the paradoxes. To understand the manner in which each paradox facilitates or inhibits creativity, it is necessary to use a more differentiated description of the process, and we will do this by returning to a seven-phase model. At the very beginning, Preparation must be sub-divided into Preparation (familiarity with a field is acquired – it is impossible to generate effective novelty in a field about which you know nothing, except perhaps through a lucky fluke), and Activation (problem awareness develops). Brown (1989) reviewed the extensive discussion of the importance for creativity of becoming aware of problems (i.e., Activation), including Guilford's emphasis on 'sensitivity to problems' in the original modern discussion (Guilford, 1950, p. 449). Other researchers such as Miller (1992) and Mumford and Moertl (2003) have also discussed the role in creativity of dissatisfaction with the status quo. One of history's most prolific inventors, Edison, was never satisfied with his invention of, for instance, the incandescent light bulb, and over the course of time took out more than a hundred patents on improvements to it.

Wallas's description of Incubation is also problematic. It seems intuitively clear that some kind of processing of information is necessary in creativity, whether this is done sequentially or in a churning mish-mash. However, in reviewing a number of relevant studies Howe, McWilliam, and Cross (2005) showed that many researchers deny that this involves working through ideas until something good suddenly pops up. They emphasised heuristic processes such as set-breaking or construction of neural networks. Simonton (2007, p. 329) contrasted 'Darwinian' or non-monotonic processes (blind variation and selective retention leading to sudden jumps – like an incubated chicken emerging as a fully formed, if immature, bird) with monotonic processes (step-by-step improvement based on, for instance, systematic and sequential application of expertise to a series of intermediate products, each of which is closer to the final product than the previous one). Our purpose here, however, is not to define the precise nature of creative thought, but to emphasise that some

kind of mental review of information (however this occurs) is one element of the process. Thus, we refer to Generation, which may involve
both non-monotonic and monotonic processes (i.e., it is more general
than Incubation in Wallas's sense).

In the case of functional creativity (see Chapter 3) in particular – creativity that achieves some effect in the external world – Wallas's stages do
not go far enough. More is needed than simply arriving at a solution and
checking that it works. The results of the generation of a creative product
must be manifested, utilised, or exploited in some way. In the case of business this involves developing and marketing or implementing a product or
process, and is usually referred to as involving 'innovation'. Consequently,
Cropley and Cropley (2012) proposed two further phases covering
exploitation of a creative product: at the end come Communication
(after Verification the result of the creative process is made public), and
Validation (the final phase in which the external environment responds to
the product of which it has been made aware through communication).

Dasgupta (2004, p. 406) summarised the need for Communication
very aptly: 'To be judged creative, a product must reach a sufficient
state of maturity or completeness to be manifested publicly.' Of course,
Communication involves very different tools, skills, and products in different fields, such as physics or art. Dasgupta gave concrete examples of
what public manifestation involves: in the case of a scientist it might be
a series of papers in which experiments are written up, in technology it
might be a set of plans or an artefact, and in literature a novel or poem.
Even schoolchildren publicly manifest the results of their efforts, for
instance, in artworks, performances in drama, music, and the like, but
also in project reports, effectively surprising solutions in maths, essays in
English, or even simply in unexpected questions or answers to teachers'
questions.

As Csikszentmihalyi (e.g., 1999) has stated strongly, such products only
achieve the status of creativity when they are judged by external authorities to involve effective surprise (not, for instance, ignorance, tomfoolery,
or deliberate disruptiveness). In other words, not only is Communication
necessary, but the approval of others too: we call this final step Validation.
We have suggested elsewhere (e.g., Cropley and Cropley, 2008) what we
call a 'universal aesthetic of creativity' – a set of criteria for validating products of any kind in any domain, including crime.

When applied to crime, Communication and Validation have a somewhat different quality from what they involve in the case of, for instance,
industrial innovation. For criminals, Communication involves carrying

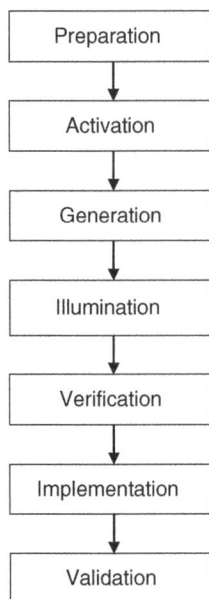

Figure 4.1 Phases of creativity

out some kind of criminal activity. Thus, the label 'Communication' does not seem to get at the essence of this phase in crime, and in this context we prefer Implementation: the putting into practice of actions conceived and planned in earlier phases. 'Validation' may also seem to be an ambivalent term in the present context, as it may seem to imply only approval. What we mean by Validation is that the product, when implemented, proves its worth in its own milieu by being not only novel but also *effective* and possibly elegant and generic. In the case of crime, Validation would involve not, let us say, the successful acquisition of a patent or the acceptance of a painting for exhibition in the Tate Gallery, but successful acquisition of ill-gotten gains or avoidance of apprehension (i.e., 'valid' criminal creativity yields profit or causes havoc and can be carried out without detection and punishment). These considerations yield an extended model of generation of effective novelty involving seven phases. This is summarised in Figure 4.1.

Although it may not be a literal description of the way creative products are generated in real life, the phase model offers a helpful way of looking at the production of effective novelty, and emphasises that it is a *process*, rather than an event, and involves qualitatively different steps. A danger with such an approach is that it may become too simplistic, implying, for instance, a set of discrete, logical steps that can be repeated in sequence in a mechanical manner. It is important to note that in practice the process of production of an effectively novel product can be broken off in any phase, for instance, when the phase fails to yield the raw material needed for the next phase. If Generation yielded nothing, for instance, there could not be an Illumination, while without Illumination nothing could be subjected to Verification. Without Preparation (heavily dependent upon acquisition of knowledge), the process would not even begin.

On the other hand, the process can begin part way through, for instance, when longstanding knowledge is used as the raw material for Generation. The phases can also interact with each other. For instance, additional information gathered in the phase of Verification could return the whole process to the Preparation phase, leading to a new Illumination, and so on. This interaction among the phases has been described in greater detail by Shaw (1989), who referred to 'loops', giving each loop a name: to take several examples, the Arieti-loop involves the interaction between Preparation and Generation, the Vinacke-loop that between Generation and Illumination, and the Lalas-loop links Illumination and Verification.

The phases do not necessarily form a lock-step progression of completely distinct stages. There may well be interactions, false starts, restarts, early break-offs, and the like. Haner (2005, p. 289) summarised the relevant literature as showing that the phases of creativity are 'iterative and non-sequential', and occur in a recurring 'nonlinear cycle'. Writing from the point of view of organisational psychology, Gupta, Smith, and Shalley (2006, p. 693) contrasted sequential or lock-step generation of effective novelty, which they called 'punctuated equilibrium', with non-linear development, which they labelled 'institutional ambidexterity'.

An example of the complex looping that may be involved is to be seen in the work of Evariste Galois, the developer of group theory in mathematics, nowadays known as 'Galois theory'. In 1832, the Frenchman was killed at the age of 20 in a duel so uneven that he knew that he was doomed (see Rothman, 1982, for a description of Galois's life and death). The young man left a body of mathematical writings on which he worked even on the night before his death (i.e., he went to great lengths to try to *implement* the results of his work – his level of Activation was high). Because of the obvious importance that he had attached to them, after his death these writings were examined and the ideas in them pronounced to be worthless (Validation was negative). They were judged to be novel, to be sure, but Galois had not successfully shown how they could be implemented. He himself was aware of this, as he indicated in his notes that more detail was needed to flesh out his arguments – unfortunately, he did not have time to do this.

It was only after the passage of several years, during which mathematics advanced enough for the importance of Galois's work to become apparent, that their creativity was recognised. In other words, it was only after the external world was well enough *prepared* and had reached a sufficient level of problem awareness (Activation) that Validation was positive. Not only may the phases of Illumination and Verification, on the one hand, and Implementation and, finally, Validation, on the other, be separated by years, and the process re-started with a return to Preparation and Activation, but the crucial new Preparation and Activation may be carried out by people different from the original creative individual.

Interactions among the 6Ps

It is now possible to map areas in which paradoxes are apparent (Process, Personal properties, Personal motivation, Personal mood/feelings, and Press from the environment) onto the phases. This is done in Table 4.2 (see p. 88). It is important to note that the 'central processes', 'core results', and 'key factors' are not intended to be seen as unique to a particular phase.

For instance, although establishing a knowledge base may occur in any phase, it is the chief business of the phase of Preparation, and is thus a core result of this phase. Similarly, solution criteria may be worked out or elaborated in various phases, but they are at the heart of the phase of Activation, and are thus core results of this phase. Tolerance of errors may well be an important aspect of the social environment in all phases, but it is vital in the phase of Generation, and is thus of central importance here. The entries in each cell are examples only; sheer space makes an exhaustive list impossible.

As the table shows in, let us say, the phase of Preparation, acquisition of knowledge via convergent thinking is of central importance, whereas in the phase of Activation, where problem awareness develops, divergent thinking is crucial. To turn to the phase of Generation, major motivational elements are risk taking and absence of drive for closure (closely linked to intrinsic motivation), whereas in the phase of Implementation motives such as desire for recognition or hope of reward are important – these are linked to extrinsic motivation. Similarly, in the personality

Table 4.2 *Core elements of creativity in different phases*

Phase	Core result (Product)	Central Process	Key motivation	Key Personal properties	Most important Press
Preparation	A knowledge base is established	Perceiving facts, learning, remembering (convergent thinking)	Willingness to take over information provided by others (mainly extrinsic)	Diligence Acceptance of authority	Guidance on core information Resources for acquiring information Incentives for acquiring information
Activation	Problems are identified Goals are defined Solution criteria are established	Divergent thinking	Curiosity Dissatisfaction with the status quo Desire to find solutions (mainly intrinsic)	Openness Rebelliousness (non-conformity)	Open goals/ open-ended tasks Non-authoritarian leadership
Generation	One or more candidate solutions are generated	Boundaries are broken Remote associations are made Existing ideas are extended (divergent thinking)	Risk taking Delay of closure Willingness to work under conditions of uncertainty	Tolerance for ambiguity Flexibility	Tolerance of errors Withholding of judgement Rewards for novelty, not just correctness

Illumination	A solution that the person recognises as promising emerges	Convergent thinking	Willingness to back one's own judgement	Intuitiveness Openness to the new Self-confidence	Support of even 'odd-ball' ideas Protection of the person who is 'different'
Verification	The solution above is explored by the individual and judged to be appropriate (or not)	The novel configuration is evaluated. If necessary further steps are identified (Convergent thinking)	Drive for closure Drive for accuracy	Self-critical attitude Objectivity Persistence	Provision of realistic, differentiated feedback on both novelty and effectiveness
Implementation	Appropriate judges become aware of the proposed solution	The apparent solution is made available to other people	Desire for recognition Hope of reward (Extrinsic)	Courage Communication skills Commitment to a solution	Openness to novelty Protection from excessive criticism Support in presenting novelty
Validation	A novel product that appropriate judges accept (or reject)	Appropriate judges evaluate the novelty	Willingness to accept the judgement of others	Toughness	Provision of objective and differentiated feedback

domain flexibility is necessary in the phase of Generation, sensitivity in the phase of Illumination, whereas the apparent opposite of flexibility (commitment to a particular solution) is necessary in the phase of Implementation, and the apparent opposite of sensitivity (toughness) in the phase of Validation. Tolerance for ambiguity is necessary in the stage of Generation, the opposite (desire for closure) in the phase of Verification. The crucial idea here is that both poles of the continua sketched out in Table 4.1 on p. 80 (divergent vs convergent thinking, extrinsic vs intrinsic motivation, sensitivity vs toughness, tolerance for ambiguity vs desire for closure, to give a few examples) are needed for production of effective novelty (hence the apparent contradictions), but not necessarily at the same moment (phase) in the process; the creative person may alternate between poles such as those just listed, according to the demands of the particular phase of the process of production of effective novelty, showing, let us say, willingness to take risks in one phase (especially Generation), drive for accuracy and closure in another (especially Verification). In early research, Hudson (1968) showed that people with a marked preference for convergence nonetheless displayed high levels of creativity in some situations. Facaoaru (1985) showed that engineers rated as creative by colleagues showed properties from both poles of the paradoxes. According to Koberg and Bagnall (1991, p. 38) this involves moving between 'alternating psycho-behavioral waves'. As Csikszentmihalyi (1996, p. 47) put it, they *combine* 'tendencies of thought and action that in most people are segregated'. Martindale (1989, p. 228) described this moving backwards and forwards from one pole of a paradox to the other in the course of generation and exploitation of effective novelty as 'oscillation'. In cricket-playing countries, such people are described in everyday language as 'all-rounders', while in baseball terms until recently they might have been known as 'switch-hitters'.

Practical implications of the paradoxes

An important implication of the paradoxes of creativity is that the generation of relevant and effective novelty is more complex than might have been imagined. It consists not of a single bolt from the blue, nor of a lucky break, nor even of careful planning of the implementation of divergent ideas, but of successful negotiation of a large number of 'nodes'. Each cell in Table 4.2 (p. 88) represents a node; for instance,

Process in the phase of Activation (Process/Activation) or Personal properties in the phase of Generation (Personal properties/Generation), and so on. In order to be effective in the generation of novelty that successfully achieves a desired effect (i.e., is relevant and effective) the creative individual has to negotiate a thicket of apparently conflicting requirements from node to node, or, as we express it, to deal with 'paradoxical' requirements. Some of these involve ignoring, defying or violating societal Press, and this can be a tricky problem for the creative individual, especially the one who is interested in profiting (legally or illegally) from his or her creativity.

The stereotype of the defiant creative individual is a familiar one: such a person cannot fit in or conform (good in some nodes, disastrous in others), and may live a chaotic even unsavoury life marked by conflict with the establishment, damaged personal relationships, wild living, perhaps drug, alcohol, or sexual excesses – lack of 'control' – and may justify this as a necessary accompaniment to creativity. Indeed, a certain amount of contrariness is highly desirable, but only in the appropriate node (e.g., Personal properties/Activation, Personal motivation/Generation, where it would favour generation of novelty). However, as Gamman and Raein (2010) pointed out, a substantial number of creative individuals are interested in making a living from their creativity, which requires what they called 'taking ideas to market' (p. 161). Thus, they must not only generate novelty and identify good solutions, but must also present the novelty to the external world (Implementation) and gain recognition (positive Validation). This means that they are involved in 'functional' creativity (see Chapter 3, pp. 52–54), not just purely 'aesthetic' creativity (Cropley and Cropley, 2005).

The Phases of Implementation and Validation are of great importance for functional creativity, such that it is necessary to operate effectively in nodes such as Process/Implementation or Motivation/Validation, which are central to taking ideas to market and coping with Press. Contrarian characteristics such as those mentioned above (chaotic lifestyle, conflict with authority, poor personal relationships, substance abuse) are disastrous in this phase, because they would, for instance, impede making the results of creativity accessible to other people in an understandable and tolerable way (Implementation) or accepting and profiting from feedback from such people (Validation). In other words, creative individuals need to be capable of being contrarian in nodes where it is advantageous, but also of 'alternating' (Koberg and Bagnall, 1991, p. 38) or 'oscillating'

(Martindale (1989, p. 228) and switching to other properties such as good communication skills, orderliness and plausibility in others, especially in nodes connected with Implementation and Validation. This requires meta-cognitive skills such as recognising when it is appropriate or necessary to switch nodes, knowing how to do this, or judging the effectiveness of a switch.

The resourceful criminals on whom this book focuses are also generally interested in functional creativity, not aesthetic creativity (i.e., they wish to bring their efforts to market and profit from them), so that it is important for them to successfully carry out all phases from Information to Validation (functional creativity). The node approach suggests, however, that various phases can be disrupted by failure in perhaps as few as one of the nodes. For instance, the criminal who does not acquire the requisite knowledge in the node of Preparation/Process or fails to display persistence in the node Verification/Perpetrator properties is unlikely to generate effectively novel crime, even if some other nodes are well mastered (e.g., boundary breaking in Generation/Process, courage in Implementation/ Perpetrator properties). This has implications for working out methods of opposing crime: for instance, it may not be necessary to disrupt the process of the emergence of an effectively novel piece of crime at every point, or even at an early stage. Disruption of a single node may conceivably suffice. Furthermore, the nature of effective disruptive actions by law-enforcers may be different in different phases. It is also quite possible that effective disruptive actions focused on specific phases may be quite different from typical law-enforcement activities (taking down details after a crime has occurred, investigation, apprehension and punishment of guilty parties).

The Committee on Science and Technology for Countering Terrorism (CSTCT) and Wilks and Zimbelman (2004) called for adoption of novel procedures for opposing crime (see Chapter 1, p. 9). Moving between alternating psycho-behavioural waves or combining tendencies of thought (oscillation or alternation) may be needed for law-enforcers to be more creative in identifying threats and devising responses capable of frustrating them, as called for by the CSTCT. However, this may be especially difficult for law-enforcers, who are committed to one way of looking at things as a result of a range of factors discussed in Chapter 10, such as police personality (preference for repeating the same procedures, unwillingness to take risks, lack of flexibility) or the law-enforcement environment (error-avoidance, protection of the rights of criminals, respect for privacy).

Creativity theory thus suggests that acknowledgement of the existence of oscillation and understanding of what it involves, plus instruction in how to oscillate while remaining within the special limits to which law-enforcers are subject, should be an element of police training. This is one of the issues discussed in Chapter 10.

CHAPTER FIVE

General enchantment with creativity

Creativity is often treated as inherently good, for instance, by definition, because it is a principle of nature underlying all growth and regeneration, or because it is inextricably linked to generation of beauty. It is also seen as good because it is spiritually good for the individual or for the society, for instance, by promoting psychological wellbeing or social cohesiveness. Finally, it is regarded as good because it has valuable concrete effects such as improving quality of life, generating new jobs, increasing prosperity, improving health care or other similar aspects of life. However, the general positive attitude to creativity raises problems; for instance, the public may be ambivalent about some crime because it has a creative component and thus be unwilling to support counter-measures, which are almost seen as spoil-sport. Nonetheless, there seems to be a threshold of badness beyond which the creative aspect of crime can no longer compensate for its degree of evil: this would explain why, for instance, the World Trade Center attack was almost universally excoriated, despite its novelty and effectiveness.

We have discussed social sciences and crime, and have shown that psychology, and especially its analysis of the role of the Perpetrator, plays an important role in understanding crime. We have discussed creativity, and seen, among other things, that the role of the Person is also extremely important in creativity; and, indeed, it appears that people who generate positive creativity share many traits in common with creative criminals, people we have dubbed 'resourceful criminals'. Before we can explore this phenomenon more fully, however, we need to explore some conceptual hurdles in the field of creativity that limit our ability to link it with crime. We characterise the hurdle as involving a general enchantment with creativity. In this chapter we will explore this hurdle, and in the following chapter we will then develop a conceptual 'crane' that helps lift our thinking and expand our understanding. It will be no surprise that this conceptual crane will be the idea that creativity has a dark side.

Failure to consider the negative dimension of creativity

Kampylis and Valtanen (2010) reviewed 42 modern definitions of creativity and no fewer than 120 terms typically associated with creativity (collocations), and concluded that the vast majority of definitions do not take any account whatsoever of the positive/negative dimension, while collocations are rarely negative.[1] In fact, one of the most striking things about discussions of creativity is that it is almost universally regarded as good. As the Nobel Prize winner Herbert Simon (1990, p. 11) put it: 'Creativity is thinking. It just happens to be thinking we think is *great*' (emphasis added).

This assumed goodness has two aspects:

1. Creativity is simply good and no reason need be given, or
2. Creativity is good because it delivers benefits.

The almost universal attribution of goodness to creativity will be examined in more detail in this chapter. However, the purpose of the chapter is not to evaluate, support, or reject any particular view of creativity or to argue that particular good aspects of creativity identified by various writers really do or do not exist, but to draw attention to the views that have been expressed in the relevant literature and the beliefs that exist about creativity's inherently benign nature. It is people's convictions about creativity that are important for the purposes of this chapter. Thus, when, let us say, Maslow's view of creativity is briefly described our purpose is not to debate whether he was right or wrong but to present his basic ideas as an example of a view of the value of creativity for the individual that is well known and widely accepted.

The bright side of creativity

Creativity is good by definition

Some writers have argued that by semantic definition the term 'creativity' refers exclusively to things that are good: actions, processes, personal

---

[1] This situation has changed somewhat in the last few years as greater attention has been paid to the dark side of creativity. A well-known negative collocation in everyday use would be the term 'creative accounting'. More recent (but relatively uncommon) negative collocations in scholarly discussions include 'negative creativity' (James, Clark, and Cropanzano, 1999), 'malevolent creativity' (Cropley, Kaufman, and Cropley, 2008), and 'cantankerous creativity' (Silvia, Kaufman, Reiter-Palmon, and Wigert, 2011).

properties, motives, feelings, or products must have a benevolent component or the label 'creative' simply cannot be applied to them, any more
than the label 'apple' can be applied to an orange, except in a poetic,
metaphorical, ironic, or just plain erroneous way. Sternberg (2010), for
instance, argued that generation of relevant and effective novelty only
involves creativity if the novelty is aimed at promoting the common good.
Otherwise it involves no more than production of variability and is thus
no more than pseudo-creativity in the sense outlined in Chapter 3. Eastern
conceptions of creativity often include goodness as a prerequisite. To be
regarded as creative a person must display moral goodness and harmony,
and the person's actions must benefit society (e.g., Chan, 2011). McCann
(2005) drew attention to the fact that among indigenous Australians, as
is also the case with the Maori people of New Zealand, First Nations in
Canada and Native Americans, creativity implies benefitting other members of the community.

Even among commentators who adopt a less lofty view, the terms 'creativity' or 'creative' have been automatically associated with the good, and
have become terms of praise. We have already referred to Henning (2005),
according to whom creativity is based on 'integrity, sincerity and trustworthiness', and is aimed at fostering 'beauty', 'self-respect', 'love', 'peace',
and 'education'. This idea is also to be seen in Csikszentmihalyi's (e.g.,
1999) systems view of creativity, according to which experts in a field use
the term to refer to things they regard as exceptionally good and worthy
of admission to the canons of the field. As McIntyre (2006, p. 202) put
it, a creative product constitutes 'a *valued* addition to the store of human
knowledge' (emphasis added). Creativity is also sometimes seen as so good
that it is able to compensate for other shortcomings, such as in an expression like: 'It looks terrible but it is very creative!' An example of this is
perhaps the dissertation of the later-famous French mathematician Henri
Poincaré, which became increasingly chaotic and unintelligible after the
first twenty pages but was passed by examiners anyway, on the grounds
that it was highly creative

The crucial point here is that Poincaré's examiners made the implicit
assumption that creativity is a symptom of 'goodness'. Therefore, they
concluded, whether consciously or not, that, 'The thesis is creative, and
creativity is always good, therefore Poincaré's thesis must be good (and
should pass)', and not, for example, that Poincaré was crazy (and in the
case of Poincaré they were undoubtedly right). In fact, this is an example
of a deductive argument in logic (All men are mortal, Socrates is a man.
Therefore Socrates is mortal); however, we would do well to remember

that the conclusion in deductive logic is only true if the premises are true. Our point is that the premise in Poincaré's case – that creativity is always good – is open to question, and may in fact be false. If that is the case, then the conclusion drawn may be false. Of course, hindsight tells us that we are being grossly unfair to Poincaré in this case, and yet the point still stands. The assumption that creativity is universally good can lead us to draw conclusions that are false.

An important issue here is the possible conflation of 'creativity' and 'creative acts' (i.e., treating mere participation in any activity usually acknowledged as creative – such as story writing or daubing paint on canvas – as 'being creative' and regarding any product of such activity as 'creative'). At best this involves confusing Process with Product, and even this only occurs when the act labelled 'creative' really does involve generation of at least some effective novelty. Writing stereotyped stories or picking aimlessly at the keys of a piano do not involve creativity, even though writing and music are regarded as creative activities and the stories and sounds being referred to only recently came into existence. This is possibly summed up as: 'All artistic activity is creative. All artistic endeavour is good. Therefore all creativity is good.' The problem seems to be that 'creativity' in this sense means 'production of anything at all' and not 'production of effective novelty'. Using the former definition, producing anything, no matter how routine, ineffective, inelegant, or lacking in genesis, is a creative act and therefore involves creativity.

A counter-example to the Poincaré dissertation is to be seen in a more recent dissertation in the area of fine art for which one of the present authors was external examiner: after a brief text of two or three pages, the dissertation consisted of exactly the same picture, identical with absolutely no change, repeated fifty times from page to page, with no explanatory text or anything else on the pages or between them. There were then a few closing sentences, explaining that people viewing the fifty consecutive presentations of the same picture would begin to see it differently by the twentieth or thirtieth repetition (for instance, as boredom set in), and that this would prove without any need for explanation by the doctoral candidate that creative works are dependent upon the perceptual processes and the moods of the viewer. The art professors were astonished by the daring and unconventionality of this work and judged it to be highly creative and therefore to constitute a brilliant academic contribution, and the dissertation was passed (with one dissenting vote). This seems to be an example of how 'creativity' is misappropriated to mean nothing more than 'engaging in artistic activities, i.e. the creative arts' or even as simply doing something unexpected (pseudo-creativity, as we expressed it earlier). Scales such as Besemer and O'Quin's (1999) *Creative Product Semantic Scale* or Cropley and Cropley's (2008, 2010a) *Creative Solution Diagnosis Scale* offer ways of assessing in a relatively objective way the extent to which such products really are creative.

Creativity fosters beauty

Creativity is also often regarded as being more or less synonymous with beauty: over the centuries, painters, sculptors, poets, musicians, writers, actors, and other workers in similar areas, as well as critics and scholars, have frequently discussed creativity from an aesthetic point of view, mainly focusing on works of art. Just how people make aesthetic judgements is the subject of discussion. The perceptionist view is that such judgements are directly determined by the properties of the object, event, or experience, which enter the brain as sensory stimuli. Thus, according to a pure perceptionist model, a sound that hurt a listener's ears would be adjudged not beautiful, since it is an unpleasant sensation. James Mill (1829) extended this by arguing that it is not necessarily the direct effects of the object on the sensory apparatus that determine whether it is adjudged beautiful or not, but the associations the stimulus activates in the perceiver's mind. However, the aesthetic properties of a stimulus are regarded as inherent in the stimulus itself.

The contrasting view to perceptionism is the cognitive argument that aesthetic judgements are a construction in the mind of the beholder. Certain properties activate previously learned aesthetics stored in the mind of the beholder, and an object or experience is classified and evaluated according to these schemata. The beholder thus infers that something is beautiful or not on the basis of learned categories of pleasingness/displeasingness. To take an example, the cognitive approach argues that an intrinsically unpleasant sound such as atonal music might not be regarded as ugly but as beautiful by a beholder who had learned that this particular sound is beautiful, for instance, through training and experience in a particular culture at a particular time, say, by studying music.

The cognitive schemata according to which aesthetic judgements are made contain the stored results of the beholder's earlier experience and training, and are thus dependent upon the particular experience of the individual (i.e., they are subjective) as well as upon what the particular society has taught the individual is aesthetically pleasing or displeasing through formal training or life experience in the culture or a combination of both (i.e., they are relativistic). This suggests, among other things, that expert observers may judge an object differently from inexperienced ones, for instance, because the experts have been trained to see beauty in objects the inexperienced typically find ugly or repulsive, or to recognise and focus on aspects of objects that are not apparent to untrained observers such as transformation of traditional materials or accordance with a particular school or style. When the painting *Woman in a Landscape* by Russell Drysdale was awarded a major art prize in Australia in 1949 experts hailed it as a great work, whereas newspapers printed numerous letters from non-expert readers saying that it was too ugly even to be regarded as creative.[2]

The link between creativity and beauty has been extended to non-artistic domains. Zuo (1998), for instance, concluded that creative problem-solving involves finding *beautiful* problems and *beautiful* solutions, through the application of 'aesthetic sensibility'. On the basis of case studies of well-known creative individuals such as Albert Einstein and Charles Darwin, Zuo argued that it is aesthetic considerations that guide creative problem solvers to a solution; the nascent solution is so beautiful that the creators' 'aesthetic awareness' tells them that it must be right. To take another example, Kay (1996) concluded that creative people are driven to move from less beautiful to more beautiful understandings of the world. At the very least, creativity is seen as inextricably tied in with beauty.

There is evidence that the level of agreement on aesthetic judgements among beholders increases with age, apparently as the result of increased use of cognitive judgements with increasing cognitive maturity (as against reacting directly to the raw sensory stimulus, as a small child would) and of the homogenisation of cognitive schemata within a group such as a society or social class as a result of shared experience in a similar environment. This phenomenon suggests that people from different social backgrounds (including cultures) are likely to have different

---

[2] Indeed, the whole issue of expertise in relation to the judgement of creativity is an open question in psychological research. Researchers such as Amabile (e.g., Hennessey and Amabile, 1999) or, more recently, Kaufman and Baer (2012) suggest that experts do indeed judge creativity differently from novices, while Cropley and Cropley (2010a) and Cropley, Kaufman, and Cropley (2011) have explored the possibility that lack of expertise can, at least to some degree, be overcome with the use of appropriate rating scales.

(learned) ideas of what is beautiful and thus, through the conflating of beauty and creativity, of whether a particular object or course of action is creative.

The tendency to regard things labelled 'creative' as beautiful and vice versa and the tendency to regard anything that is creative as good raises special problems in the area of creativity and crime, which will be discussed below. Put briefly, it is difficult for people to define the same object, action, process, or procedure as simultaneously beautiful (creative) and ugly (criminal). This may result in people being ambivalent about crime that involves a high level of novelty generation or that reveals personal properties, motives, attitudes, and the like resembling those described in Chapter 3 as 'creative': being 'soft on crime', in fact.

Creativity encapsulates the essence of humanity

Early in the modern creativity era, some writers adopted a metaphysical view of creativity, seeing it as a primal force of nature underlying growth and rebuilding in all organic systems, and thus automatically good. Henning (2005) referred to it as 'the *dynamic process* of the universe' (emphasis added). According to Maslow (1973), creativity is part of a natural, built-in tendency of human beings to seek self-actualisation. According to May (1976), it gives them the courage to deal with uncertainty and alienation in their lives. Grayling (2003) summarised the philosophy of Camus and Sartre as involving four ways human beings can give meaning to human life, which they saw as inherently meaningless and absurd. One of these was creativity.

Toynbee (1962) described creativity as the fundamental resource available to human beings that leads to social progress and the improvement of life. Bruner (1962) saw it as the last bastion of the truly human in a world where intelligent machines are taking over thinking and reasoning, even design and innovation. The importance of creativity in this regard (preventing a takeover of human life by technology, especially information technology) was vividly stated by Rorty (1979, p. 351), who argued along the lines that if creativity dried up, society would stop developing and 'ubiquitous technocratic totalitarianism' would lead to all societies becoming drab identical copies of each other. He referred dramatically and strikingly to the problem of a world without creativity as involving the '*non*human world which squirms out of our conceptual net'.

Creativity is of divine origin

Some thinkers have even elevated creativity to the level of the godlike or divine. Nietzsche (1968, p. 428) argued that creativity involves '*deification of existence*' (emphasis added), while very early in the modern creativity era, Gammel (1946) emphasised that for many people creativity functions as the new way of finding spiritual solace in an imperfect world. For some, it seems to have what McLaren (1993) called a 'quasi-religious function' (p. 139). Apart from creativity's divine function, many writers have reported that the actual contents of creative ideas are of divine origin. For instance, they were attributed by Plato to the muses or some other 'divine influence' (McLaren, 1993, p. 137, citing Plato), or to the action of 'some divine principle' (McLaren, 1993, p. 137, citing Tsanoff). According to McIntyre and McIntyre (2007, p. 15), Henry Miller believed that the ideas for his writing came directly from the 'celestial recording room', and Ray Bradbury reported that he received 'lighting strikes' from on high that had to be written down immediately. Probably the best known modern popular exponent of the divine origins approach to creativity is Cameron (e.g., 2002). She asserts that creativity comes from God and emphasises the importance of 'spiritual electricity'.

Cameron (2002) and other writers who emphasise the divine origin of creativity seem to adopt the position that no effort is required for creativity, no phase of Information or of Evaluation, but simply being open for gifts from on high. Indeed, there are historical anecdotes that seem to support this position: Henri Poincaré, the French mathematician already mentioned, is now remembered as one of the most creative mathematicians of all time. In 1881, as he was about to enter a coach for a sightseeing trip during a conference, he was not thinking about mathematics at all (see O'Connor and Robertson, 2003). Suddenly, the Fuchsian functions (nowadays known as 'automorphic functions') came unexpectedly into his head. Refinements of the equations came later in a second burst, while he was having a relaxing walk by the sea. The crucial thing seemed to be that Poincaré was relaxed and open. However, Cropley and Cropley (2009) pointed out that Poincaré had been working on the problem of the Fuchsian functions for years and had invested hundreds if not thousands of hours into thinking about them. These authors argued strongly that effortless creativity coming as a gift from heaven is an attractive myth, although this point will not be developed any further here, because the purpose of this section is not to evaluate the idea of God-given creativity but to draw attention to the existence of this notion about the source and nature of creativity.

The benefits brought by creativity

Benefits for the individual

In addition to being regarded as good in itself, creativity is also often praised as being good for the individual, for example, by fostering mental health or leading to personal fulfilment. The perceived benefits of creativity for the individual are of central importance to our discussion because it is probably this focus which has given rise to the modern association of creativity with goodness, by contrast with earlier views which connected it with, for instance, deception (e.g., Plato) or madness (e.g., Lombroso).

According to Maslow (e.g., 1973), creativity is an essential element in growing into a healthy and fully functioning human being. He saw it as involving a special ability to understand the world in a rounded way that fosters independence, self-confidence, openness to experience, sense of humour, and the ability to deal with ambiguity and complexity, among other things. The core of Maslow's approach is the idea that people have 'needs', which are arranged in a hierarchy of levels ranging from the lowest level of physiological needs for things that are necessary for survival (e.g., the needs for air and nourishment) to the highest level involving the need for self-actualisation. According to him, striving to achieve self-actualisation is the natural built-in purpose of life, and creativity is a process that is vital for moving towards such self-actualisation.

Rogers (1954) was even more direct. He too saw the purpose of life as being self-actualisation and regarded the essential nature of living creatures as involving doing as well as possible: it is in our nature as living things to do the very best we can. This is why people try through creativity to improve things that are not perfect. According to May (1976), we live in a world that is constantly in a state of change. This causes many to experience a sense of alienation and purposelessness as what they know and the ways they act become meaningless. People have two choices: either to withdraw and panic, or to develop themselves psychologically. The second choice requires discovering new forms, ideas, patterns, symbols, and the like, (i.e., creativity). Ultimately, creativity requires the courage to defy the greatest change of all – death. One way to achieve this is by living on through creative products.

Benefits for the society

Quite apart from the assumed inherent goodness and the benefits for the individual outlined above, creativity is often looked at as also good in a more concrete way, because of the beneficial effects it produces for society. It involves a variety of beneficial results, not just concrete products such as works of art, machines, processes, systems of ideas, and similar forms of effective novelty, but also desirable social conditions such as peace and harmony, tolerance, fair-mindedness, and similar goods. A good example of beneficial effects simultaneously at both a down-to-earth practical level and also an abstract more spiritual level is to be seen in the value of production of artworks for indigenous Australians. The sale of artworks generates income of about half a billion Australian dollars a year for them but, in addition to the obvious benefit of monetary income, creativity is said to promote pride, enhance self-esteem, encourage maintenance and transmission of indigenous culture, and promote inter-generational learning among the members of this minority group (Commonwealth of Australia, 2008).

Interest in creativity as a socially useful phenomenon goes back to the ancient world. About 2,500 years ago in his *Ion*, Plato discussed the contribution of creative artists to society, albeit in a rather sarcastic and uncomplimentary way. The Chinese Emperor, Han Wudi, who reigned until 87 BCE, was intensely interested in finding creative thinkers and giving them high rank in the civil service, and he reformed the method of selection of mandarins to achieve this. Both Francis Bacon (1909 [1627]) and René Descartes (1991 [1644]), two of the founders of modern science, saw scientific creativity as involving the harnessing of the forces of nature *for the betterment of the human condition*. Nowadays we would recognise in this the human capital approach, and this view of creative people has become well known (e.g., Walberg and Stariha, 1992). McWilliam and Dawson (2008, p. 235) gave a summary of the discussions on the '*dollar value* of creative capital' (emphasis added).

In a 2009 speech, José Manuel Barroso, President of the European Commission, identified creativity as essential for collective and individual wellbeing, long and sustainable economic growth, and finding answers to the current financial, economic, and social crisis. As Oral (2006) put it, creativity is vital 'for shaping ... future orientations and actualizing reforms in political, economic and cultural areas' (p. 65). Elaborating the idea of 'creative capital', Florida and Goodnight (2005, p. 124) were unequivocal about the idea of creative people as capital: 'A company's most important asset is not raw materials, transportation systems, or political influence. It's creative capital – simply put, an arsenal of creative thinkers whose ideas can be turned into valuable products and services.'

Thus, creative people are thought to be good for a society because, among other things, they are good for business. For instance, economic theory suggests that returns on investments in rich countries should have been lower during the second half of the twentieth century than during the first half, because the stock of capital was rising faster than the workforce. However, the fact is that they were considerably higher. The decisive factor that defeated the law of diminishing returns and added greatly to an explosion of human material welfare was the *addition to the system of new knowledge and technology*, i.e., creativity. In fact, at the turn of the present century the successful application of relevant and effective novelty in manufacturing, business, engineering, science, and the like was accounting for more than half of economic growth (*Economist Technology Quarterly*, 2002, p. 13).

One of the most obvious areas that scarcely needs further elaboration is information and communications technology. Other emerging technologies, notably biotechnology and nanotechnology, are further examples of the good things that creativity is thought to bring for society. In addition, it is thought that creativity will help deal with issues that are demographic (e.g., ageing of the population, changing family patterns), social (e.g., inequality, adaptation of labour migrants and refugees), environmental (e.g., global warming, gene-modified crops), political (e.g., terrorism, achieving fairness in international relations), or industrial (e.g., offshore manufacturing, globalisation). The fear is that without sufficient creativity societies will stagnate, even deteriorate. Benefits of creativity for society of this kind were summarised in general and abstract terms by Haseman and Jaaniste (2008) as involving:

- creating and promoting an atmosphere of innovation;
- buildings the skills required in a future innovative workforce;
- creating new knowledge;
- promoting entrepreneurial activity.

Innovation

The mechanism through which creativity benefits society in the way just outlined is innovation. Bledow et al. (2009, p. 305) defined this as the development and intentional introduction into practice of new and useful ideas by individuals, teams, and organisations. The term 'value innovation' (e.g.,

Kim and Mauborgne, 2004, Dillon, Lee, and Matheson, 2005) is somewhat more explicit: it focuses on innovation as a process through which organisations find novel and effective ways of serving their current customers and identifying new markets, thus linking innovation to what customers value. This terminology makes it clear that at the level of organisations, innovation is not just a matter of coming up with a new idea but requires a valuable product, although 'product' is not confined to technological devices or even tangible objects, but covers the full value chain, including marketing, market research, sales, advertising, distribution, and customer service. In recent years, it has become almost axiomatic that this process is a key one: at the *macro* level (for instance, national innovation policy) it is accepted as vital in meeting the challenges of the early twenty-first century arising from technological advances, social change, globalisation, and now the global financial crisis, while at the *meso* level of the individual organisation it is 'a key to organisational effectiveness and competitive advantage' (Davis, 2009, p. 25) and thus ultimately to commercial success and creation of wealth.

Bledow et al. (2009) saw the complete process of innovation as involving novelty *production* (in effect, creativity) plus *implementation* of the newly generated novelty. This approach is similar to the phase model outlined in Chapter 3, with implementation resembling what we called 'Implementation' and 'Validation' there. West (2002, p. 356) stated the matter quite explicitly: 'Creativity is the development of ideas, while innovation … is the application of ideas.' West also envisaged the joint action of creativity and innovation implementation as sequential: 'Innovation then can be defined as encompassing both stages – the development of ideas – creativity; *followed by* their application' (emphasis added). However, more recent organisational theory does not see the interplay between creativity and innovation implementation as strictly sequential, with creativity always preceding innovation implementation and being completely separate from it. Haner (2005, p. 389) concluded that 'both creativity and innovation processes need to be seen as complex, *partly iterative* and *partly simultaneous* efforts' (emphasis added). Of central importance for present purposes, however, is not the nature of the interaction between creativity and exploitation of ideas but the argument that creativity is essential to innovation, which is in turn vital for the welfare of the nation.

Education

In the educational field there is a very substantial literature on the benefits of creativity dating back at least to Torrance (e.g., 1965). For instance, it is thought to facilitate learning, promote positive motivation, and foster favourable attitudes, thus improving both academic achievement and also classroom discipline and atmosphere. There are large numbers of teaching methods and materials whose aim is to help teachers promote creativity, reviewed by, for instance, Cropley (2001). In a recent review of Australian education, Ewing (2011) drew attention to possible benefits of creativity-facilitating teaching methods for traditional school achievement: she listed benefits such as better grades and higher overall test scores. However, she warned against assuming the existence of a direct cause-and-effect relationship between creativity and higher achievement. Indeed, Winner and Hetland (2000) reviewed ten meta-analyses of research on this topic and reported that seven showed no such effects. However, Cropley (2012) summarised research suggesting that the use of creativity-fostering teaching methods ('creative pedagogy') has benefits that are more general than simply academic achievement. Some of these are not directly part of academic work at all (e.g., reduced likelihood of dropping out of school early, less boredom, and a more positive self-concept), although the indirect effects of staying on, finding schoolwork interesting, or having confidence in one's own ability on school learning are obvious.

O'Brien and Donelan (2008) gave a good overview of personal benefits thought to derive from participation in creative activities in schools, listing improved self-esteem, learning to work cooperatively, improved planning and goal setting, developing the ability to make and accept constructive criticism, and better expression of emotions. These authors also discussed the value of creativity for promoting the personal well-being and academic achievement of 'disempowered and disenfranchised' students. O'Brien (2011) concluded that children benefit 'in multiple ways'. These include personal benefits such as becoming more well-rounded and possessing better life skills (e.g., conflict resolution, stress management, and empathy). English and Jones (2003) also gave examples of what incorporation of creativity into the general curriculum would entail, apart from direct enhancement of creativity: in addition to creativity-facilitating cognitive processes such as combining elements, lateral thinking, problem definition, and idea generation, they emphasised personal properties such as imaginativeness, willingness to take risks, or openness to the new.

The benefits that have been reported as flowing from deliberate incorporation of creative approaches in the classroom are summarised in Table 5.1.

Table 5.1 *The educational benefits of creative pedagogy*

Area of benefit	Nature of benefit
General life benefits	Fewer school drop-outs Fully realised individual potentials Better life skills Better stress management More empathy Greater personal wellbeing
Classroom atmosphere benefits	More active involvement in learning More interesting lessons, less boredom Reduced inattention, absenteeism Lessons more effective Better grades and higher test scores
General process benefits	Cooperative work habits Improved planning and goal setting Ability to make and accept constructive criticism Use of the imagination Production of ideas
Cognitive skill benefits	Improved questioning skill Recognising inconsistent information Recognising need for additional information Using more than one pathway Generating multiple solutions Combining concepts Making broad associations Seeing unusual perspectives Displaying daring thinking Recognising pattern Creating analogies Crossing domain boundaries Exploring alternatives Solving problems
Self-related benefits	Improved self-esteem Better expression of emotions More positive self-concept Openness to the new Spontaneity
Motivational benefits	Willingness to challenge received opinions Inquisitiveness Increased willingness to take risks Willingness to express unusual ideas Willingness to change Inclination to seek novelty Desire to develop new skills Desire to understand things

Ambivalence about creativity

Nonetheless, despite the contents of the earlier sections of this chapter, the general approval of creativity may not be unlimited and unconditional, or even limited to the dichotomy good/bad. On the basis of an extremely dramatic example (the invention, construction, and use of the atomic bomb in 1945), Hecht (2010) drew attention to the 'more complex cultural meaning' (p. 73) of even such an apparently terrifying application of creativity for undeniably malevolent purposes. Hecht cited, on the one hand, Boyer (1985, pp. 13–14), who referred to the 'unutterably shattering effect upon civilization' of the bomb, but also identified awe and celebration among public reactions to it. The bomb was quite commonly regarded as God's work, and many people saw it as ushering in a new era in which war would be obsolete, while others hailed the ability of atomic energy to deliver cheap power and lauded it as about to produce a brave new world of plenty and rapid social progress: what Hecht called 'atomic utopia' (p. 75). According to Hecht, reactions to the bomb went far beyond judging it simply 'good' or 'bad'. He referred (p. 76) to 'dynamic, confusing and paradoxical images and meanings of [negative creativity]'.[3]

For instance, generation of effective novelty that is regarded as creative in one era or society can be seen as uncreative in another. Brahms was unable to obtain the post of director of the philharmonic orchestra in Hamburg because his music was initially judged to be too conservative, and he had to go to Vienna to find acclaim, eventually settling there in about 1872, although he never forgave Hamburg. In Georgian England, Shakespeare's plays were regarded as indecent and had to be edited to make them respectable – in 1818 Dr Thomas Bowdler published the *Family Shakespeare*, in which he removed expressions that could not with propriety be read aloud in the family (he *bowdlerised* Shakespeare's work, as we now express it). The social environment sometimes identifies people who generate novelty as eccentric, mentally ill, or criminal. If society applauds the novelty a person generates, the person is regarded as creative, but if it frowns upon the behaviour, the person is regarded as criminal or crazy – all this despite the fact that the behaviour in question may essentially be the same, just carried out in different places or in different eras. It is not so much the actual deviation from the usual itself that determines creativity, but how the environment reacts to the deviation.

---

[3] Actually Hecht wrote 'atomic energy' here, but we see his remarks as applying to negative creativity in general.

A case in point is Nicolaus Copernicus's formulation, published in 1543 in *De Revolutionibus Orbium Coelestium*, of a heliocentric cosmology, which displaced the Earth from the centre of the universe and replaced it with the Sun. What is striking about this example is that Copernicus had completed the manuscript some ten years earlier but resisted publishing it, despite the encouragement of his close friends, because he feared that the ideas were too novel and would be widely scorned. In fact, the book was *not* poorly received; however, it *was* many years before his ideas became widely known and adopted. Thus, there was neither hostility to the novelty of the heliocentric model, nor enthusiastic adoption, but simply a strong measure of ambivalence or uncertainty. It was almost as if the members of the scientific community of the time wanted to wait and see how others reacted before declaring their own hands.

In particular, the precise social group in which the person in question displays the deviation may be decisive. For instance, someone who was active in a setting where unbridled expression of impulses and ignoring the conventions were regarded as odd or incompetent (let us say, an engineer) would be treated differently for the same behaviours from someone in a setting where such behaviour was admired – in, perhaps, avant-garde theatre or dance. The second person might be fortunate enough to have the behaviour accepted as not only surprising but also effective, and thus creative. By contrast, generation of novelty through application of a high level of technical skill might be highly prized among engineers, but regarded as boringly conventional in the dance or theatre groups just mentioned.

Ambivalence in school settings

In school, too, there may be ambivalence about creativity. In addition to divergent *processes* such as those outlined in Chapter 3 (making unexpected combinations, seeing unusual implications, generating a variety of possible responses, etc.) creative children display *personal properties* like boldness and self-confidence, *motivational states* such as dissatisfaction with received wisdom or the drive to fill gaps in knowledge and *resistance to social pressure to conform* to classroom norms. These are tricky for teachers, partly because they may lead to behaviour that is difficult to tell apart from misbehaviour. It is sometimes hard to distinguish between creativity in the classroom and disorderliness or disruptiveness, or even sheer wilful naughtiness. Creative children's attempts to understand things more deeply or from a different angle and express this via apparently strange questions, unexpected answers to the teacher's questions, apparently nonsensical remarks in classroom discussions, choice of exotic contents in classroom exercises, or selection of strange topics in homework or projects can disrupt lessons, and if not stopped by the teacher can seem to other students to involve tolerating misbehaviour, thus encouraging these children to misbehave too. In short, creativity by its very nature represents a potential threat to good order in the classroom. Indeed, as Cropley (2009) concluded, especially, but not only, in countries where there is strong emphasis on good order and respect for authority, teachers often see creative children as defiant, chaotic, disruptive, or even psychologically disturbed.

A problem is that, although creative children display many highly positive personal characteristics such as autonomy, ego strength, tolerance of ambiguity, or openness, as a group they are also significantly more introverted, more self-willed, less satisfied, and less controlled than children who display lower levels of creativity. Other characteristics associated with creativity also include lack of concern for social norms, and antisocial attitudes, as well as psychopathological tendencies. To put it plainly and briefly, creative students can sometimes seem to teachers to be 'weird', defiant, aggressive, self-centred, or antisocial, characteristics that make them disturbing, even threatening, and this is apparently an inherent part of being creative, at least in some people. Evariste Galois was one of the most creative mathematicians who ever lived. His prodigious mathematical talent was already visible at school, to be sure, but there was what would now be called a 'downside': he refused to study anything except mathematics! His teachers described him as 'original', but they also judged him to be 'singular', 'withdrawn', even 'bizarre'. On the other hand, teachers know that creativity is universally regarded as a good thing so that they have to cope with the paradox that the 'best' students may not display the characteristics most admired in schoolchildren by teachers (orderliness, accuracy, ability to repeat conventional knowledge, etc.).

Problems arising from intoxication with creativity

Even studies that examine negative applications of creativity may regard them as fundamentally benevolent. To take a single example, Brisman (2010) explicitly discussed 'creative crime', but saw its purpose as *good*: to 'undermine … repressive structures' in society' (p. 215). He pointed out that people breaking the law for such purposes not infrequently see themselves as social reformers striving to expose injustice, abuse, and violence on the part of, for instance, government agencies, the police, or large corporations. Thus, breaking the law creatively may be seen as having something good about it, despite the disruption, mayhem, and damage it often causes. Singer (2010) gave two simple examples of negative creativity in incarcerated criminals that tempt us almost to smile indulgently, despite the fact that there is clearly no socially benevolent intent involved. She described the ingenious way incarcerated prisoners make small (but forbidden) cooking stoves out of materials that are readily available in prison (in this case toilet paper and toothpaste). The stoves do not seem to do any great harm and add greatly to the comfort of prison life, and thus seem more admirable than abhorrent, even though they are forbidden. Even in the case of knives made from unexpected materials such as a toothbrush, the generation of novelty seems somehow admirable, despite the fact that the knives are not made for benevolent purposes at all.

At a more theoretical level, a number of researchers have discussed the inherently *antisocial* nature of creativity, but have still concluded that it is a good thing. Moustakis (1977) characterised creativity as the pathway to living your own life your own way. Barron (1969) concluded that creativity requires *resistance* to socialisation, and Burkhardt (1985) argued that the creative individual must fight against society's pathological desire for sameness. Although they were writing about giftedness, Sternberg and Lubart (1995) gave this fight the easily understandable label 'defying the crowd', and called the tendency of certain creative individuals to resist society's pressure to conform 'contrarianism' (p. 41).

The general intoxication with creativity may be summarised as involving the following assumptions:

- benevolent outcomes are a necessary consequence of creativity;
- benevolence enables or facilitates creativity;
- benevolence is the intent of creativity;
- a benevolent environment stimulates creativity;
- creativity produces a benevolent environment.

These assumptions do not simply impose blinkers that limit the way creativity is looked at, but have effects in a number of areas. For instance, they have restricted the kind of research that has been done in this area. A more important effect from the perspective of crime is that admiration of creativity may influence society's response to crime and law-enforcement.

Difficulty taking a stand against crime

The modern broad assumption that creativity is good for you has no doubt influenced people to focus on evidence supporting this view and is an example of the psychological phenomenon of 'confirmation bias' (e.g., Nickerson, 1998), which leads people to interpret all experience as confirming what they already believe is true, if necessary taking note only of conforming evidence and ignoring contradictory evidence. Trivers (1985, p. 420) also speculated about this and concluded that: 'There is a tendency for humans consciously to see what they wish to see. They literally have difficulty seeing things with negative connotations while seeing with increasing ease items that are positive.'

It appears that the tendency to see the bright side even of law-breaking and the resultant tendency to focus on its 'good' side is part of a more general human trait of optimism. According to Tiger (1979), optimism is part of the biology of our species and is one of our most defining and adaptive characteristics. Tiger proposed that optimism is an integral part of human nature, selected for in the course of evolution, and that it is developing along with our cognitive abilities and indeed the human capacity for culture. Tiger even speculated that optimism drove human evolution. Because optimism entails thinking about the future, it first appeared when people began to think ahead. Once people began anticipating the future, they could imagine dire consequences, including their own mortality. Something had to develop to counteract the fear and paralysis that these thoughts might entail, and that something was optimism. According this view, optimism is inherent in the make-up of people, not a derivative of some other psychological characteristic. Tiger went on to characterise optimism as easy to think, easy to learn, and pleasing – what modern evolutionary psychologists describe as an evolved psychological mechanism (Buss, 1991).

From a more psychological point of view, Taylor and Brown's (1988) literature review of research on positive illusions described a variety of studies showing that people are biased toward the positive and that the only exceptions to this rule are individuals who are anxious or depressed. Taylor (1989) elaborated on these ideas and proposed that people's pervasive tendency to see themselves in the best possible light is a sign of wellbeing. She distinguished optimism as an illusion from optimism as a delusion: illusions are responsive, albeit reluctantly, to reality, whereas delusions are not.

A study carried out by Kaufman, Cropley, Chiera, and White (forthcoming) with nearly 600 US college students mostly aged between 18 and

30 cast considerable light on the tendency to be less disapproving of crime when it displays aspects of creativity. These researchers investigated the perceived creativity of various courses of action in 'scenarios' (hypothetical situations) where the person in the scenario had to solve a problem (e.g., obtaining cash when short of money) and the alternative courses of action involved increasingly socially disapproved behaviour. In the scenario just cited (obtaining cash), for instance, the actions whose creativity was to be rated included, among others, begging money from friends, gambling in the hope of a big win, pawning personal belongings, borrowing from a bank, taking unauthorised work, burgling a stranger's house, embezzling money from a relative's business, or robbing a bank. Another of the scenarios involved persuading the authorities to take action to remedy some injustice. Alternative courses of action included handing in a petition, carrying out a protest/demonstration outside a government building, making and distributing a subversive video, vandalising a government building, or setting off a bomb under various circumstances (e.g., in a deserted place, during off-peak hours, at a time when the likelihood of civilian casualties was at its highest). The respondents' task was to indicate how creative the various courses of action were, and how 'evil' they were.

The study's findings showed that the respondents were able to differentiate between good and bad courses of action and that they interpreted the goodness/badness of the courses of action in a reasonably differentiated way: a particular course of action was not perceived simply as entirely good or entirely bad. For instance, respondents differentiated between the simple legality/illegality of a course of action and its level of violence, and also differentiated between morally or legally *ambiguous* acts and those that were clearly entirely legal or entirely illegal. Respondents also judged creativity in a fairly differentiated way: the courses of action rated most creative tended to be those that were perceived as morally or legally ambiguous, with those that were rated either entirely legal or moral and those that were rated as utterly immoral and/or illegal (but not violent or destructive) seen as less creative. However, in cases of extreme violence or destructiveness, this relationship no longer held. This is an example of the well-known U-shaped relationship between variables that is often seen in psychological research and has been demonstrated by Martindale (1989) in connection with the link between creativity and knowledge.

This relationship suggests that there may be a *threshold* of badness, *below* which increasingly malevolent behaviour is seen as increasingly creative, that is, the novelty is the main source of evaluative judgement. However, *above* the threshold of badness perceived creativity *decreases* with increasing malevolence, that is, above the threshold the level of badness is the main source of judgement. The threshold is located somewhere around the point of 'legal ambiguity'. Courses that are unequivocally legal (e.g., borrowing money from a bank to cover a debt) lie below the threshold, whereas robbing the bank to cover the debt lies above the threshold. Norm-breaking courses of action that are legal or merely morally or ethically dubious (as against clearly wicked) may be accepted as creative and may escape public censure, whereas those that are perceived as undeniably illegal or highly destructive and/or murderous may be adjudged not creative, regardless of novelty, effectiveness, and the like.

This may explain the almost universal excoriation of Bernie Madoff, despite the effective novelty he generated, as against the near admiration of the Great Train Robber, Ronnie Biggs, who was seen as not really having hurt anybody apart from a railroad and an insurance company (i.e., there was ambiguity about the badness of his actions, since big corporations and insurance companies do not enjoy unconditional positive regard among the public) and as having displayed quick wit, ability to see things in a new light, a novel approach to escaping apprehension, an unexpected trick for avoiding extradition (he married a beautiful and much younger Brazilian woman and had a child with her, thus making himself ineligible for extradition – a novel, effective and elegant solution to his problem), and so on. In fact, Madoff displayed several of the properties revealed by Biggs, but these did not excite admiration, presumably because some of his victims were highly socially approved organisations such as charities. The combination of moral ambiguity and substantial generation of effective novelty produces grudging admiration and unwillingness to condemn behaviour, that is, softness on crime.[4]

Apparently, operating fully within the law imposes a framework of constraints that may limit the potential for generation of effective novelty. However, while operating with complete disregard for the law may open up the possibility of generating large amounts of effective novelty, it makes it easy for observers to condemn the novelty and negates the indulgent-smile effect. In addition, excessive violence and destructiveness are seen as inelegant. Morally/ethically ambiguous courses of action, on the other hand, offer the greatest potential for getting away with negative creativity. The

---

[4] Although it is a repugnant and offensive idea, the events of 11 September, 2001 may have aroused secret admiration in some observers (apart from Al-Qa'ida supporters). The terrorists went about their crimes in a way involving creative aspects (novelty, ingenuity, effectiveness), but the admirableness of these was cancelled in most people's minds by the very high level of badness of what they did – in our view, rightly.

question that now arises is whether the low perceived creativity of courses of action above the threshold is a result of creativity-related criteria such as novelty, relevance and effectiveness, elegance, or genesis, or of a general intolerance of norm-breaking behaviour, which could unkindly be labelled 'conformism'. The latter explanation implies that as the constraints of law and ethics/morals are softened, the opportunity for creativity is heightened. This would imply that strong moral/ethical codes are the enemy of creativity, and if creativity is invariably a good thing and leads to the benefits that have been outlined in earlier sections, morals/ethics would have a negative function by placing an upper limit on the amount of production of novelty that is tolerated. In the next chapter we will begin to move into establishing a less ambiguous link between creativity and crime by beginning an examination of the dark side of creativity.

CHAPTER SIX

The dark side of creativity

In order to study the link between creativity and crime it is necessary to understand that not everything about creativity is good. One dangerous or destructive component is the Personal properties that help people generate effective novelty: these may be antisocial or even lead to self-harm. Another is the creative Processes, which may make it difficult for creative people to fit in with the norms of the social environment. Turning to Products, people with good intentions may work on projects clearly serving evil ends because they are deceived, blinded by curiosity, or overwhelmed by the desire to create something new. There are also many instances where effective novelty is generated for the specific purpose of breaking the law more effectively. Paradoxically, such creativity is not completely bad, since it benefits somebody (the perpetrator), and may even excite grudging admiration from some people because of the society's mistaken tendency to regard all creativity as basically good. This tendency may have negative consequences for law-enforcement.

As was shown in Chapter 5, in both everyday usage as well as scholarly discussions it is almost axiomatic that creativity is good. Indeed, there is no denying that it often leads to beneficial advances in art and literature, science, medicine, engineering, manufacturing, business, and other areas (the bright side). Nonetheless, creativity has what James, Clark, and Cropanzano (1999) called a 'negative' side or, as Cropley, Kaufman, and Cropley (2008) put it, its 'malevolent' aspect. This is seen in Product, but also in Process and Person, as will be shown below. Thus, the first step in understanding the role that creativity plays in crime is to overcome the natural, human tendency discussed by Tiger (1979) and Trivers (2011) and discussed more fully in Chapter 5, to accentuate the positive and ignore the negative. This requires a conceptual framework that allows for the fact that creativity can be applied both to positive and to negative ends.

The dark/light balance

Despite its dark side, in a certain sense creativity really is inherently good: as Jasper (2010) pointed out, relevant and effective novelty (creativity) always brings benefits to someone (otherwise it would not be relevant and effective). The problem as identified by Jasper is thus not the presence or absence of benefits resulting from creativity – since there are always benefits for somebody – but the distribution of the benefits. If the advantages all flow in one direction and the disadvantages all flow in the other, then the creativity is positive for one side, but negative for the other. Hilton (2010, p. 134) takes a similar view in that he sees creativity as 'naturally' leading to both good and bad, and regards the good or evil of creativity as lying in the balance of the two elements. Once again we see a paradox of creativity: in a sense it really is always good (for someone), although dark creativity may simultaneously do great harm.

The subjectivity of benevolence

Singer (2010, p. 178) used the term 'subjective benevolence' to distinguish benevolence in the eyes of only a single person or a small group of observers (i.e., a form of benevolence where the benefits accrue to an individual or minority, or the balance is in favour of the few) from benevolence that is acknowledged by a wide range of people (presumably 'objective' benevolence), where the benefits accrue to the majority or the balance is in favour of the general group. This approach conceptualises benevolence not as differing qualitatively (e.g., of the subjective *kind* or of the objective *kind*), but as lying on a continuum ranging from benevolence for a few at one pole to benevolence for many at the other, so that the crucial factor is the amount of benevolence for whom, or what we call 'relative' benevolence.

Sternberg (2010, p. 318) extended this two-dimensional approach (benefit for the few vs benefit for the many) by discussing *three* dimensions:

- *intrapersonal* benefit (benefit for one person only – usually the person generating the effective novelty);
- *interpersonal* benefit (benefit for other people as well as oneself);
- *extrapersonal* benefit (benefit for the context or setting such as one's city or country or the environment).

Extrapersonal benefit has obvious links to the P of Press and is reminiscent of the ecological nature of creativity. These three dimensions help to make the difference between creative crime and positive creativity clearer: in the first instance, crime is benevolent relative only to the purposes of the perpetrator(s) or a particular group of people who support them, i.e., it involves only *intra*personal benefit, and indeed often leads to harm for others (in the *inter*personal sense it is usually not benevolent or is even malevolent). Consideration of the third dimension of relative benefit (*extra*personal benefit) also brings out the negative effects of crime: the effects of worldwide drug dealing, human trafficking, and terrorist disruption of normal life, or destruction of rain forests, pollution of waterways, or over-fishing are examples of crime that does substantial extrapersonal harm. Even though it may bring considerable intrapersonal benefit, or even interpersonal benefit, for instance to large numbers of shareholders in a company profiting from illegal logging or waste disposal, and may thus seem to be benevolent, it is clear that in the extrapersonal sense such crime is malevolent.

Kampylis and Valtanen (2010, p. 209) summarised theories of the origins of creativity in a historical way. They identified three 'main eras':

1. the *metaphysical* era, from antiquity to the Renaissance, in which a few geniuses were considered able to *create from nothing* through divine (or other) inspiration;
2. the *aristocratic era*, from the Renaissance to the middle of the twentieth century, in which a few charismatic geniuses were considered able to *create from something*;
3. the *democratic era*, from the middle of the twentieth century up to today, in which anyone is considered able to *create from anything*.

However, Kampylis and Valtanen pointed out that all three of these approaches focus on the individual and place little emphasis on the consequences of creativity for other people or for the society in general. In other words, they ignore the interpersonal and extrapersonal domains just outlined. Kampylis and Valtanen went on to argue that a more holistic approach – we have called it an 'ecological' approach – would take account of the consequences of creativity for others, and called for a new era of 'conscientious creativity'. An emphasis on the consequences of a person's creativity for other people and/or the society in general is highly productive for an analysis of creativity and crime, as will show in later chapters, especially Chapter 7.

The balance of benefit

The crucial point in this discussion is not so much that benevolence/malevolence is subjective or objective, because, in the last analysis, these judgements are all dependent on the opinions of those affected: benefit is always subjective – benevolence and malevolence are relative to the actors involved. Thus, and of great importance, a 'product' can be both benevolent and malevolent, depending on the point of view taken. However, it also has an absolute quality defined by its impact. Thus 9/11, for example, in absolute terms was malevolent – thousands of people were intentionally killed and billions of dollars of property destroyed. In *relative* terms, a very large number of people saw it as malevolent, to be sure, but some people saw it as benevolent in the sense that it fulfilled their particular, albeit warped, goals.

Hilton drew conclusions for practice from his analysis (see above), and suggested that dealing with negative creativity can be conceptualised as involving correctives that 'tip the balance' in a desired direction. In the case of crime, this would mean in the direction of law-enforcers or non-criminals or, at the very least, away from criminals. Creative crime is yet another paradox: it yields intrapersonal benefits for the criminal, so that in a sense it is actually *good*, as perverse as that sounds. However, the flow of benefits is asymmetrical – only to the criminal at the expense of the law-abiding or even of the social, economic, or physical environment. Thus the balance of good and evil is unequal, and in this sense the creativity is negative (despite being regarded by some observers as good).

The reaction of the surrounding environment to crime (Press) usually involves widespread condemnation of one side (the criminals), while there is lopsided support of the other (the law-enforcers), so that, in a further paradox, the light side of the dark side may be overlooked: the creativity of crime may go unrecognised. However, most people would probably regard this as right and proper. On the other hand, it is also possible for the paradoxical light side of dark creativity to lead people to overlook its negative aspects, or to be only half-hearted in opposing them. A less obvious positive aspect of negative creativity in crime is that the perpetrators' creativity may enable law-enforcers to see a situation in a new way, in effect introducing a new paradigm through the phenomenon of genesis (see the relevant discussion and Table 3.1 in Chapter 3, pp. 52–54). To take an example: the World Trade Center attack of 11 September, 2001 was highly effective, to be sure, but led the 'opposition' (Homeland Security) to introduce changes that have prevented a repetition.

The concept of *relative benevolence* can be seen in situations like, for instance, the July plot against Adolf Hitler. When the July plotters attempted to assassinate Hitler by exploding a bomb in the conference room of his headquarters near Rastenburg in East Prussia (the so-called *Wolfsschanze*, or Wolf's Lair) in July 1944 they were clearly breaking prevailing German law. Millions of Nazi true believers were probably genuinely appalled, would have regarded[1] any creativity involved as negative and any benevolence in the plotters' actions as existing only in the plotters' own minds (i.e., as being entirely relative to the goals of the plotters). Despite this, at the time there was widespread support both inside and outside Germany for the plot, and a very large number of people would have agreed that the plotters' motives were benevolent *relative to the needs of the whole world*, that is, in the extrapersonal sense, even though they were highly malevolent with regard to Hitler. If we looked at benevolence in a purely *absolute* sense we would be unable to deal with this situation, since the attack was highly illegal in terms of prevailing German law, definitely meant to do harm to Hitler (and was therefore malevolent relative to him), but would have been regarded by most people as benevolent in the extrapersonal sense, since Hitler's early death would have saved millions of lives, while the balance of benefit in the interpersonal sense (i.e., the relative benefit) would also have been markedly skewed in the direction of approval, outside the Third Reich at least.

In the case of the World Trade Center attack, the balance in the distribution of perceived 'benefits' – in this case, the deaths of over 2,000 non-combatants – was very much in favour of one side, the state of affairs where, as Jasper (2010) and Kaufman, Cropley, Chiera, and White (submitted) showed, creativity becomes questionable. However, that side was not confined to a relatively small group of people, as in the case of the July plot (remaining loyal Hitler admirers). There would have been widespread perception in some parts of the world of the relative benevolence of the highly effective novelty of the attack. Thus, the uneven split in the flow of benefits from the highly effective novelty was not a clear-cut matter of only a single person or a handful on the one side, everyone else on the other (an enormously disproportionate split), but of a large number of people on both sides, even if far more on one than the other.

This means that it may be hard to define just when the balance of benefit – the relative benefit – becomes unacceptably one-sided. General Wolfe's highly effective novel tactic of scaling the cliffs under cover of darkness to win the Battle of the Plains of Abraham at Quebec City on 13 September 1759 brought huge benefits for the British (the conquest of Canada), a disaster for the French.[2] That makes Wolfe's effective and relevant novelty

[1] Whether or not the plot was creative is irrelevant to the present discussion.
[2] It also brought Captain James Cook, who made the first European contact with the Hawaiian Islands and the eastern coast of Australia, to prominence as a navigator par excellence. He surveyed the St Lawrence River, making it possible for the attack to be carried out.

positive relative to the British, negative relative to the French and, from the French point of view, not creative at all.[3] A discussion of the subjectiveness of right and wrong or of factors such as the point at which the imbalance in benefits becomes one-sided enough for relevant and effective novelty to become negative or malevolent, or even cease to be regarded as creative at all, would go beyond the limits of the present discussion, so that we will focus here on the dark side as we define it below.

The dark side

James et al. (1999) pointed out that the range of situations in which the dark side of creativity can manifest itself is large. Unfortunately, the enchantment with creativity is so intense that, as these authors complained, people – including researchers – 'typically ignore the fact that a great deal of creative effort is done in service of negative ends' (p. 212). This means that little has been worked out about the 'triggers, processes, outcomes' (p. 212) of the dark side. The result is that approaches to issues such as recognising the dark side, avoiding circumstances that foster its growth, discouraging its manifestation, redirecting it, or protecting against it are not well developed. The purpose of this section is to increase awareness of the dark side and increase understanding of the forms and processes of negative and especially malevolent creativity, and set in motion a discussion of how to deal with it in practical settings. It has already been pointed out that the initial approach to creativity in this book is via *products*, especially products that do harm to others. Nonetheless, it is obvious that such products result from processes carried out in the minds of people, so that any consideration of the dark side must go beyond the P of Product and include the Ps of Process, Person, and Press. These will be looked at in the following sections.

The dark side of Product

McLaren (1993) contrasted the extremely positive view of creativity spelled out in Chapter 5 with the facts of its misuse in, for instance, (a) advertising, where it is employed to promote the sales of, among other things, unhealthy food or dangerous products, (b) entertainment, where it is used to promote repulsive values, glorify crime, etc., (c) politics, where it

---

[3] Even today there would be disagreement between French Canadians and Anglo Canadians about the extrapersonal benefit of General Wolfe's tactic!

has been used to promote, for instance, racial hatred, or (d) science and technology, where it is applied to developing and building weapons of mass destruction (see the discussions of the development of such weapons in Zaitseva, 2010 and Hecht, 2010), or polluting the environment. Interestingly, McLaren pointed out that the harm generated by technological creativity is not confined to physical destruction. He referred to eighteenth- and nineteenth-century figures such as Coleridge, Dickens, and Victor Hugo, who already then were warning of the destructive *social* effects of technological innovation. To these can be added (e.g., James et al., 1999) negative use of creativity in (e) business or production, for instance, to evade regulators or to steal competitors' secrets, (f) social life or at work, for instance, to avoid work, curry favour, gain unfair advantage, or steal from an employer without being detected, (g) crime in general, or in (h) war or (i) terrorism (e.g., Cropley et al., 2008).

Unfortunately, even creative products intended to be entirely benevolent may have a dark side in the form of unintended or unforeseen negative consequences: for instance, the discoveries of Jenner and Pasteur, although extremely beneficial for all humankind, laid the foundation for germ warfare. McLaren (1993) gave a quite different example: the building of cathedrals in the Middle Ages. These may still stand as creative triumphs of architecture and civil engineering that add beauty to the world even today, but their dark side is that they often caused great misery and hardship to the poor at the time of their construction, even though the intention of the builders was to save souls and give people access to the joys of paradise.

A more concrete example is given by Cadbury (2004): the advent of steam locomotion resulted in the need to build tunnels to facilitate the opening up of rail networks. Often these tunnels were plagued by flooding during tunnelling. The solution was to pressurise the excavations. This prevented the inflow of water and made it possible for tunnellers to continue working without water leaking into the works. A similar problem occurred in the construction of the foundations of large bridges and this problem, too, was solved using pressurised caissons to allow workers to dig foundations and pour concrete on the beds of rivers – the use of pressurised air was a novel, effective, elegant, and even generic solution which fitted all our criteria of creativity (see pp. 52–54). However, when workers finished their shifts and returned to the external environment they began to suffer the effects of nitrogen bubbles released in their bloodstream – they suffered from the 'bends'. It took some years and a number of deaths before the problem was understood and a solution found. It is impossible

to ascribe any evil intent to the engineers who devised the creative procedure of using pressurised air to facilitate this kind of work but, despite being effective, novel, elegant, and generic it also resulted in harmful
outcomes.

Even where an undesirable outcome is clearly foreseeable, negative creativity is not necessarily the result of deliberately evil intentions. Some
people even create evil despite having benevolent motives. They may, for
instance, be unable to, unaware of, or unwilling to anticipate the dark side
of their work, deliberately or subconsciously blinding themselves to negative consequences. This may occur because of, for instance, their patriot-
ism or their loyalty to a political regime, their fascination with the work
they are doing, or because they are deceived or coerced by factors like the
prospect of money and fame.

Zaitseva (2010) showed how this happened with some participants in
the Soviet Union's programme for the development of weapons of mass
destruction: although some of the scientists were aware of the monstrous-
ness of the work they were doing, others believed that it would all have a
beneficial end, while yet others simply went about their interesting, even
exciting, work as well as they could without considering the consequences.
Brower and Stahl (2011) described the case study of Leni Riefenstahl, who
made propaganda films for the Nazis. In 1932 she made what these authors
called 'perhaps the most notorious documentary ever filmed' (p. 319) and
described as 'a masterwork' of propaganda. After the Second World War
Riefenstahl was imprisoned by the French and spent almost four years in
prison. Despite the tremendous effect of her artistic masterwork in favour
of evil, she maintained that she had never supported the Nazis but had
only made very good films.

Unfortunately, it is not uncommon for people to generate negative creativity, knowing full well that it will have negative consequences for others.
James et al. (1999) gave the example of a person finding a creative way to
get others to do the hard work in a factory. This may be regarded by observers as no more than annoying cunning. More obviously dark, however, is
the application of creativity to manipulate other people or to profit at other
people's expense, without regard to possible negative consequences for the
people concerned: an obvious, legally permitted example would be the use
of creativity to persuade children to eat foods that are harmful to their
health (as in advertising), where ill health for children is not the primary
purpose of the creativity but merely an unfortunate spin-off.

Most obviously dark is the application of creativity with the conscious
and deliberate intention of doing harm to others, the harm being the

main purpose of the creativity, not just a spin-off. This is what Cropley et al. (2008) called 'malevolent' creativity (see the discussion of this topic in Chapter 1, pp. 14–20). Major examples of such creativity may be seen in business, as well as in war. Fully intended negative creativity may be widely applauded as positive by one side (often the victors), even though it is devastatingly negative for the other. One example from war is Admiral Lord Nelson's highly effective novel tactic of sailing inshore of the French fleet at the Battle of the Nile in 1798, which brought the loss of twelve out of fourteen French ships of the line (adjudged good by the British but bad by the French) and death or captivity for thousands of French sailors (again good to the British but bad to the French). Another is the dropping of the atomic bombs on Hiroshima and Nagasaki in 1945 (see Hecht, 2010), which was greeted with delirious gladness by some – especially allied soldiers whose lives it may well have saved – but ultimately killed hundreds of thousands of Japanese civilians.

The dark side of Process

Runco (2010) argued strongly that the creative process, like evolution, is inherently blind: it can lead to good or bad results, but it is the results that are good or bad, not the process. However, Cropley (2009) argued that the creative Process has an *inherent* dark side, which is independent of the Person or the Product. In fact, we have already mentioned a number of researchers who see creativity as inherently *antisocial* (e.g., Barron, 1969; Moustakis, 1977; Burkhardt, 1985). Its purpose is to deviate from what already exists and this involves refusing to accept the status quo, thrusting forward alternative possibilities, and possibly belittling or frightening other people or making it impossible for them to function in the usual way. While it is easy to imagine situations where this is good, because the status quo needs to be shaken up, this does not mean that the process is not risky or disruptive, even in those cases where the ultimate result is good.

To use an analogy: driving along the street on whichever side you choose, for instance because you are dissatisfied with always driving on the same side, want to make society change, or enjoy the thrill of being different, does not have a bad result unless you hit something. Thus, it could indeed be argued that there is nothing inherently bad about wrong-side driving. However, the fact that it is the *results* of the wrong-side driving which can be negative, not the actual act of driving itself, does not mean that there is nothing inherently bad about wrong-side driving. It has a much greater potential for danger than driving on the correct side, opens up risks that would not exist if the driver stayed on the correct side of the road, exposes the driver and passengers to increased danger, and causes greater inconvenience, not to say danger, for other people. There is an inherent risk in wrong-side driving, even if other drivers succeed in getting out of the way: the success of other drivers in avoiding a collision does not mean that it is perfectly all right to drive wherever you please. The wrong-side driving may have unpleasant consequences for other people even when the direct result is not negative: an example would be the extra care that people in Britain must exercise when driving in areas where American tourists commonly drive on the wrong side of the road, and the concern and uncertainty this causes even when no collision occurs.

Gamman and Raein (2010) offered a related perspective by summing up divergent processes as involving 'rejection of mechanical approaches' (p. 157). As these authors pointed out, a focus on 'non-mechanical' processes is sometimes associated with failure to master 'mechanical' ones such as making fine distinctions, being accurate or, indeed, adhering to the law. The creative Process involves procedures like seeing the known in a new light, shifting perspective, making unexpected combinations, or opening up risky possibilities (often referred to as 'divergent' processes). These are admirable, but not without their problems. They can spill over into behaviour that is destructive for innocent bystanders. Evariste Galois, whose case has already been mentioned (Chapter 4, pp. 86–87), was expelled from secondary school not as a more or less innocent victim of the unreasonable attitudes, values, or demands of those around him, but because his behaviour disrupted the teaching of other children and intimidated some teachers, even though there is no doubt that Galois was an extraordinarily creative mathematician.[4]

Baucus et al. (2008) identified four aspects of the creative process that have substantial potential for causing harm. These involve:

- breaking rules and standard operating procedures;
- challenging authority and avoiding tradition;
- creating conflict, competition, and stress;
- taking risks.

Cropley (2010) discussed the problems with aspects of process such as these using the example of education. He pointed out that such processes

---

[4] This is not to suggest that creative processes are bad, but rather to make the point that they are capable of causing havoc and that their negative side is inherent.

shake the foundations of the received classroom order and may even create the impression that teachers are favouring disruptive troublemakers, consequently bringing uncertainty for pupils (and parents) about what is really required for classroom success, questioning the value of laboriously acquired knowledge and skills, threatening loss of status and authority for teachers, and conceivably weakening teachers' self-image by, for instance, placing their role as authoritative sources of worthwhile knowledge in question. Thus, it is hardly surprising that, despite lip service to the contrary, many teachers dislike creative pupils or, in their subjective definitions, link creativity with unruliness or even pathology; Cropley (2009) gives examples of studies that demonstrate this phenomenon in a wide variety of countries.

In fact, it has been suggested since ancient times that creative people display processes that we would now say involve mental illness. Writers typically cited as examples of those who expressed this view prior to the modern era are Plato and Lombroso. More recent research summarised by Cropley (2001) has shown that there really are some similarities between schizophrenic thinking processes and creative thinking, schizophrenics making more remote associations and thus thinking more divergently than most people and in this sense resembling creative individuals. Rothenberg (1983) showed that Nobel Prize winners, creative college students, and schizophrenic patients all showed patterns of thinking processes that were more divergent than those of less creative students. However, the creative people also differed from the schizophrenic patients, so that although creativity and schizophrenia share some characteristics, they are not identical. Thus, in some respects the relationship of creativity and mental illness is reminiscent of the intersection of creativity and crime; they have some shared attributes but are different. We are not suggesting, however, that criminals are mentally ill (although some undoubtedly are).

Cropley and Sikand (1973) explored this latter point in greater detail and showed where the differences lie. When they compared architects, writers, and musicians with schizophrenic patients they found that the members of both groups made more remote associations than the members of a control group. However, although schizophrenic thinking generated novelty through unexpected combinations, this novelty frightened schizophrenic patients, whereas it was positively motivating for the creative people. This is consistent with Barron's (1972) finding that creative writers and architects were in the upper 15 per cent on all pathology scales of the Minnesota Multiphasic Personality Inventory, but that they also displayed high ego strength, which made it possible for them to make use of the unusual associations and elevated mood they displayed to generate effective novelty.

Goncalo, Vincent, and Audia (2010) drew attention to another dark aspect of the creative process: past creativity may actually block further creativity. Successful production of effective novelty in the past may lead a person to continue to work along a particular line of attack that has ceased to be novel in the present. Thus, in a sense, one of the numerous paradoxes of creativity may be that creativity itself is a danger to creativity. Goncalo et al. (2010, pp. 118–24) identified three psychological explanations for this phenomenon: cognitive, affective, and social. For instance, successful creative achievement may lead to 'cognitive framing': it may be assumed that all new solutions will be variants of the earlier successful creative solution. A successful creative solution may be associated with strong positive feelings so that the person continues to operate within the framework of the old solution because of the good feelings this arouses. In the social area, a successful creative solution may lead a person to be 'typecast' as the person who invented a particular solution, and they may be expected to produce more of the same. The successful creative may accept this and play the social role of the person who solves problems by repeating over and over again whatever led to the original creative solution. Goncalo et al. gave the example of Art Fry, the inventor of the Post-It note, who was typecast as 'the Post-It man' and, indeed, after acquiring this reputation subsequently apparently saw all new problems as requiring a new kind of sticky message label or ticket, thus never making any further paradigm change.

As Jasper (2010, p. 93) put it, creativity may 'take on a life of its own' that the creator cannot control. He called this the 'sorcerer's apprentice dilemma'. More mundanely explained, people are reluctant to abandon what was once a creative solution because they may have invested a great deal in it. The investment is possibly physical and financial, but of central interest for us is that it is also psychological: the person is familiar with it, it may have delivered substantial benefits in the past, may have brought praise and excited admiration, and is perhaps part of the individual's public persona. Jasper explains this in terms of risk avoidance, referring to 'the perils of unknown factors' (p. 93), although it is also consistent with theories of self, with dissonance theory, openness (or lack of it), learning theory (a behaviour that has repeatedly been positively reinforced in the past will be repeated), or with Mednick's (1962) hierarchy of associations (responses to a stimulus are arranged in a hierarchy of likelihood of being activated, associations frequently made in the past being high in the hierarchy and those made infrequently low).

A further paradox arises from the fact that, as Amabile (1983) and Csikszentmihalyi (1996) pointed out, a product is only publicly acclaimed as creative when it is accepted by those who are knowledgeable in a field and it becomes integrated into the field. Thus, creativity not infrequently changes the current paradigm in a field and thereafter redefines the norm, on the one hand ceasing to be novel itself (the process of acclamation as creative makes a product familiar, and therefore no longer novel, at least to insiders), and on the other hand not only rendering redundant earlier products which may, in their own time, have been novel, but also destroying the novelty of potential (possibly as yet unknown) new products in their cradle, as it were, by anticipating them, making the paradigm they represent obsolete, or directing attention in a new direction and thus denying them the seal of approval.[5]

Hull, Tesner, and Diamond (1978) made an interesting examination of this phenomenon (yesterday's creativity is the enemy of today's) at the level of the field rather than of individual creatives by analysing acceptance of Darwin's theory of evolution in the years around 1860. Although their empirical findings were not clear-cut, they reviewed a number of discussions of the difficulty existing paradigms pose for novel ideas and the resistance to such ideas they arouse. Put plainly, once a piece of effective novelty becomes the paradigm in a field it takes on the status of orthodoxy in that field and provokes resistance to subsequent effective novelty; some of the reasons for this have been discussed above with a focus on individual experts. According to Max Planck (1948), the older generation of true believers in the old orthodoxy (which was at one time itself creativity) must die out before new novelty can prevail. Thomas Huxley went so far as to suggest – presumably with ironic intention – that all scientists should be strangled on their sixtieth birthday before they become 'clogs upon progress' (see Huxley, 1901, p. 117). Huxley argued that the problem is worse in proportion to the level of creativity of the earlier contribution of the elderly scientist: the greater the creativity of the earlier product, the worse the clogging effect on future Process.

An example is that Darwin's theory of evolution required that the Earth be hundreds of millions of years old, whereas prevailing opinion held that it was only a few million years old. Resolving this issue was impeded by the fact that the towering scientific figure of Lord Kelvin (who published

---

[5] One consolation is that a new product can re-open assessment of the creativity of a product previously dismissed as uncreative, for instance, by making observers look at the old product in a new way.

661 papers in his career and accumulated 69 patents) opposed Darwin's view and indeed 'With the passage of time Kelvin would become more forthright in his assertions and less correct' (Bryson, 2004, p. 107). Such resistance led to Darwin withdrawing his very specific calculations from the third edition of *On the Origin of Species*, despite the fact that he was far closer to the truth than Kelvin.

The dark side of Person

The essence of creativity is going against the crowd. The development of an individual identity by each person also involves becoming different from the crowd by 'creating' an individual self and a unique identity. However, at some point the process can go awry. The positive, desirable breaking away from the conventional to form a unique personal identity can cross the line and become pathological, leading to maladjustment and neurosis, or manipulation, antisocial behaviour, crime, or terrorism. Simonton (2010) examined this relationship and concluded that there is some truth to the idea that creativity is connected with mental illness. However, there is no simple, linear causal relationship, according to which mental illness makes people creative (the more serious the illness, the greater the creativity) or creativity make people mentally ill (the more creative the person, the more acute the illness).

Negative consequences of creativity have been connected with negative phenomena in the area of Person by many researchers: for a summary see Simonton (2010) and Gabora and Holmes (2010). Creativity appears to be linked with both cognitive disturbance, as in schizophrenia (e.g., Schuldberg, 2000–2001), and also mood disturbance, as in bipolar disorder (e.g., Andreasen, 1987; Jamison, 1993). Jamison studied famous artists and authors and concluded that manic-depressive disorders are six times more common in such people than in the general public. She concluded that elevated mood (as in the manic phase of manic-depressive disorder) is vital for creativity. However, mood disturbance does not directly *cause* creativity: rather, both creativity and mood disturbance seem to derive from emotional lability and increased sensitivity to external stimuli. This is highly reminiscent of Eysenck's (1995) General Arousal Theory of Criminality, which is discussed more fully in Chapter 7 (p. 154).

Ludwig (1998) reported that there are exceptionally high rates of mental illness among creative artists but not among creative scientists. This led him to conclude that there is no direct cause-and-effect relationship between creativity and mental illness, but any link that exists is moderated by the characteristics of the particular field involved. For instance, severe personal conflicts or drug-induced distortions of reality might provide insights that can be applied in artistic creativity but be highly disruptive to creativity in physics or physiology. Ludwig concluded that the more informal, imprecise, subjective, and emotive a particular field, the greater the chance that mental illness will facilitate creativity.

Kaufman, Baer, Cropley, Reiter-Palmon, and Nienhauser (in press) looked at ratings by experts, quasi-experts, and novices of the creativity of two kinds of task differing along the continuum of formality and precision versus informality and imprecision identified by Ludwig (1998): creative writing, on the one hand, engineered products, on the other. They showed that although experts, quasi-experts, and novices differ in both domains, they are closer for the rating of creative writing than for the engineering products. The reason suggested for this is that 'expertise' in creative writing is more blurred because the domain does not have the same well-defined set of criteria of expertise compared with engineering (for example). One effect of this would be that, in simple terms, a quasi-expert can more easily pass for an expert in creative writing than in engineering, because it is easier to fake expertise in the former.

In a field that is towards the softer end of Simonton's (2009) continuum of domains or Ludwig's precision–imprecision continuum (i.e., the field is less formal, less precise, and the boundaries between expertise and quasi-expertise and non-expertise are more blurred, more overlapping), it is more likely that crazy ideas can give the appearance of creativity. One result is that there is more opportunity for an idea induced by mental illness to be regarded as creative. In something like physics, pseudo-creativity is much more easily recognisable.

Some concepts, such as mood and impulsivity, illustrate ways that creative individuals may be more at risk of moving over to the dark side. Averill and Nunley (2010) analysed the relationship in a closer and more differentiated way by examining the nature of the link between creativity and neurosis. Essentially, they concluded that neurosis is creativity gone wrong, that is, neurosis is an example of the dark side of creativity. Focusing on literary creativity, Gabora and Holmes (2010) examined the 'shadowy swamplands of the creative mind' (p. 277). They reviewed the connection between creativity and 'depression, alienation and self-abuse' (p. 277), especially creativity and substance abuse, and gave the numerous examples of twentieth-century poets, writers, musicians, and painters who committed suicide already outlined in Chapter 1. Gabora and Holmes (2010) also reviewed discussions of the question of whether creativity causes psychological disturbance or psychological disturbance leads to creativity. One possible dynamic of the relationship is that creative artists may delve deeply into the unconscious in a process of 'deep mining into the darkness' (p. 285), and bring to the surface material that uncreative people – wisely – leave undisturbed. Gabora and Holmes suggested that precisely this process of going where others fear to go may lead to an 'allure of darkness' (p. 283) that makes the dark side attractive to some creative individuals as well as to some of the people who admire their work, but with the danger of ultimately destructive results.

Moral darkness

Early in modern thinking, Amabile (1983) emphasised that creativity does not occur in a vacuum but in a social context. It always involves subjective judgements made by observers. These judgements may involve formalist qualities (e.g., unity, harmony, or complexity), or technical properties (e.g., high quality of construction, skilfulness, or professional finish), as Slater (2006) pointed out, or practical considerations such as usefulness, practicability, or marketability. However, the approval of external observers also results from a creative work being judged beautiful or pleasing (i.e., aesthetic criteria), as well as admirable and worthy of emulation (moral criteria). Morality, in particular, involves judgements of good and bad, virtuousness or wickedness.

Although he was not concerned with crime but rather the difference between genuine creativity and mere production of variation, Sternberg (2010) argued that, in fact, it is the *moral* dimension that is decisive. Only moral effective novelty involves creativity. Otherwise the effectively novel actions of disgusting criminals would have to be recognised as creative. Sternberg gave the examples of Hitler and Stalin, who presided over regimes which developed highly effective novel systems for killing people by the millions. In the absence of moral goodness, such monsters cannot be called creative. Martin (2006) also argued that creativity should be morally valuable, as did Gruber (1993). Craft, Gardner, and Claxton (2008) called for creativity that derives from wisdom, accepts and exercises responsibility, and is moral in nature. Otherwise, the danger is that it will become self-indulgent, egotistical, materialistic, and wasteful of resources. They regarded such 'unbridled' creativity as 'dangerous' (p. 169). However, the situation is not so clear-cut: McLaren (1993) gave the example of the building of magnificent cathedrals in the Middle Ages that are still regarded as monuments of human architectural and engineering creativity, despite being self-indulgent, egotistical, material-istic, and wasteful of resources.

Runco and Nemiro (2003) made the interesting point that, once again, there is what we would call a paradox here: creativity implies deviance from the conventional, whereas morality implies a special form of con-formity. This paradox leads to ambiguity about issues such as which rules can be broken, when they can be broken and under what circumstances, how dramatic the rule-breaking may be, and who is permitted to break the rules (Baucus et al., 2008). Indeed, moral precepts are not physical laws or forces of nature such as gravity, but are ideals that have been worked out by philosophers, religious authorities, or other thinkers, and in this sense they reflect the influence of religion or philosophy, culture, family, and friends, are subjective, and liable to change over time or in dif-ferent societies. They are a matter of subjective internal conviction rather than concrete evidence or physical or even legal coercion. Nonetheless, moral precepts seem to go beyond this and to demonstrate their worth in people's practical experience of life (as the evolutionary view of morals discussed below particularly emphasises).

Although there is obviously a connection between them, morality and law are not the same thing. We have already given the example of the use of creativity to persuade children to eat foods that are harmful to their health (as in advertising). This is legal, but of dubious morality. On the other hand, cheating on your tax return is illegal, but is regarded by many people (perhaps most) as moral. Although moral transgressions may be punished by condemnation, rejection, public shaming, or other external sanctions, they are discouraged at least as strongly by internal sanctions such as pangs of conscience or feelings of shame. The truly moral person behaves in a moral way out of personal conviction.

Nonetheless, some ethical values transcend cultural, religious, or eth-nic differences, and thus involve something approaching a universal moral worldview. According to Plato, for instance, there are four 'cardinal' virtues (courage, temperance, prudence, and justice) that should guide actions. All other virtues are thought to spring from these. Immanuel Kant argued that there is a 'moral imperative' to treat other people with dignity, and never to exploit them as instruments of one's own satisfaction. According to John Locke, no-one should act in such a way as to harm anyone else's life, health, liberty, or possessions. For Locke, these were natural rights, given by God. Although the time dimension discussed by Salcedo-Albarán et al. (2009) must be borne in mind (what is moral at one time may not be at another time), there do seem to be some moral universals. Examples are responsibility, fairness, concern about the wellbeing of others, good citizenship, integrity, sincerity, trustworthiness, generosity, and fortitude, all of which are mentioned by numerous writers in the area. These writers are not all representatives of the Western, Aristotelian tradition. The Confucian construct of *ren*, for instance, is an example of a broad definition of what is right and good that is widely accepted in Asian countries and beyond. *Ren* can be translated as 'righteousness'. It includes moral virtues such as loyalty, consideration, conscientiousness, or altruism, which are easily recognisable to people raised in the European–North American traditions.

Among other things, moral actions are responsible, promote fairness and the wellbeing of others, lead to justice, and contribute to good citizenship. The implications for creativity are obvious: moral creativity seeks to generate benefits for all, and is motivated by the wish to promote the common good. The idea that moral creativity can be defined in such a straightforward and yet broad and sweeping way as generation of effective novelty that seeks the common good may seem excessively simplistic. However, it is consistent with the views of philosophers who have wrestled with the issues at stake. Immanuel Kant defined creativity as 'the aspiration to create a perfect world *for everyone*' (emphasis added). Henning (2005) worked out a number of 'obligations' for moral creativity from the writings of Alfred North Whitehead: the obligations include beauty (to bring about the *widest possible* universe of beauty [emphasis added]), love (to maximise the intensity and harmony of oneself and *everything within one's sphere of influence* [emphasis added]), and peace (to avoid destruction). All of these obligations involve a responsibility to avoid doing harm to others and to promote the common good of the larger society. All of these approaches focus on the benefits flowing from creativity and especially the *distribution* of the benefits. The concepts of intrapersonal, interpersonal, and extrapersonal benefit (see p. 117) are helpful here: creativity centred on the common good involves emphasis on extrapersonal benefit, whereas creative crime focuses on intrapersonal benefit (benefit exclusively for the person generating the effective novelty).

What is needed are guidelines on how to recognise moral creativity. Sternberg (2010) offered insights into the distinguishing characteristic that renders creativity moral: according to him the crucial element is what he called 'wisdom'. When creativity is tempered by wisdom it is of necessity moral. The central characteristic of wisdom is concern for the common good: a wise person seeks to maximise the common good, not just to seek his or her own advantage. Sternberg's emphasis on creativity requiring effective novelty that benefits the common good (extrapersonal benefit) is reminiscent of Jasper's (2010) discussion of negative creativity as creativity where the benefits flow only in one direction instead of being shared by all players in a situation. The common good can be understood as involving a flow of benefits in the direction of other people and not just the person generating the effective novelty (i.e., interpersonal and extrapersonal benefit, not just intrapersonal benefit). From an American point of view, the 9/11 attack can then be seen as not creative, since its intention was not to serve the common good,[6] or as involving creativity, to be sure, but deliberately dark creativity (malevolent creativity) in which all benefits (whatever they were) flowed in one direction, thus making it reprehensible.

A second aspect of the negative moral side of creativity is described by Hilton (2010). One person's creativity may inspire another person's antisocial behaviour. An obvious example is the copying of evil deeds depicted in imaginative works. Hilton gives the examples of a murder committed using a technique described in the novel *Shibumi* and a double murder committed by copying a scene in a Clint Eastwood film. Another example is the 'Werther effect': a wave of suicides inspired by Goethe's book *The Sorrows of Young Werther*, which caused the book, a masterpiece by one of the world's greatest authors, to be banned in several countries. Ramsland (2010) gave an example that is in a way the mirror image of the two just given: a filmmaker made a movie about a killer who lured men into a trap with false ads on the Internet offering a liaison with a woman. Later, he began practising the same scheme himself using the same bait, and actually completed one real-life chainsaw murder before being caught. Thus, an artistic creation that is successful in entertaining, even informing or inspiring readers, listeners, beholders or even the creative individual him- or herself (the bright side), may simultaneously encourage, promote or provide models of wicked behaviour (the dark side). It seems plausible that the more effective the creativity in such situations, the greater the likelihood that it will promote antisocial behaviour, so that, perversely, the stronger the bright side, the worse the dark side.

---

[6] Nonetheless, it may well have seemed (rightly or wrongly) to the attackers to be advancing the common good of some other ethnic or national group(s), so that even wisdom is obviously relative. Disagreement among beholders on what is dark and what is bright does not negate the general principle that creativity can have a dark side.

The social utility of moral creativity

Moral creativity can bring great benefit for human beings and their environment, but immoral creativity can bring great harm. Thus, it seems to lie in the public interest that creative people possess positive moral values and apply these to their own behaviour. How does this occur? Some evolutionary biologists and socio-biologists believe that morality develops as a result of evolutionary forces. Seeking justice, fostering the wellbeing of others, showing courage, cooperating with others, and similar behaviours are not the only behaviours of which people are capable. Unfairness, lack of concern about others, or exaggerated individualism are also possible (and indeed, are not especially uncommon in real life). The widely accepted morality outlined above is thus not absolute, but relative, and in theory any set of values could be adopted. However, properties such as justice, concern about the wellbeing of others, cooperation, and courage enhance the survival both of the individuals who display them and also of the collective to which the individuals belong. As a result, such moral values have come to prevail through the process of natural selection. Simple versions of what humans regard as morality are seen, according to biologists, in all species. The greater complexity of human moral systems is attributable to their greater brain size, living in larger groups, and more complex interactions among individuals and groups.

In closing this chapter, it can be said that creativity is not all sweetness and light. It has long been linked in popular imagination with dissatisfaction, disquiet, restlessness, defiance, and deviance. Although essential for personal development and individuation, such wrestling with the status quo also has a dark side for the individual, such as the frustrations and inner torments of creative individuals that may even lead them to delve into the dark shadow-lands of the mind, with disastrous consequences for their physical and psychological wellbeing. Creative behaviour may also have negative consequences for the society, such as the shaking of the foundations of stability and good order brought about by questioning of received opinions and habits – although these need to be shaken up regularly for progress and renewal to occur, questioning them can arouse resistance in guardians of the status quo and even lead to conflict between generations. Individuals can see the basis of their identity and sense of order and wellbeing swept away and their achievements belittled as no longer relevant or meaningful, as in Thomas Huxley's (1901) undoubtedly ironic but nonetheless pointed remark about the need to strangle scientists on their sixtieth birthday. At a more concrete level, the Products of creativity can have more specific negative consequences and, indeed, effective novelty can even be generated for the specific purpose of achieving negative ends. Chapter 7 will begin the exploration of this fusion of creativity and deliberately blameworthy behaviour, especially crime.

CHAPTER SEVEN

Creativity and crime

All creativity involves products that deviate from the norm, processes that also involve deviation – both in thought and action – and personal properties such as openness, daring, or confidence. These processes and personal characteristics may generate products that receive social approval – in which case they may be labelled 'creativity' – or disapproval, in which case they are often labelled 'crime'. At a fundamental level, however, both kinds of product are manifestations of the general phenomenon of generation of effective novelty (i.e., creativity). This link means that there is a fine line between the positive and the negative application of creativity. In fact, some researchers argue that creativity is of bio-psychological origin, and involves an evolutionary predisposition to personality traits such as, for instance, sensation seeking, impulsiveness, and risk taking. As a result, we would say that creative individuals are 'vulnerable' to crime. Because of the fact that positive creativity is of great benefit to society, it is important to understand the differences between positive creativity and crime.

Although they are far less common than discussions of the virtues and benefits of creativity, discussions of the creativity–crime link stretch over many years (e.g., Lynn, 1971; Johnson, 1983; Wilson, 1984; Eisenman, 1991; Brower and Stahl, 2011). In a discussion of terrorism/ counter-terrorism, Cropley (2005) drew parallels between the results of creativity as a competitive enabler in business and its usefulness in crime, arguing that the same competitive benefits that businesses hope to draw on through creative products are also available to people and organisations with less benevolent motives (such as terrorist organisations or criminals). It is clear that, while creativity is normally regarded as a tool for enabling positive, affirming change, there is no reason in principle why it cannot be used for negative, destructive purposes. As Salcedo-Albarán et al. (2009, p. 4) put it, 'perverse creativity' can be used to serve wicked ends. These include crime, and the purpose of this chapter is to examine the fusion between the two manifestations of creativity.

It is true, as Runco (2010) pointed out with the metaphor of a hammer, that it is the use that creativity is put to that is decisive for goodness or badness, not the process of creativity itself. In other words, the obvious difference between positive creativity and creative crime lies in the Ps of Product and Press (environmental reaction to the product): social acclaim of the product as positive on the one hand, condemnation as criminal on the other. In this book, however, we go beyond Product and Press to look more closely at the actual generation of relevant and effective novelty, including Process and Person – and especially the interaction or the *ecology* of the factors involved. Generation of relevant and effective novelty – or creativity in its broadest sense – is by its very nature especially suitable for achieving ends that societies regard as misuse, such as manipulating people or gaining unfair advantage, and is particularly potent when it is misused for what we call 'resourceful' crime (see Introduction, p. 3). However, it does not cease to be creativity when it is misused, and can be understood using the same principles as when it is applied for socially approved purposes. Indeed, despite the clear difference between creative crime and acclaimed creativity in terms of Product and Press, there are marked *similarities* between the two phenomena in other Ps of creativity, especially Process and aspects of Person.

Process

The crucial essence of the generation of effective novelty is deviating from the customary way of doing things. At the very least, the creative Process involves breaking implicit social rules or informal agreements on what is right and what is wrong. It is thus inherently deviant and disorderly. As a result, the line separating creativity for *socially approved* purposes and creativity for *disapproved* purposes (or positive vs negative creativity, dark vs light creativity or malevolent vs benevolent creativity, as we have labelled the distinction in earlier chapters[1]) may be difficult to spot or may be placed in a different position by different individuals or groups, or in different eras; norm-breaking inherent to creativity is constantly at risk of crossing the line from social approval to social disapproval. The example

---

[1] These terms are not synonyms or simply confused ways of referring to the same thing, but represent a step-by-step refinement of terminology, ranging from the broadest sense (positive vs negative creativity) to the most precise (malevolent vs benevolent creativity).

of an artist in Britain who stole human body parts so that he could use them in artworks is a good demonstration of this.[2] Many observers would probably find this abhorrent or disgusting or as showing disgraceful disrespect for the dead or those mourning the person's death, but the artist himself was indignant at the interference with his work, and some commentators found the results of the theft artistically powerful and technically daring. The Crown Prosecutor saw the case as simple: the body parts had been stolen, so the whole matter was a straightforward case of theft – for one side, art, for the other, crime.

Despite this, it is important to note that deviance, as the term is used here, is not inherently reprehensible: since norms are specific to a particular society, behaviour that is regarded as abhorrent in one society may be perfectly acceptable, or even admirable, in another. Mixed nude bathing or shared male and female showers in a sports club may be completely unremarkable in one society (e.g., Japan or Germany), lead to imprisonment for crime in another (e.g., Iran), or perhaps be regarded as a daring social innovation in a third, and hence as creativity (e.g., Australia). Thus, the same behaviour may be customary, criminal, or creative, depending on the reaction of the external environment.

This lack of clarity about when deviance becomes negative in the eyes of observers is complicated by the fact that the criteria of what is acceptable change not only from society to society but also from era to era within a given society. Brower and Stahl (2011) gave an informative case study that shows how the fate of deviance depends strongly on the zeitgeist; similar acts carried out with similar motivation may be labelled 'crime' or 'creativity', depending on society's values at a particular time. They compared Lewis Carroll and Egon Schiele, who both used nude, under-age girls as models; Carroll photographed them and Schiele painted them. Schiele was jailed for lewdness but Carroll was not. Carroll did his work in the nineteenth century, a time when people did not see sexual implications in nudity in young girls, but Schiele worked in the early twentieth century at a time when young children had come to be seen as objects of sexual desire. Brower and Stahl attributed the difference in attitudes to the work of Freud. Even more striking are the views expressed by H. G. Wells in 1902 in *New Republic* that in this utopia 'inferior' races would have to be killed off in order to prevent 'propagating weakness'. Such views were perfectly acceptable in 1902, although they would be regarded with horror today.

---

[2] www.independent.ie/world-news/parts-of-bodies-stolen-for-art-casts-452817.html. Downloaded on 20 April 2012.

A more recent example that illustrates several of the points just made is Andres Serrano's photograph 'Piss Christ' (referred to in Chapter 1) which involves a crucifix submerged in a glass of the artist's own urine. Many lay-people might find this product of the creative process disgusting and in some countries it might even be prohibited by law, whereas some experts found it daring, paradigm-breaking, and highly effective, and it won a visual arts award from the South-eastern Center for Contemporary Arts. In some countries it could have led to prosecution and in an earlier era it might well have been regarded as crime in many countries. Nonetheless, it seems unlikely that Serrano wanted to do harm with his artwork, but rather that his deviance was intended for artistic effect.

Another example with links to a major theme in later sections of this book, terrorism, involves the smashing of the Buddhas of Bamiyan, two huge sixth-century statues carved into the side of a cliff in the Bamyan valley in Afghanistan. After surviving for around 1,500 years, the statues were destroyed by order of the Taliban Mullah Mohammed Omar, starting on 2 March 2001. The announcement of the Taliban's intention to destroy the statues set off huge protests from many governments that regarded the statues as works of art of overwhelming cultural significance. The Taliban, however, justified the smashing of the statues on the grounds that destroying them was in the interests of propagation of virtue and prevention of vice. What was art for one side – the overwhelming majority – and had to be preserved at all costs, was sin for the other, and had to be destroyed at all costs.

The social environment and deviance

The relationship between the surrounding social environment and creativity may be looked at from both qualitative and quantitative points of view. One possibility is that very large departures from the usual are labelled mental illness or criminality, moderate departures, on the other hand, as creativity (i.e., that it is the *amount* of deviation that is decisive for the public reaction to creativity). It is also possible, however, that it is not so much the amount of departure from the usual, but the *kind* of departure that is decisive in determining whether variation is condemned or acclaimed. The society can tolerate only a certain amount and a certain kind of variability. The social setting thus determines what kinds of new ideas emerge by setting limits on both the amount and also the kind of divergence that is seen, or by guiding creative thinking into particular channels. The interaction of amount and kind of deviance and social reaction to deviation was directly linked to creative crime in the study by Kaufman et al. (submitted) already described in Chapter 5 (pp. 112–113). The study's findings showed that respondents were able to differentiate between good and bad courses of action (qualitative criterion) but that the perceived goodness/badness of a course of action was also influenced by the *amount* of badness (quantitative criterion). In fact, these authors concluded that there is a threshold *amount* of badness, above which behaviour is not seen as being of a creative *kind*.

Gabora and Holmes (2010, p. 281) proposed an analysis of creativity in terms of the social environment that shows the link to crime. They distinguished between 'consensus reality' and 'self-made reality'. The former is what most people agree constitutes 'reality'; the latter involves an idiosyncratic view of reality constructed by certain people strictly on the basis of their own experiences. As a result of the deviation of their self-made reality from consensus reality the views of such people come to deviate more and more from the accepted norms. This means that they seem very interesting to *some* observers (and are likely to be labelled 'creative' by these observers), but exasperating or even threatening to *others* (and thus likely to be labelled 'criminals'). Gabora and Holmes interpreted the 'deviant' behaviour of such people as giving them a feeling of 'connection' with the external world and a sense of some measure of control over it, either through socially approved acts (such as production of socially approved products) or through disapproved products (frequently crime). In both cases, the people involved are 'doing something' about the world they live in, acting upon it and not just passively accepting whatever it has to offer.

Person

Some discussions of the application of creativity to crime study the relationship in terms of personality traits, the P of Person. Put briefly, creative individuals may turn to crime as the way of expressing their creativity because of the kind of person they are. Brower and Stahl (2011) argued that rebelling against the standard way of doing things is a perfectly normal, even desirable part of growing up. Indeed, according to them, deviating from standard ways confirms a person's individual identity and also provides a way of opposing impersonal conformity. However, Gascón and Kaufman (2010) pointed out that there is an essential tension between individualism and conformity, between behaving the same as others and breaking out of established patterns (of action and thought). People who fail to conform may strengthen their own individuality and sense of self, but may be seen as rebels or deviants by other people. Thus, individuality and independence define a place where the socially positive and socially negative aspects of creativity meet; just as deviance from the norm may lead to positive creative ideas, so too can it lead to crime.

Creative personal traits and crime

The commission of crimes is often linked to *psychological deficits* within the individual person. Krohn, Lizotte, and Hall (2009) gave an overview of such deficits, including (a) inefficient cognitive processes, such as inappropriate social learning or self-referential ideation; (b) defective coping skills, such as inability to deal with stress; and (c) weakness in aspects of personality, such as self-control. These may be exacerbated by unfavourable social factors, such as negative labelling, social disorganisation, or institutional anomie. However, conceptualising crime purely in terms of deficits cannot account for the ingenuity, resourcefulness, willingness to take a calculated risk, self-confidence, and determination of people like Shirley Pitts, Ronnie Biggs, or Bernie Madoff (as unpalatable as it is to use such terms in describing Madoff).

For instance, the psychological study of, in particular, psychopathy has drawn attention to properties among offenders of this kind that are typically regarded in a *positive* light, such as high intelligence, advanced verbal skills, or highly developed social skills (e.g., Hare and Neumann, 2006). Consequently, resourceful crime requires more than a deficit model in order to be understood. However, psychopaths also display glib and superficial charm, grandiosity, pathological lying, inability to empathise, high levels of deceit and manipulation, lack of remorse, callousness, poor behavioural controls, failure to accept responsibility for their own actions, anger, egocentricity, goallessness, and deficient affect (Hare, 2006). Positive characteristics are present, but are outweighed by characteristics associated with harmful effects for other people.

Turning to actual crime (as against deviance as a test score), Johnson's (1983) overview of the relationship between criminal behaviour and personality traits led him to conclude that findings are inconclusive, with support for the existence of a link being weak on the whole. Narrowing the focus even further by concentrating on convicted criminals, Eisenman (2008) summarised research as indicating that, as a group, these people display *low* levels of creativity, and are poor at solving problems. Furthermore, actual prisoners rated by guards and other inmates as behaving creatively generated little or no effective novelty, but merely showed lack of inhibition and low levels of social conformity (pseudo-creativity). Although easy to confuse with creativity, these characteristics are more typical of daily physical and property crime or expressive crime (see Introduction, p. 2), i.e., uncreative crime.

Thus, it appears that criminals *as a group* are not characterised by high levels of creativity as a general or overall personal characteristic. This may well reflect the fact that actively creative criminals constitute a (small) subgroup within the population of criminals (as indeed actively creative people do in the general population) so that the effect of their presence on trends within the total group of offenders would be hard to detect using statistical procedures based on aggregated data (e.g., correlations, mean differences). Nonetheless, Eisenman (2008) reported that prisoners did reveal creativity on the Thematic Apperception Test (TAT), but only when telling stories about crime. They tried to think up ways of operating that were creative (novel and highly effective) in their area of specialisation – crime. Such confinement of creativity to a specific area is consistent with a good deal of research (for a summary, see Baer, 2011) showing that creativity is often domain specific, and thus does not negate the idea that criminals can be creative. Crime seems to be their domain, just as science is the domain of a scientist, who might not be creative in the arts, or even other sciences. This all suggests that, although when the creativity of criminals is assessed across the entire group or outside their domain their creativity may be less apparent, within their specialty (crime) they may be more creative. In this, they would not differ from other specialists.

Negative personal traits and creativity

Just as negative behaviour in the form of creative crime is associated with positive personality traits, as has just been shown, there is also evidence that positive behaviour acclaimed as creative is associated with negative traits. In an early but comprehensive review, Johnson (1983) showed that there was weak evidence that acknowledged creative individuals are not only non-conformist, unconventional, and radical (traits that many would admire, even if with reservations), but also rebellious, troublesome, cynical, and vindictive, less admirable traits. He concluded that creatives as a group tend to be self-centred and to lack ego control.

More recent studies have related creativity to self-centredness, self-justification, lack of concern about others, arrogance, and dishonesty (e.g., Silvia, Kaufman, Reiter-Palmon, and Wigert, 2011; Gino and Ariely, 2012). Nebel (1988) even linked it to destructiveness. However, there is some disagreement about these characteristics: for instance, Silvia et al. carried out a highly differentiated analysis in which they were at pains to avoid conflating disagreeableness and hostility, and concluded that low agreeableness has often been mistaken for hostility. They argued, in fact, that creative people are often not even disagreeable, but simply *pretentious* or, to reinterpret Johnson (1983, see previous paragraph), affected by self-aggrandisement.

Walczyk, Runco, Tripp, and Smith (2008) looked at a characteristic more obviously linked to crime – lying – and showed that people who scored high on a creativity task were more likely to lie. Gino and Ariely (2012) went further and reported greater 'moral disengagement' (p. 454) among creative individuals (i.e., lack of scruples or conscience), which conceivably 'triggers dishonest behaviour' (p. 446). Gino and Ariely proposed an actual cause-and-effect relationship between creativity and dishonesty. They started by drawing attention to the phenomenon of 'the dishonesty of honest people' (Mazar, Amir, and Ariely, 2008, p. 633). Dishonest behaviour seems to be acceptable to even honest people provided that they can preserve their self-concept as a solid citizen. They gave the example of cheating on tax returns, which seems to be widespread but does not make people feel like law-breakers. Creative people may be particularly prone to this effect, with creativity encouraging them to be dishonest in two ways: (1) high levels of divergent thinking (Process) may help them to find loopholes that can be exploited with the help of creativity, while (2) greater flexibility (Person) may help them to rationalise their behaviour, for instance, by interpreting it in a way that makes it seem justified and thus preserves their positive self-image. To put it bluntly, crime may be facilitated in creative people by their ability to think up effective ways of breaking the law and still feel good about themselves.

Motivation and feelings/emotions

Gino and Ariely (2012) argued that the phenomenon just described (breaking the law but preserving a feeling of being a good person) is particularly strong when people are highly motivated. We pointed out in Chapter 3 that dissatisfaction with the status quo and high motivation to change it is a characteristic of creative people: motivation to eliminate defects, close gaps, and the like, as well as to complete tasks, produce a finished product, etc. This aspect will be discussed in greater detail in the following section. Creative people show a combination of motivation to introduce novelty, special skill in the processes for doing this, self-serving and self-righteous moral judgements, a low level of concern about the effects of their behaviour on other people, and the flexibility to reinterpret events in their own favour and avoid a bad conscience, a complex of properties that places them at greater risk of crime than less creative people. Creative people could be described as *vulnerable* to crime. This is particularly apparent, for example, in cases of fraud, where these characteristics may combine to make creative people, given a sufficiently strong need, more susceptible to stealing from their employer (or better equipped to do so).

Many acknowledged creative individuals have described their discontent with the existing state of affairs and their use of creativity to resolve this discontent; we have already given the examples of Albert Einstein and Thomas Alva Edison. Both creatives and criminals may use risky strategies for achieving ends, and are apparently willing to challenge the status quo, probably in the belief that they can pull it off (whereas others cannot). Lemert, Lemert, and Winter (2000, p. 93) referred to cheque forgers' 'life on the edge'. This willingness to live on the edge suggests a lower level of anxiety in the face of threat. Gamman and Raein particularly emphasised the 'need to be different' (p. 164), the associated urge to 'do something', and willingness to take risks, the latter encouraged by self-belief or the conviction by members of both groups that they are luckier than other people, that is, that they will get away with it.

The role of excitement in crime is encapsulated in Gamman and Raein's (2010) case study of Buster Edwards, one of the Great Train Robbers – and thus an accomplice of Ronnie Biggs, who has been mentioned several times. This robbery was organised in an innovative way and was carried out with daring and panache. Edwards had been a soldier, a boxer, and a nightclub owner before he turned to crime; he was not a social outcast or a person who had moved in crime circles all his life, but consciously chose crime as a pathway to 'the good life', not because he did not know how to do anything else, lacked social or job skills, was subjected to irresistible pressure from his peers, or simply lived according to the deviant norms of his subculture. After serving time in jail for the robbery, Edwards was released in 1975 and made his living by running a flower stall outside Waterloo Station in London. In a television interview he said that he missed his life of crime because it had been *exciting*, whereas life on the right side of the law was *boring*. Thus, for him, crime seems to have been a way of doing something that satisfied his need for arousal. Gamman and Raein also mention that there is evidence that even some hate crimes, which seem to encapsulate antisocial pathology, may be seen by the perpetrators as above all an exciting way of escaping boredom, that is, of raising their arousal level.

Dunne and Raby (2001) used the concept of 'dark' creativity in their concept of 'design noir'. They made the interesting point that humans seem to have a capacity for *enjoying* illegal activities, giving the example of hackers, who inflict sometimes massive damage on other people not out of malevolence but apparently out of sheer enjoyment of their own wickedness. Dunne and Raby also emphasised that human beings have the potential to form not only, in our terms, bright relationships with things in the world, but also dark relationships. They gave the tragic example of a fifteen-year-old girl who was bullied by mobile phone, clearly a dark use of communications technology whose inventors, developers, and designers probably envisaged only its bright side during their creative work. Eventually, the girl committed suicide. She left a suicide note, which she recorded as a text message on her mobile phone! This seems like an ultimate act of irony, but may well constitute perfectly 'normal' behaviour in a system involving a dark relationship with telephone technology.

What may be crucial when creativity is used for negative or malevolent ends is self-control. This is a stable personal characteristic that becomes discernible at an early age and persists over the life span. Gottfredson and Hirschi (1990) showed that people with low self-control often act out of impulse, with resulting deviant behaviour. According to Gottfredson and Hirschi and Longshore, Turner, and Stein (1996), individuals with low self-control tend to be self-interested and impulsive, to seek instant gratification, to lack persistence, to be risk-seekers, and to be insensitive to others' needs. Lynam and Miller (2004) showed that such people, whom they described as 'impulsive', often do not weigh up right and wrong, and frequently trivialise the consequences of their actions for other people. Such characteristics are favourable for rule-breaking, norm-defying behaviours that may, as has been shown in earlier sections, lead to positive or negative creativity.

In a discussion of the active role of the individual transgressor in his or her crime, as against being a passive acceptor of whatever the environment ordains, Agnew (2011) emphasised the phenomenon of *control*, referring to such control as involving 'agency'. Agentic individuals possess properties related to creativity such as flexibility (Personal properties), desire for change (Personal motivation) and ability to imagine a wide range of options (i.e., divergent thinking – Process). Agnew specifically mentioned the link of such characteristics with creativity. Agentic people behave in ways that are unpredictable and deviate from the customary, sometimes in the form of crime, but sometimes in the form of law-abiding behaviour. Thus, he links both creativity and crime to agency or, as we have put it, control. However, despite sharing problems with self-control with criminals, positively creative individuals seem to be better able to cope with these problems, because they are more agentic.

The fine line between crime and creativity

The material just reviewed suggests that creativity is associated with both positive and negative products, even where intentions are basically good. Gamman and Raein (2010, p. 172) gave a number of examples of acknowledged contemporary artists who really did use 'transgressive behaviour' as part of their way of making what they saw as an artistic statement: for us, these involve walking the fine line. The examples include an artist who kidnapped a model and mistreated her to create good perspectives for his work, a woman who stalked people in order to expose the evils of surveillance, a man who shoplifted and displayed the stolen goods in a gallery to make a statement on ownership, an artist who, in order to protest against rejection of his work by a gallery, issued a press release falsely reporting that his parents had been beheaded in their bed and that he had committed suicide, and another who stole human body parts and made plaster casts of them as sculptures – this latter was frowned upon in artistic circles because plaster is considered an inferior medium for sculptors to work in! The line between creativity and crime is certainly blurred in these cases.

Although resourceful offenders do not, as a rule, aim at making a creative statement, but at achieving profit for themselves (however they understand profit), they do seem to share a number of characteristics with people whose work is socially acclaimed, such as creative artists. Julius (2002) outlined a number of similarities: these include the ability to scan the environment and spot and exploit a favourable situation. Both artists and resourceful criminals also make use of divergent thinking in order, for instance, as Gamman and Raein (2010, p. 162) put it, 'to "do" something' practical. De Grave (1995) gave examples of the self-confidence of female confidence tricksters. In a much more recent study, Andrews Bonta, and Wormith (2006) identified 'adventurousness' as an aspect of the big four psychological characteristics of criminals. Such properties are typically associated not with crime but with socially acclaimed *creativity*. Gamman and Raein (2010) emphasised the feeling in both people acclaimed socially as creative and those condemned as criminal of being outsiders, or, as Gladwell (2008) puts it, of being social 'outliers' who consciously stand outside the everyday and seek opportunities of exploiting it for their own purposes: in the one case to make an artistic statement, in the other to make a profit.

The lure of self-aggrandisement

Gabora and Holmes (2010) made the interesting point that some people may actually have a vested interest in blurring the differences between, for instance, artistic creativity and socially marginal if not antisocial behaviour. Established creative individuals may make their own lives seem more rational and more meaningful or more romantic and exciting by endorsing 'myths' about the social-outcast status of the creative, their natural eccentricity or their artistic licence to ignore traditional social norms. This role playing, posturing, or even self-aggrandisement may also be seen not in widely acclaimed creatives but in would-be creatives, where the real problem may be lack of talent or knowledge, idleness, or fecklessness. They may cast themselves as being part of a creative tradition serving a noble cause, even if society fails to give them due recognition or even rejects them. It is easy to imagine criminals also adopting and promulgating stereotypes about themselves for the purpose of self-justification or to make themselves seem like almost romantic figures, for instance, by claiming that they are forced into crime by the unfavourable circumstances of their life, are victims hitting back at their oppressors or fighters against injustice, or are actually social benefactors exposing weaknesses of the system for the good of other people.

Indeed, it is commonplace for people to do precisely this. Examples include people who engage in activities like 'cultural jamming' (Brisman, 2010, p. 210), for instance, defacing advertising billboards in ways designed, according to them, to reveal the true and sinister manipulative purpose of the advertising, 'interventionism' (interfering in the daily life of the community by, for instance, disrupting traffic, in order to demonstrate communal ownership of the streets), and 'sabotage' (for instance, wrecking animal labs or logging mills). The purpose of such acts is reformist; to 'undermine … repressive structures' in society (Brisman, 2010, p. 215): the perpetrators see themselves as social reformers striving to expose injustice, abuse, and violence, no matter how misguided they may seem to some observers. Recently, the various Occupy movements (Occupy Wall Street, Occupy London, Occupy Moscow, and the like) have indeed developed novel and effective forms of protest behaviour such as the tent cities they have constructed. However, British courts have cast doubt on the purity of the pro-social motives of some of these people by sentencing them to prison terms for being rioters, looters, and arsonists, and for carrying out violent assaults on uninvolved members of the public, treating them not as social benefactors but as criminals.[3] It is clear that perceptions may differ.

It has been common in recent years for internet activists to claim benevolent motives for destructive actions such as hacking into industrial, military, or social service websites and destroying files, altering or deleting information, or otherwise causing chaos, inconvenience, or even sometimes huge financial damage to the individuals or organisations on the receiving end. To take an example, in November 1988, Robert Morris, a hacker in the USA, infected thousands of large company computers with a virus and caused millions of dollars in damage. He claimed that the 'worm' was activated for research purposes, but was convicted and fined despite this. In other words, as far as the court was concerned, his work had crossed the line and become crime, even though he claimed a benign intention. Websites such as the well-known Wikileaks obtain and publish private confidential/classified material regardless of possible harm to some of the people involved, doing this in the service of what they see as a higher good, such as exposing government machinations. Despite the alleged good intentions, many authorities regard their work as crime. It may be hard to decide if they are heroes or villains, especially as their media statements sometimes make a personal impression of self-righteousness and self-importance.

The similarities – overview

The fine line between using creativity for benevolent purposes and for crime may indeed be vague and shifting, may be placed differently by different parties such as the people generating the novelty and various groups in the society such as law-enforcers, or may even be deliberately or at least self-servingly obfuscated for purposes of self-glorification or self-justification. Nonetheless, there are striking psychological similarities, summarised in Table 7.1.

The table is organised around the four of the Ps presented in detail in Chapter 3. The personal properties listed in the table enhance people's ability to generate creativity regardless of whether it leads to socially approved or negative products. It is apparent from Table 7.1 that many of

---

[3] We are not making a judgement about the worthiness of the crime involved in this or the immediately following examples, or about their possible ultimate pro-social effects. Our purpose is merely to give examples of crime whose perpetrators claim to be using crime to do good, whereas others may see the matter differently.

Table 7.1 *Properties shared by creatives and resourceful criminals*

P of Creativity			
Process	Personal properties	Personal motivation	Personal feelings
Environmental scanning	Ego-centrism	Dissatisfaction/ discontent	Feeling of being an outsider
Recognising opportunities	Low arousability	Sensation seeking	Self-confidence
Seeing remote possibilities	Openness	Urge to take action	Confidence in success
Redefining the problem	Ingenuity	Rebelliousness	Optimism
Making unexpected links	Resourcefulness	Need to be different	Excitement
Recognising effective strategies	Flexibility	Appetite for risk	
Trying something out	Opportunism	Adventure seeking	
	Lack of inhibition		
	Non-conformity		
	Willingness to break norms		
	Moral disengagement		
	Courage		
	Self-confidence		
	Self-centredness		
	Resourcefulness		
	Toughness in the face of resistance		

the properties of creative individuals really are likely to encourage them to cross the line: examples include ego-centrism, moral disengagement, impulsiveness, rebelliousness, or the feeling of being able to pull it off. Gamman and Raein (2010) pointed out that some artists sometimes really do cross the line in full knowledge of the fact that the actions in question involve crime but in the belief that the crime will serve society and ultimately the common good by breaking down taboos or exposing the dark side of the society. Much the same can be said about people such as the social activists or internet activists given above. What this means is that people engaged in both aesthetic as well as functional creativity are in danger of crossing the line or, as we put it, the properties highlighted in Table 7.1 make them 'vulnerable' to crime.

Common source of positive and negative creativity

In fact, the overlaps between positive and negative creativity are so notice-able that some researchers have proposed that they have a common biological origin. Of particular interest in this context are approaches according to which the biological underpinnings of both forms of creativity are the same. In a nutshell, both creative criminals and socially acclaimed creatives are acting out the same biologically based drives but are doing it in different ways, the different results (Products) being more socially acceptable (creativity) or less acceptable (crime).

Evolutionary psychology
Kanazawa's (2003) evolutionary psychology research and theory is confined to males, because their numbers are very much larger in the ranks of both criminals and acknowledged creatives. This is not to suggest that females cannot be either criminals or creatives, and it seems that his ideas are capable of being applied to females, *mutatis mutandis*, although such a discussion would go beyond the limits of this book. According to Kanazawa, both crime and creativity are expressions of young men's competitive drives derived from the *ancestral environment*. The original function of the competitive drive was to increase reproductive success and, because it was rather successful, the genes for competitiveness have been handed on to many descendants, even though society now has relatively peaceable norms, and agencies specifically empowered with preventing excessive displays of aggressiveness, seizure of other people's possessions, elimination of other people who get in the way or are annoying, and so on (law-enforcers). Today, men can express their competitiveness 'in evolutionarily novel ways in science, music, art and literature, *if they have talent*' (emphasis added) (Kanazawa, 2003, p. 265). Those who are able to act out their competitive drive in socially approved ways – often regarded as involving expression of talent or high ability – achieve social acclaim and are regarded as creative or at least as successful. Those who lack socially approved talent but are perhaps tough and strong or quick to spot vulnerability in an environment (such as lack of safeguards or a good chance of getting away with it) can achieve 'success' through crime.

Men who act out their competitive urges in one way or another are not consciously aware of what is happening. As Kanazawa (2003, p. 265) put it, 'Organisms (including humans) are usually not privy to the evolutionary logic that placed the psychological mechanisms in the brain to solve adaptive problems [of the ancestral environment]. Criminals [and creatives] are therefore unaware of the ultimate causes of their behavior; they are not consciously pursuing reproductive success.' Thus, although young criminals want to assert themselves in empowering ways, *they do not know why*. This is also true of creatives – the literature on motivation and creativity already reviewed indicates that creative individuals report a general dissatisfaction with the status quo and an urge to do things better. Some people engaged in art, music, literature, or other aesthetic fields report a desire to make a name for themselves or to change the world for the good (i.e., to the way they think it ought to be). An attempt to understand either positive or negative creativity in a purely environmentally driven way, as is especially the case in most sociological, anthropological, or ethnological explanations of crime, is thus certain to remain only partial, and cannot be elucidated in narrative interviews, autobiographies, and the like.

Like other evolutionary psychologists, Kanazawa (2003) cannot conduct experimental or even quasi-experimental research, since he is drawing conclusions about events some of which took place aeons ago. He relies instead on correlational findings. In his research, however, he does this with great ingenuity, drawing on modern data pertaining to two interesting pairs of phenomena, age and creativity/crime, on the one hand, and marriage and creativity/crime, on the other, thus drawing together data from two disparate domains and displaying divergent thinking, building of broad categories, the making of remote associates, and the like. He showed in a nutshell that both law-breaking and creativity are young men's games and that they are also single men's games. Naturally, because he is dealing with correlational data (a) cause-and-effect conclusions are merely logical inferences and (b) the findings do not refer to everybody (some older men are creative and some older men break the law; some married men are creative and some are criminals).

Kanazawa's review of research shows (p. 264) that although there are 'life-course persisters', the majority of criminals are 'adolescence-limiters', while his own study of 280 creative scientists (mainly male mathematicians, physicists, chemists and biologists), nearly all from the eighteenth century to the present, showed that two-thirds had made their most significant contribution by their mid-thirties and 80 per cent by around forty. The mean age was 35.4. Kanazawa reported that this relationship between age and creativity was repeated among male jazz musicians, and that the relationship is also true for painters and authors. Although their analysis was much more differentiated, in a study of 173 classical composers, Kozbelt and Meredith (2011) reported that the musicians tended to produce their best work at about the age of forty. Furthermore, marriage also leads to a decrease in creativity. A very high proportion of scientists desist from further highly creative work shortly after their marriage, whereas unmarried scientists as a group continue to make creative contributions. Indeed, the age–creativity relationship may be at least in part a confounding of age and marital status, since the mean age of peak performance is around ten years higher in unmarried men.

Turning to the topic of crime, Kanazawa (2003) reviewed existing findings on age and crime and marriage and crime, and showed that the relationships are very similar. Both ageing and marriage lead to sharp reductions in crime, although life-course persisters are also seen, as is the case with creatives. The same is true of other risk-taking behaviour: in creatives, phenomena such as tolerance for ambiguity and openness to the novel decrease, as Planck's principle (see Chapter 6, p. 128) and Huxley's tongue-in-cheek suggestion that all scientists should be strangled on their sixtieth birthday imply, while in criminals mindless high-risk offences such as risky driving or involvement in motor-vehicle accidents reduce substantially with increasing age (Kanazawa, 2003, p. 270). Kanazawa's explanation is that the same mechanism is at work in both creativity and crime, essentially a genetic urge among young men to gain status and power in order to increase success as a breeder, an urge which was so successful in the ancestral environment that the genes involved were selected for survival and persist today. The drop in such behaviour after marriage (the desistance effect) occurs because, 'having resigned from the competition for breeding partners by getting married, men focus more on looking after their existing young than on seeking to impregnate additional women' (p. 269), something which was particularly wise in the caves, where 'competition with childless younger men was literally dangerous'.

Kanazawa counters social arguments, such as that decreases in creativity after marriage are due to changed social roles, with men nowadays expected, for instance, to share household chores, by pointing out that the desistance effect is clear to see in men who were active in the eighteenth and nineteenth centuries, a time when men were almost completely free of responsibility for caring for the children or running the household. Cropley (1995) reviewed other social explanations, such as changing roles (from young tearaway to fatherly mentor, from norm-breaker to norm-enforcer, from doer to administrator – often at a much higher salary). All of these role changes would be facilitated by retiring from the competition for breeding partners, although it must be admitted that not all high-achieving males seem to behave according to this dictum. In essence, Kanazawa's thesis is that 'both crime and [creativity] are expressions of *young* men's proximate competitive desires, whose ultimate function in the ancestral environment would have been to increase reproductive success' (p. 265).

General arousal theory

A clearly related approach is to be seen in Eysenck's (1995) General Arousal Theory of Criminality, in which he proposed a biological link between creativity, crime and deviance, rule-breaking, and the like. He argued that a property of the central nervous system (low arousability) impels some people to engage in impulsive, risk-taking and sensation-seeking behaviour in order to raise their arousal to a comfortable level. Some achieve the necessary exposure to uncertainty, risk, or surprise through actions that are hailed by observers as 'creative', others by engaging in behaviours that society regards as crime. Nonetheless, according to Eysenck, the same physiological disposition is involved, so that creativity and crime have a common biological origin (and, interestingly, this disposition has been shown to be highly heritable). Other researchers have examined this relationship empirically and have provided some support for the idea of a link between arousability and crime (e.g., Lynam and Miller, 2004; Aluja and Garcia, 2005).

Gamman and Raein (2010) gave a brief summary of research on brain functioning and deviance/creativity/crime and concluded that there really are grounds for regarding all three as social labels attached to behaviours emanating from the same neurological 'pathology', some arousal-seeking behaviour attracting praise as creative, some attracting criticism as crime. Kuszewski (2009) pointed out that researchers are now using MRIs, PET scans, and EEG measures to investigate the neurology of creativity by investigating differences in pathways and levels of cortical activity in creative and non-creative individuals through measures of cerebral blood flow and neural activity. Researchers are also investigating the genetics of creativity and crime through studies in, for instance, molecular genetics. Reuter, Roth, Holve, and Hennig (2006) reported identifying the first candidate gene for creativity. Kanazawa (2003) – see above – also referred to research moving towards identifying a creativity gene or gene constellation. However, some commentators have raised the question of whether success in this search would be a benefit or a disaster for humankind: gene manipulation might be capable of eliminating the crime gene, but might simultaneously eliminate creativity. This is a potential example of one aspect of the dark side of creativity: well-intentioned research on the dark side could lead to an unintended danger for creativity itself.

Where do the differences lie?

Are there no differences, then? In view of the benefits of creativity both for the individual and society outlined in Chapter 5, inability to differentiate between creative crime and positive creativity would cause serious problems if preventive measures were undifferentiated. As Hilton (2010) pointed out, if everyone carefully imagined and weighed up any and all possible consequences of every piece of novelty production, creativity might cease altogether. Creativity is an instrument of social renewal and refreshment in the arts, philosophy, religion, politics, science, engineering, technology, industry, commerce, and health care, to give some examples. Creativity is indispensable and negative creativity may be an almost unavoidable price societies pay for the beneficial results of generation of effective novelty. The ability to distinguish between the two thus becomes extremely important, and will be discussed in more detail in this section.

Although it can have disruptive social effects, the fact is that most European/North American societies, at least since the Reformation, have been prepared to tolerate some deviance. Tiger and Fox (1971, pp. 52–4) pointed out that societies will generally tolerate their 'radical politicians, bloody-minded intellectuals, criminals, religious maniacs, unconventional artists, military geniuses, visionary poets, reformist priests, and revolutionary philosophers'. The reason for this is fairly straightforward: it is because sometimes 'their innovative behavior pays off' (p. 54). We have (Chapter 5, p. 100) already cited Rorty's (1979, p. 351) conclusion that, without creativity, societies would stop developing and 'ubiquitous technocratic totalitarianism' would lead to them all becoming drab identical copies of each other.

Fortunately, there do seem to be recognisable differences between people generally regarded with approval as creative (or at least tolerated) and those condemned as criminals. To take a crass example, most people would probably see clear differences between Mahatma Gandhi and Adolf Hitler, even if they could only express them in general terms: 'Hitler was evil; Gandhi was good'. In this section, we will examine such differences more systematically in terms of the 6Ps, and work out a system for recognising them.

Process

We have already emphasised the common features of Process in positive creativity and crime – deviation from the norm, breaking of rules, doing things differently, that is, law-breaking. Even here, however, Salcedo-Albarán et al. (2009) have argued that there is a major difference. According to these authors, from the point of view of the social environment, positive creativity and crime (which they call 'illegality') are in fact 'polar opposites' (p. 2) of a *single dimension* involving the process of rule-breaking. At one pole comes the breaking of statutory rules, which society labels 'crime' – although for our purposes it is still creativity – at the other comes the breaking of customary rules, which may be labelled 'creativity', but can also be seen as just eccentric, self-willed, irritating, or crazy. From our point of view, it is important to note that rule-breaking is part of creativity, whether the society approves of the result or not; creativity can be applied for malevolent or benevolent purposes, as we will show in greater detail in Chapters 8 and 9.

According to Salcedo-Albarán et al. (2009), creativity and crime are thus simultaneously the same but also different. They see the differences as involving:

- the kind of rule that is broken (positive creativity breaks only informal, non-statutory rules such as social conventions or the rules of art, music, commerce, and the like, whereas illegality involves breaking formal statutory rules);
- the role of social benefit in the rule-breaking (positive creativity often produces benefits for society – or at least is usually aimed at such benefits – whereas illegality has no such aim and often produces harm for society).

Writing in the context of organisational innovation, Bodankin and Tziner (2009, p. 549) made a similar point by distinguishing between 'destructive' and 'constructive' deviance, and emphasised the importance of the latter for progress and development. Mainemelis (2010, p. 559) referred directly to '*creative* deviance' (emphasis added) and gave examples of an extreme form in organisational settings involving direct defiance of specific instructions from managers that eventually led to acclaimed creative products such as LED bright lighting technology – this was developed by a scientist who repeatedly ignored orders to abandon the project.

Gamman and Raein (2010) believe that in their rule-breaking generally *artists* seek to conquer taboos and prejudices in the service of what they regard as the general good, and are thus group-oriented (even if the group does not agree with them), so that their rule-breaking is pro-social and well intentioned, whereas *criminals* pursue their own selfish ends without any thought of the good of others. Indeed, some criminals are not only indifferent to the good of others but may deliberately seek to do harm, terrorists being an obvious example.[4] These authors see this difference

---

[4] We refer to such *deliberate* evil-doing (as against, for instance, mere indifference to the common good) as 'malevolent' (see the discussion in Chapter 1, pp. 14–20).

(motivation arising from hope of achieving social change through deviance versus lack of any such hope, indifference or even malevolence) as reflecting a fundamental *pessimism* in criminals: whereas the optimism of people who engage in positive creativity leads them to believe that they can achieve something worthwhile by breaking the rules, criminals see no such prospect, and concentrate instead on their own narrow immediate ends. Put plainly for the purposes of a discussion of creativity, crime, and intent, positive creativity usually involves rule-breaking with *benevolent intent*, crime with malevolent intent.

Personal properties, motives, and feelings

Indeed, the issue of motivation was squarely put by TenHouten (1999, p. 800), who called for close attention to the 'reciprocal relations between creativity and intentionality'. In an extensive discussion of how to distinguish between positive and negative creativity, Kampylis and Valtanen (2010) also emphasised the *intentions*, *plans*, and *values* of the individual (i.e., the Ps of Personal motivation and Personal feelings/values). Following a similar line of argument, Gamman and Raein (2010, p. 173) concluded that, generally speaking, publicly acclaimed top creatives often exhibit a *high* level of empathy, whereas criminals show low levels. According to them, artists are frequently high in empathy and low in parasitism, whereas the reverse is true in the case of criminals. The outstanding example of the latter (lack of empathy in criminals) is provided by psychopaths who are callous, remorseless, and without feelings for others (Hare, 2006).

A related approach that leads to similar conclusions is based on research suggesting that positive creativity and crime are both related to personal characteristics such as impulsivity, sensation seeking, and self-control, but not always in the same way: Kipper, Green, and Prorak (2010) reported that impulsivity is negatively correlated with creativity, while sensation seeking is positively correlated with it, while Dacey and Lennon (1998) showed that self-control is positively correlated with positive creativity. By contrast, although both positive creativity and crime are positively correlated with sensation seeking, impulsivity is positively correlated with crime and self-control is negatively correlated with it. Thus, both acknowledged creative individuals and criminals are sensation-seekers, to be sure, but they differ in that creatives are better able to control impulses and are better at self-control in general.

Table 7.2 *Major differences between positive creativity and crime*

P	Positive creativity	Crime
Product	Socially *responsible*	Socially *irresponsible*
	Morally *valuable*	Morally *valueless*
	Non-exploitative	Exploitative
	Beneficial product	*Harmful* product
	Benefits from publicity	*Harmed* by publicity
Process	*Constructive* deviance	*Destructive* deviance
	Breaking *non-statutory* rules	Breaking *statutory* rules
Personal	*Optimistic* explanatory style	*Pessimistic* explanatory style
properties	*High* empathy	*Low* empathy
	High self-control	*Low* self-control
Motivation	*Benevolent* intent	*Indifferent* or *malevolent* intent
	Low impulsivity	*High* impulsivity
	Able to set boundaries	*Unable* to set boundaries
	Seeking publicity	*Avoiding* publicity
Press	*Low* parasitism	*High* parasitism
	Group orientation	*Individualistic* orientation
	Orientation towards *general* good	Orientation towards *individual* good
	Orientation towards *benefitting* society	Orientation towards *harming* society
	Public knowledge is *beneficial*	Public knowledge is often *harmful*

The major differences between the generation of effective novelty in creativity and crime are summarised in Table 7.2 in terms of the usual Ps framework presented throughout this book.

It must be admitted that the entries in the table are over-simplifications or at the very least idealised descriptions, which run the risk of becoming stereotypes according to which acclaimed creatives are very good and criminals very bad. For instance, some acknowledged creatives are undoubtedly highly impulsive and unable to set boundaries, despite the fact that the table describes them as low in impulsivity and able to set boundaries, while some criminals actively seek publicity or even, in special cases such as terrorism, may depend almost entirely on publicity for the success or failure of the novelty they generate. Nonetheless, the table offers a generalised overview of the dominant tendencies in the Ps listed, and draws a sharp contrast between the two groups. Thus, the Ps model of creativity makes it possible to discriminate psychologically between creative crime and positive creativity and offers insights into how to oppose the one without discouraging the other. This issue will be taken up in Chapter 10.

CHAPTER EIGHT

Consumer and corporate fraud
Scams, hustles, and swindles

Fraud is a phenomenon that has existed for thousands of years. From the time of ancient Babylon, through the Middle Ages, and into modern times, we see documented cases of creative fraud. In the modern world it is very big business, partly due to the rise of information technology. It often involves generation of novelty that is at least effective and may be elegant and generic: thus it involves creativity. It can be looked at particularly from the point of view of the creative Product and the creative Person. This way of looking at fraud suggests approaches to protection against fraud such as looking at the elements of an organisation that offer special opportunities for creative individuals to generate harmful creativity, adopting surprising and unexpected counter-measures, or identifying employees who are vulnerable to crime (as outlined in Chapter 7) and adopting appropriate measures.

Since the late 1990s, anyone with a computer connected to the Internet has probably received an email similar to the one below:

Dear Sir,

First, I must solicit your strictest confidence in this transaction; this is by virtue of its nature as being utterly confidential and top secret. I am the Legal adviser of the Contract Review Panel instituted by H. E. President Olusegun Obasanjo to probe/review all Contracts executed and payments made during the regime of late General Sani Abacha. My colleagues on the Panel have mandated me to seek your assistance in the transfer of the sum of US$18.5 Million into your Bank Account.

As you may know, the late General Abacha and members of his government embezzled billions of dollars through spurious contracts and payments to foreigners between 1993 and 1998 and this is now the subject of probe by my Panel. In the course of our review, we have discovered this sum of $18.5 Million, which the former dictator could not transfer from the dedicated account of the Central Bank of Nigeria before his sudden death in June 1998. It is this amount that my colleagues and I have decided to acquire for us through your assistance. This assistance becomes crucial because we cannot acquire the funds in our names and as government officials we are not allowed to own or operate foreign bank accounts. We have thus developed a, fool proof, legal and totally risk free scheme through which the fund can be transferred to your nominated bank account within a very short time. The scheme is to use our position and influence on the Panel to represent you as a foreign Contractor beneficiary of the funds. We shall arrange all documentation to support this claim and get Approval for the transfer of the funds for your benefit on our behalf. The scheme is perfected to be 100% risk free and we are sure the funds can arrive your Account within 10 working days from when you agree to assist us. You should acknowledge the receipt of my mail through the above e-mail address so we can further discuss the modalities of your cooperation and negotiate the charge for the usage of your Account. You definitely have a lot to benefit from this transaction as we are prepared to give you between 20% of the total funds as soon as you secure it in your account.

Please, endeavor to send me an e-mail indicating your interest as to enable me furnish you with my confidential telephone/fax number through which we can communicate with you in confidence (in your response) as the need for secrecy is great to this transaction. We expect your urgent response.

Yours faithfully,
DR. INU ZEMEDE (MB.BS, PH.D, FNMA.)

Known variously as a 'Nigerian Letter', 'Nigerian Scam' or 'Nigerian 419 Scam', this example from March 2001 (source: www.potifos.com/fraud/) is a form of what is widely classified as consumer fraud that is now familiar to many people. The letter is one of over 500 that have been documented over the last decade and is a form of *advance-fee fraud*, the purpose of which is to invite consumers to advance sums of money to the fraudster in the expectation that they will subsequently realise a much larger financial gain.

Fraud is widely understood to be dishonesty, deliberate deception, trickery, or cheating calculated or intended for advantage or gain. It is a domain that is ripe with examples at the intersection of creativity and crime. It is not our intention, nor is it necessary, to construct or defend a legal definition of fraud, either in its general sense or in the sense of either consumer or corporate fraud. Rather, we seek here to draw attention to an example of resourceful crime that is characterised not by overt violence and threats to life and property, but predominantly by those behaviours by which 'one person intends to gain a dishonest advantage over another' (Comer, 1977, p. 1). In particular, we wish to focus on activities in which either individual consumers or businesses and organisations are the victims of tricky dishonesty calculated for advantage or gain. Consumer fraud can be defined as: 'Deceptive practices that result in financial or other losses for consumers in the course of seemingly legitimate business transactions' (The Free Dictionary: www.thefreedictionary.com/). Corporate fraud, by contrast, sees the victim as a business entity rather than an individual.

Fraud through the ages

According to the KPMG Fraud and Misconduct Survey 2010, in Australia and New Zealand alone, some US$345 million was lost to fraud across organisations participating in the survey. Where an organisation experienced at least one incidence of fraud, the average loss doubled from US$1.5m in 2008 to US$3m in 2010, with 65 per cent of major frauds being inside jobs. The main motivator was reported as typically being greed and lifestyle. Furthermore, only one-third of losses were thought to be detected. According to the biannual KPMG fraud barometer for December 2011 (www.kpmg.com/au), drawing on figures for large frauds coming before Australian courts, corporate fraud over the last four years involved 546 cases, with losses exceeding US$1 billion. In a summary of the KPMG report (KPMG, 2011) we learn that fraudsters 'follow the money trail to the financial services sector with major banks the most common victims of fraud, followed by insurance companies, credit unions/building societies and other lenders'. Of frauds against commercial businesses, 80 per cent were committed by rank-and-file employees or managers, with gambling often cited as an important motivator.

However, writing more than thirty years ago, Hamilton, in the foreword to Comer's book (Comer 1977, p. vii) asserted that, after violence, fraud was 'the fastest rising crime in the western world'. This draws attention to the fact that fraud is not a crime that is peculiar to the Information Age, although the rise of the Internet, personal computers, and mass communication has given it a new lease of life. It also masks the fact that fraud has been a form of law-breaking that has existed ever since humans have engaged in business and trade – that is, for thousands of years!

Ancient fraud

Consumer and corporate fraud – or more colloquially, scams, hustles, and swindles – have been a threat to legitimate trade, business, and honest consumers for centuries. From at least the time of ancient Babylon, in approximately 1770 BC, we can trace attempts by unscrupulous people or organisations to exploit commercial transactions in dishonest ways in the hope of obtaining an advantage that is usually financial in nature. In relation to the ownership of slaves, for example, the Code of Hammurabi, enacted by the sixth Babylonian king of that name, anticipated attempts to defraud slave owners through incorrect branding:

> If someone has deceived the brander, and induced him to cut out a mark on a slave, that man shall be put to death and buried in his house; the brander shall swear, 'I did not mark him knowingly', and shall go free.[1]

In ancient Greece, in the mid-200s BC, we encounter the famous anecdote of Archimedes and the Golden Crown commissioned by King Hiero II (described in Marcus Vitruvius's *De Architectura* sometime in the first century BC). The king is reputed to have given a precise amount of gold to a goldsmith for the purpose of making a votive crown. After hearing rumours that the goldsmith had cheated him by substituting an equal weight of less valuable silver for some of the gold in the crown, the king engaged Archimedes to devise a method for determining whether the alleged substitution had, in fact, taken place. The challenge facing Archimedes was to make this determination without damaging the finished crown. While the story is better remembered for Archimedes' dramatic discovery of the principle named after him, whereby water is displaced by a submerged mass ('Eureka!'), and through which he was able to show that the goldsmith had, indeed, cheated the king, it is also an early example of a documented attempt to deliberately deceive a consumer for some material advantage in the course of a business transaction – i.e., consumer fraud.

The South Sea Bubble

Moving forward in time, in mediaeval Europe sophisticated systems were devised to ensure the uniformity and legality of weights and measures, in order to prevent fraudulent trade. In England, for example, the Statute of Ells and Perches, or *Compositio Ulnarum et Perticarum*, thought to date from the period 1266–1303, defined the length of various units such as the inch, foot, and yard, and also derived units such as the acre. Reyerson (1982) recounts 'the case of the dissembling pepperer' in the French town of Montpellier in the mid-fourteenth century, in which a spice merchant,

---

[1] *Babylonian and Assyrian Laws, Contracts and Letters*, by C. H. W. Johns, in 1904, one of a series called the Library of Ancient Inscriptions, from a facsimile produced by The Legal Classics Library, Division of Gryphon Editions, New York in 1987.

one Johannes Andree, was accused of using impure saffron. Unscrupulous traders, such as Andree, might try to increase the weight of saffron through wetting or the addition of other materials to bulk out their spices, in an effort to realise a greater profit. It is noteworthy not only that commercial fraud of this type occurred, but also that authorities went to considerable lengths to detect, regulate, and punish it.

The South Sea Bubble of 1720, by contrast, provides an example of a more complex case of consumer deception at a corporate level, reminiscent of the Enron affair in more recent times. An economic 'bubble' occurs when stock is traded in large volumes at prices that are significantly above the intrinsic value of the stock (its real value, as opposed to its market value). The South Sea Company was formed in England in 1711 and was granted a monopoly to trade in Spain's South American colonies. The price for this monopoly was that the South Sea Company assumed the national debt that England had incurred during the War of Spanish Succession (1701–14). The Bubble occurred as the company assumed additional national debt against an issue of new shares and a promise of lower interest rates.

In order to make the scheme work, the company engaged in a process of talking up its own stock by exaggerating the value of its potential trade in the New World. This quickly led to a wave of speculation in which the price of South Sea Company shares more than tripled in a matter of only a few months. The company further gilded the allure of the shares by 'selling' them to prominent people, including influential politicians, without requiring immediate payment. These favoured investors could simply sell their shares back to the company at any time, at the current market price, receiving the profit. This meant that these elite stockholders had a strong vested interest in driving up the stock price, while the company used the names of its prominent shareholders to draw in other buyers.

The South Sea Bubble spawned many other similar ventures as a number of other companies were floated on the stock market, often based on unlikely, if not outright fraudulent, ventures. The worst of these may be the scheme that advertised itself as 'a company for carrying on an undertaking of great advantage, but nobody to know what it is' (MacKay, 1852)! The unknown inventor of this particular scheme sought to raise £500,000 by issuing 5,000 shares of £100. He opened for business requiring only an initial deposit of £2. After selling 1,000 shares on his first day of business, raising £2,000 in deposits (equivalent, depending on the method of calculation, to at least US$360,000 today), he promptly closed up his office and absconded.[2] The most ironic subsequent scheme among a long list of bubbles that were banned by the Lords Justice of the Privy Council was a scheme 'For insuring from thefts and robberies'!

As the South Sea Company shares soared, the English Parliament stepped in to regulate these bubbles (the term originally referred to the companies and their stock, but later became synonymous with the resulting financial crisis), but this simply boosted the apparent legitimacy of the original South Sea Company, and its shares climbed higher, reaching some seven times their starting price by June 1720. The price of South Sea Company shares peaked at about £1,000 in August 1720, some ten times its starting price of barely six months earlier. Around this time, speculators began selling and the price dropped precipitously, crashing back to its starting price within only a few months. This bankrupted many people, both aristocrats and ordinary investors, who had been drawn into the scheme and who were now unable to pay off the debt they had incurred in purchasing their shares.

The South Sea Bubble had important consequences for trade, commerce, and financial regulation. One that might strike a chord with modern readers smarting from the after-effects of the global financial crisis was a proposition by Lord Molesworth in the English Parliament that the South Sea directors should be 'tied in like manner in sacks, and thrown into the Thames' (MacKay, 1852). While not fraudulent as originally conceived, and enjoying official endorsement, there is little doubt that the South Sea Company used deceit to entice investors to buy shares, ultimately defrauding many people.

More modern fraud

In the nineteenth century, improved communications and technology, as well as greater levels of legislative and financial sophistication, did nothing to quell instances of consumer and corporate fraud. In New York, in the period leading up to the opening of the Brooklyn Bridge in 1883, it became known that the steel suspension cabling supplied by the contractor, J. Lloyd Haigh, had been deliberately and dishonestly manufactured using a proportion of inferior quality steel wire (see Cadbury, 2004). While this deceit was detected, it came too late to replace the steel suspension cables already installed. It was only thanks to the wide safety

---

[2] MacKay puts this more quaintly as 'He was philosopher enough to be contented with his venture, and set off the same evening for the Continent. He was never heard of again'.

margin built into the design of the bridge by its architect, Washington Roebling, that the bridge could be used safely. In this case, while Haigh went unpunished, and the bridge suffered no terminal defect, the fact is that the owners of the bridge did not get what they thought they were paying for, while Haigh gained financially (in the sense that he avoided a substantial loss) through his dishonesty.

In modern times, possibly the most spectacular, and one of the most costly, examples of deliberately deceptive business practices is seen in the case of Enron. The company's bankruptcy in late 2001 brought about the collapse of an organisation employing approximately 20,000 staff, with reported revenues of over US$100 billion. The 'Enron scandal' also precipitated the dissolution of the accounting firm Arthur Andersen. It is acknowledged that Enron's apparent financial strength was 'sustained substantially by institutionalised, systematic, and creatively planned accounting fraud' (Wikipedia, 2012). In simple terms, Enron manipulated the financial regulatory environment in such a way as to disguise its financial liabilities and therefore to project an image of a strong and growing stock price, in order to maintain its credit ratings. Even before its collapse, Enron was criticised by many analysts for its high levels of debt, but the company was adept at dealing with such criticism as part of its practice of maintaining an image of financial strength. After bankruptcy, it emerged that many of Enron's assets and profits were either highly inflated or entirely fraudulent and non-existent. The company hid or disguised its financial losses in a manner that was deliberately intended to deceive shareholders and regulators.

Corporate fraud also occurs when dishonesty and deception are used by an individual employee for financial gain, and where the victim is the employing organisation. In 2010, in Adelaide, South Australia, we see a simple example of this at the Flinders University of South Australia. A cashier's office supervisor was charged with five counts of dishonestly taking property. Specifically, the employee of the university was alleged to have stolen sums of money ranging from AU$2m to AU$7m on five occasions over a period of approximately three months. The deception and theft only came to light after the fifth occasion, when staff at the university reportedly detected 'anomalous transactions' (*The Australian*, 23 January 2010).

Fraud, as these examples show, can take many forms and is found in all sectors of business and trade. While some are clearly and overtly an attempt to use dishonesty and deceit for financial gain, as in the case of stealing money, some are more subtle and the focus of the fraud may be a less obvious asset. It is important, however, to understand fraud in the broadest sense of dishonestly acquiring an asset, and not limit the definition simply to money.

Two examples illustrate the more subtle forms that fraud can take. First, in 1996, 'the producers of the television show of *The Simpsons* [20th Century Fox Film Corporation] succeeded in proceedings to restrain the respondent [the South Australian Brewing Company Ltd] marketing beer under the name "Duff beer", the name used in the show' (Miller, 2011, p. 1642). While arguably not done in a malicious attempt to steal from either the producers of the television show or the general public, this case nevertheless represents an example of what is called 'passing off' under Australian Competition and Consumer law. The law makes it clear that the primary purpose of defining the concept of 'passing off' is to ensure that consumers are protected from possible fraud.

The second example where deceptive practices may have led to financial or other losses to consumers is illustrated by a case taken from the provision of childhood education in 2001. 'The respondent [Black on White Pty Ltd] operated a private college [in Australia] for childhood education. The respondent [Black on White Pty Ltd] advertised that its courses were accredited with various government vocational training accreditation systems when they were not' (Miller, 2011, p. 1612). The provider was found to have breached the laws relating to misleading or deceptive conduct.

Creativity and fraud

While the idea of fraudulently exploiting consumers, whether individuals or organisations, is not new, the methods by which misleading and deceptive conduct is carried out – these scams, swindles, and hustles – continue to move with the times. Comer (1977) reinforces this view stating that 'There are very few "new" frauds, merely old ones given new leases of life by particular embellishments' (p. 15). It seems to be a characteristic of fraud, both corporate and consumer, that as the tools and methods of commerce, trade, and communication evolve, so do the methods by which scammers attempt to profit at the expense of unsuspecting consumers or organisations. It is no surprise, therefore, that as more and more business is conducted electronically, so too has consumer and corporate fraud shifted to exploit this medium. Each innovation in business, commerce, and trade spawns novel mechanisms by which criminals attempt to defraud their victims. Like any competitive activity, success depends on the ability of the competitors, both the scammer and those concerned with detecting and eliminating fraud, to devise new and effective methods by which they can achieve their ends, and outwit their opponents.

The 6Ps and fraud

In earlier chapters we proposed that creativity in a range of different domains – art, engineering, business, mental health, sport, and of course, crime – can be better understood and analysed through a conceptual framework encompassing the so-called 6Ps: Product, Process, Personal properties, Personal motivation, Personal feelings, Press (see Chapter 3, pp. 61–71). In this chapter we now apply this framework of creativity to the domain of fraud, as an example of resourceful crime, with the aim of illustrating and drawing attention to:

• the nature of fraud as the production of effective novelty;
• the variety of creative ways that fraud can be achieved;
• the dangers that creativity poses when applied to fraud;
• conclusions about how to prevent creative fraud and protect ourselves from its effects.

We will begin by outlining the nature and types of consumer and corporate fraud currently used – the fraudulent *Product* – and then show how fraud can be conceptualised in terms of the characteristics of a creative product outlined in Chapter 3 (pp. 52–54), encompassing novelty, effectiveness, elegance, and genesis. We will then examine the stages of innovation in consumer fraud – the *Process* – through which an idea in the mind of a fraudster is transformed into a working scam. This will be followed by a consideration of the characteristics of the scammers themselves (*Person*) – motivation, feelings, personal properties – and how these also characterise the resourceful criminal. The concept of a blind spot in relation to creativity and crime will also be considered here (see Kaufman, Cropley, Chiera, and White, forthcoming). We then examine the role that the environment – the *Press* – plays in relation to creative fraud. Finally, and most importantly, we will show how the characteristics of consumer and corporate fraud as resourceful, innovative law-breaking can be used to inform the practice of agencies and organisations, for example, the police, consumer watchdogs, and government agencies, as they attempt to anticipate, prevent, and mitigate consumer and corporate fraud. We will be especially sensitive to creative approaches to this prevention and mitigation.

The fraudulent Product: the things scammers do

Comer (1977) provides a comprehensive analysis of fraud types and definitions that encompasses both corporate fraud and consumer fraud. He further highlighted two important facts that have a bearing on our discussion of creativity and crime. First, 'the intricate workings of fraud are limited only by human imagination' (p. 15), and second that 'Conventional definitions of assets and liabilities do not adequately describe those goods or interests that thieves find attractive to steal' (p. 15). In everyday terms, fraudsters bring to bear great ingenuity in the task of dishonestly acquiring items of value, and what is seen to be of value is itself open to significant creativity.

The range of types of fraud to which human creativity is frequently applied includes:

- bankruptcy frauds;
- bribery and kickbacks;
- computer-related frauds;
- consumer fraud/illegal competition;
- credit card and cheque frauds;
- embezzlement;
- pilferage;
- receiving stolen property;
- insurance frauds;
- securities theft, fraud, forgery.

Under the heading of 'consumer fraud' – i.e., those schemes specifically targeting individual consumers – we see a long list of further types, including:

- advance-fee fraud;
- adult services fraud;
- investment and real estate fraud;
- unexpected prizes fraud;
- false billing fraud;
- mobile phone fraud;
- fax-back fraud.

The Australian Competition and Consumer Commission, in its 2011 publication 'Targeting Scams: Report of the ACCC on scam activity 2011' (Australian Competition and Consumer Commission, 2012), identified no less than eighteen specific types of consumer fraud that accounted for some AU$85 million (approximately US$87.5 million) in reported losses in 2011. By comparison, the Global Economic Crime Survey (PricewaterhouseCoopers, 2011) reported that 34 per cent of nearly 4,000 respondents from across the globe had 'experienced economic crime in the last 12 months' (p. 16). Among the highest levels of reported fraud were the United Kingdom (51%), Australia (47%), France (46%), and the United States (45%), levels that the report suggests may be high because of both a willingness to report fraud and the effectiveness of detection methods in those countries (p. 17).

In analysing the fraudulent *Product* – the method by which the fraud was perpetrated – we can draw on the well-established characterisations of creative products described in Chapter 3. Product creativity is a combination of *effectiveness* (the product must do what it is designed to do), *novelty* (the product is new, original, and/or surprising), *elegance* (the product is complete, fully worked out, and skilfully executed) and *genesis* (the product must move beyond the immediate problem, opening up new perspectives and drawing attention to new elements of the problem). These elements may be present in a product in different proportions; however, a prerequisite for considering a product creative is the presence of effectiveness and novelty. Elegance and genesis add further value to the product, but without novelty and effectiveness as a minimum, the product cannot be considered creative.

It is tempting to leap to the application of these characteristics to the fraudulent product, and there may be some value in doing so. However, such an approach may also fail to contribute to our larger purpose of informing the practice of law-enforcement. The application of the characteristics of a creative product to the many examples of fraud will yield, at best, an interesting taxonomy of consumer and corporate fraud, but one that may do little to contribute to anticipating, preventing, and mitigating these examples of resourceful crime. Such an approach is also likely to be relevant only in hindsight – the example above of a Nigerian scam was certainly unusual and surprising, and it was effective in that many people fell for it and lost millions of dollars – merely recognising the presence of novelty and effectiveness *ex post facto* is of limited value.

A more promising approach that draws on the characteristics of a creative product and offers more scope for law-enforcement first requires us to understand the fraudulent product a little better. By decomposing the fraudulent product into its key elements and then analysing these for their creativity, we shed much more light on what makes fraud creative, on how this creativity contributes to the success of fraud, and on how to take action to negate this creativity for the purpose of disrupting the

fraud. Comer (1977) set out a framework for categorising and understanding the range of types of fraud. The framework is based on three
parameters:

- Opportunity:
  - the existence of an asset, real or intangible, to steal;
  - the asset must be able to be separated from its rightful owner;
  - a means of obtaining the asset must exist;
  - a high chance of success and a low chance of detection must exist.
- Method of Concealment:
  - none – larceny. Simple, opportunistic theft;
  - falsification of a reality – misrepresentation of personal, physical, or
    commercial facts, before, during, or after theft, to assist or conceal a
    loss;
  - falsification of an account – manipulation of documentary evidence
    such as an accounting record, before, during, or after theft, to assist
    or conceal a loss;
  - force, blackmail/coercion – extortion. Threats made against someone
    in order to conceal a loss.
- Level of risk (Source):
  - internal criminal – an employee of an organisation at risk from cor-
    porate fraud;
  - external criminal – a fraudster *not* employed by an organisation at
    risk from corporate fraud;
  - business contact – a fraudster with some level of access to an organ-
    isation's or individual's assets;
  - opportunist – fraudsters who are neither an employee of an organisa-
    tion at risk from corporate fraud, nor business contacts of an at-risk
    organisation or individual;
  - organised criminal – fraudsters operating with a level of organisation,
    planning and resources that set them apart from opportunists and
    individuals.

Comer's (1977) decomposition of fraud now serves as the basis of a framework for analysing creativity in the context of fraud. Figure 8.1 shows the
necessary interactions between the three elements of the fraudulent product (see next page). Creativity as it applies to fraud can now be seen as
occurring across three different aspects of the product. Effective novelty
may be generated in relation to the opportunity, the method of concealment, or the source. In the case of 'opportunity' this may, for example,
involve the generation of effective novelty in relation to:

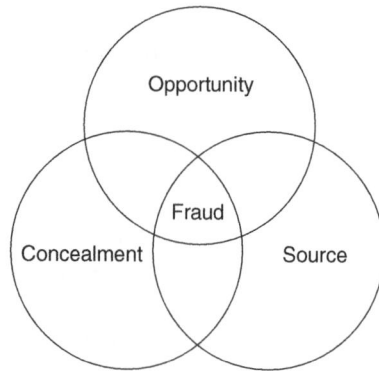

Figure 8.1 The three elements of the fraudulent Product

- the identification of a new 'asset' – identifying an asset for which there is a demand, and which is worth the while of the fraudster to steal;
- a novel approach to what can be separated from its owner;
- a creative means for obtaining the asset.

Each of these then has the potential to inform law-enforcement practice in much more specific ways. For example, recognising that the identification of assets worth stealing requires a degree of creativity, law-enforcers can direct their own proactive effort towards identifying assets as a precursor to identifying mechanisms to make those assets harder to separate from their owners. We will discuss this concept further in Chapter 10 as a form of 'red teaming' (see p. 270).

We diverge slightly, however, from Comer's (1977) fourth point regarding 'opportunity'. He states that 'The thief must perceive a high chance of success, coupled with a low chance of detection' (p. 22). However, we see this as a function both of the opportunity and the concealment method. Thus, an effective opportunity and a good method of concealment dictate what constitutes a high chance of success and a low chance of detection. In relation to creativity and law-enforcement practice, this draws attention to the value that the creativity criterion *effectiveness* adds to the fraudulent product. Disrupting the effectiveness of any of the aspects of opportunity reduces the overall chance of success and raises the probability of detection, hopefully to the point that the fraud no longer presents a viable opportunity to the thief.

Successful fraud, the Product, requires an opportunity (an identified, separable asset and an effective means for obtaining it) coupled with appropriate, effective concealment, and an effective source. By bringing these elements together, the fraudster creates a product with an assessable level of likely success and likely detection. The application of creativity – the generation of effective novelty – in the development of the product gives the fraudster the means to improve the likelihood of success and to lower the likelihood of detection by seeking original, surprising solutions. These *solutions* will be characterised by the identification of new forms of asset and new markets for those assets, original conceptualisations of what it means for an asset to be separated from its owner, and novel methods by which assets can be separated from their rightful owners. Such solutions will be recognisable through their novel conceptualisations of concealment and their original approaches to achieving that concealment. Finally, they will be noteworthy for their fresh approach to identifying and utilising sources.

Concealment (or a lack thereof) emerges as a critical element of fraud. As Comer states, 'concealment is an essential ingredient of most large-scale or prolonged frauds' (p. 19) and 'he [the fraudster] will strive to conceal fraud in the best way available to him' (p. 18). It follows that, while most forms of fraud are not new, the 'new lease of life' Comer refers to will usually be found either in the method of concealment, or the source, or both.

Comer (1977, pp. 20ff) uses the factors *Concealment* (sub-divided into four groups: *no concealment, misrepresentation, manipulation,* and *extortion*), and *Source* (sub-divided into five groups: internal-management, internal-operations, external-business contacts, external-opportunist, collusive-organised), along with the assumption that an *Opportunity* exists, to categorise seventeen different forms of fraud. These categorisations highlight the fact that *larcenous fraud* (i.e., fraud with no attempt at concealment) falls into the category of impulsive (non-resourceful) crime, and is outside our intended focus. Examples of this range from a spur-of-the-moment decision by an employee to steal, let us say, a box of paperclips, through to a delivery driver pocketing a screwdriver left on a workbench as he drops off a package at a company.

Comer (1977) also gives a large number of examples of fraud in categories that are of direct interest for our purposes. These range across the concealment strategies *misrepresentation, manipulation,* and *extortion*, and the various source types, highlighting the fact that where the victim is an organisation and where the source is internal (i.e., an employee) we can speak more generally of corporate fraud. In cases where the source is external to the victim (whether a business or an opportunistic individual), we find cases both of consumer fraud and corporate fraud, depending on the status of the victim (individual or organisation). In some cases, the fraud may be both, affecting both an organisation and individuals (e.g., a fraud in which people pass themselves off as official representatives of a company, and perform, for instance substandard maintenance of a product. In this case, the organisation is a victim because its reputation and potential sales are damaged, while the individual consumer is also a victim, receiving poor quality or defective work).

Implications for law-enforcement practice may be manifest in several different approaches. The current focus of law-enforcement seems to rely on two avenues: *risk assessment* and *detection*. Organisations are advised (PricewaterhouseCoopers, 2011) to conduct regular risk assessments as a means of identifying fraud in an approach that they report describes as 'seek and you shall find' (p. 27). The more frequent the risk assessment, the more fraud is reported. While highly reactive in nature, this should be directed by a consideration, as a minimum, of: *who* is at risk of committing fraud (source); *what* is at risk of being stolen (opportunity); *how* it can be separated from its rightful owner, if at all (opportunity); *how* potential fraud can be concealed (concealment)?

In each case, the assessment of risk must be made through the lens of the characteristics of a creative product. On the assumption that the resourceful criminal uses creativity as an integral part of fraud, each question that forms part of the risk assessment must consider the novelty, effectiveness, elegance, and genesis of each identified source, opportunity, and method of concealment. Those that are the most creative – that is, the most novel and effective as a minimum – are likely to be the favoured approaches of the resourceful criminal. We discuss this assessment further in Chapter 10 as part of the concept of red teaming, within the context of 'thinking thief'.

Having identified risks, organisations then employ methods of detection. The PricewaterhouseCoopers Global Economic Crime Survey (2011) reports three categories of detection (p. 24):

- corporate controls – internal auditing, transaction monitoring, and management strategies such as moving staff regularly;
- corporate culture – tip-offs and whistle-blowing;
- external factors – methods that are 'beyond the influence of management' such as finding out by accident or through the media.

All three categories of *detection* are reactive in nature. They assume that the fraud will occur and cannot be prevented. The detection strategy is dependent on the quality of the risk assessment. If the risk assessment fails to identify a novel source, opportunity, or method of concealment, then detection methods that are in place are likely to miss the creative fraud. Corporate controls like internal auditing also suffer from a high degree of predictability and a lack of novelty (and surprise) and may therefore be inherently weak. Wilks and Zimbelman (2004) highlight the fact that a checklist approach to audit standards fails 'to consider how management could manipulate the cues on the checklists' (p. 176). In other words, the method of detection is described in detail to the potential fraudster, and is rigidly applied, so that resourceful criminals have every opportunity to take advantage of this situation to commit successful fraud.

As with risk assessment, detection must be informed by the knowledge that resourceful criminals are drawing on creativity to enhance their criminal activities. Creative approaches to committing fraud must be matched by creative approaches to detecting it. A third consideration for law-enforcement is *prevention*. The application of creativity to risk assessment and detection moves these activities from reactive to proactive. The identification of novel assets and ways that they might be stolen (opportunity), potential new fraudsters (sources), and new ways that fraud might be masked (concealment) transforms risk assessment and detection into prevention. The organisation proactively closes off avenues for fraud before they occur. It secures assets not previously thought of as able to be stolen or having value to potential thieves; it protects itself from previously unrecognised potential thieves by limiting their access to assets; it rules out methods of concealment that would otherwise be available to the fraudster. Creative risk assessment and creative detection are then the pillars of an effective prevention strategy. Critically, this is founded not only on recognising the potential for creativity by the fraudster, but also the need for creativity by the organisation itself. This moves the organisation from merely 'seeking and it shall find' to fighting fire with fire.

The fraudulent person: who are the swindlers?
Pedneault (2009) highlights the important role that 'motivators' play in fraud. In a corporate context, for example, there is clear evidence that generous incentive schemes of the kind seen in association with the global financial crisis in 2008/09, for example, tying executive compensation to 'incentive stock options and other financial perks directly tied to the company's stock performance' (p. 22), can provide a strong motivation to commit fraud for executives 'seeking to maximise personal gains upon redeeming his or her stock options' (p. 22). This extrinsic motivation – the

allure of the big win – is matched by the incentive to commit fraud for business owners who provide personal guarantees for financing. Here the extrinsic motivation is the fear of the big loss – 'the owner wishes to keep the bank from taking his or her personal residence and investments to repay the debt' (p. 23) and is motivated to commit financial statement fraud.

It appears that extrinsic motivation, in the form of gaining rewards and avoiding penalties, is a powerful force in relation to creative crime. Indeed, it seems as though there may be some threshold at which any innate tendency to avoid risk, and the power of one's intrinsic motivation (to do the right thing), is overwhelmed by the extrinsic reward (whether the promise of a sufficiently large reward, or the fear of a sufficiently large loss). Thus the creative personality shares key traits with the resourceful criminal. Utility Theory, Game Theory, risk, and the science behind rational decision making may provide some insight into the intersection of creativity and fraud. Daniel Bernoulli, as far back as 1731,[3] outlined the factors that come into play in evaluating any decision – including, we argue, a decision to commit fraud – and the attendant risk. As Bernstein (1996) points out in commenting on Bernoulli's work, 'Price – and probability – are not enough in determining what something is worth' (p. 103). Bernstein goes on to say, citing Bernoulli, that 'Although the facts are the same for everyone [in the case of fraud, the value of the asset to be gained], "the utility" [the value of the decision to commit fraud] … is dependent on the particular circumstances of the person making the estimate … There is no reason to assume that … the risks anticipated by each must be deemed equal in value' (p. 103).

Critically, for our purposes, this means that the extrinsic motivation to commit fraud that is provided by, for example, a possible gain of $200,000, differs for each person and depends on, at the very least, the current level of wealth of the individual, their degree of risk aversion, and their ability to shape the odds in their favour. The latter two points link to creativity because we know that the appetite for risk is a psychological trait linked to creativity, and we have asserted that creativity offers the best chance to boost the likelihood of success in fraud. We can hypothesise therefore that, given a sufficiently tempting reward, a highly creative personality is

---

[3] Daniel Bernoulli's essay *Specimen Theoriae Novae de Mensura Sortis* ('Exposition of a New Theory on the Measurement of Risk') was presented to the Imperial Academy of Sciences in St Petersburg in 1731, and formally published by that institution in 1738.

in a more favourable position to exploit this opportunity. Some examples will illustrate this.

Imagine, for example, that you are faced with the following situation. You may continue to accept a salary of $100,000, or you can commit fraud where there is a 50 per cent chance that you will successfully defraud your employer of $200,000, and a 50 per cent chance that you will be caught and lose your job (which we will consider as resulting in $0). Mathematically, the choice is between a certain $100,000 and a gamble that has a value, an *expectancy*, of $100,000 (calculated as (0.5 × $200,000) + (0.5 × $0)). Again, purely mathematically, it is reasonable to assume that people would be indifferent to the choice – that is, they would see no point in taking the risk of committing the fraud – because the expectancy is the same as doing nothing. However, we recognise, as did Bernoulli, that not everyone assesses the risk in the same way. Some of us are risk-takers, some are risk averse. If I am, at heart, a risk-taker, I might be tempted by the prospect of gaining $200,000, in spite of the risk. My decision will be influenced, among other things, by my degree of risk aversion, my ability to tilt the odds more in my favour, and by my current level of wealth.

The latter point is important to the question of motivation. Bernoulli made the critical breakthrough in his paper (cited in Bernstein, 1996) that 'utility resulting from a small increase in wealth will be inversely proportionate to the quantity of goods previously possessed' (p.105). In simple terms, the more we have, the bigger the gain needs to be to have value for us. What this means for our discussion of fraud is that the motivation to commit fraud may be shaped by the relative size of the pay-off. Defrauding one's employer of $100,000 will have a very different level of attractiveness to someone earning $50,000 compared to someone earning $500,000. It is reasonable to assume that this attractiveness – the utility of the decision to commit fraud – can be computed for any given employee.

Returning to the matter of risk aversion and creativity, in relation to the example, imagine the following. The choice is now between accepting a salary of $100,000 or contemplating a fraud in which there is some chance of successfully gaining $500,000 and some chance of being caught ($0). The choice is now between accepting a certain $100,000 and taking a gamble with an expectancy that can range between $500,000 (= (1.0 × $500,000) + (0 × $0)) and $0 (= (0 × $500,000) + (1.0 × $0)). Let us assume that in this second case there exists a point at which the pay-off is sufficiently tempting – in other words, the potential gain is attractive enough – to motivate the employee into committing fraud. Let us say that this threshold is $300,000. What is required to reach that threshold? Mathematically that would require a 60 per cent chance of successful fraud and a 40 per cent chance of getting caught. There are two variables at play, both of which have a link to creativity. A highly creative person might feel capable of devising a novel method of committing fraud (opportunity) or a novel method of hiding the crime (concealment), for example, that raises the chance of success so high that the decision to commit fraud is obvious.

Another perspective is to see fraud as a game involving two players – the employee and the employer. In a rational, 'fair' world (where the odds are 50–50) the expectation of each player's wealth after the game is equal to what they started with. The employee, for example, is faced with a 50 per cent chance of gaining $200,000, or a 50 per cent chance of finishing with $0. The expectancy is $100,000 which is what the person would have if he or she did nothing. The same applies to the employer. Bernoulli recognised, however, an asymmetry. The money the loser gives up has a greater utility than the money the winner gains. This makes a zero-sum game – one in which there must be a winner and a loser – 'a loser's game when it is valued in terms of utility' (Bernstein, 1996, p. 113).

Why, then, would a rational player engage in this game? The answer is that, unlike a game of dice, it is not a zero-sum game. In the same way that Pilzer (1994) recognised 'that technology has liberated us from the zero-sum game of traditional economics' (p. 4), technology, in the sense of both the fraudster's product and the law-enforcer's product, offers both players the ability to tilt the playing field and change the odds. If the employee can devise a sufficiently novel effective fraud scheme, the loser's game can be turned into a winner's game. Equally, the law-enforcer seeks to do the same. As we recognised in Chapter 7, there are many traits that are common to both benevolent creativity and resourceful crime. We argued (pp. 145–150) that these traits make a person vulnerable to crime. In practical terms, in the case of fraud, this may manifest itself as lowering the threshold at which fraud is judged by the resourceful criminal as being worth the risk.

Echoing Comer's (1977) framework of opportunity, concealment, and source, Pedneault (2009) describes the 'fraud triangle' (p. 54), according to which three elements must be present for fraud to occur. The first is 'opportunity' and we have already explored the role that creativity might play in relation to identifying and exploiting opportunities. The second element that must be built into the question of risk and Bernoulli's consideration of utility is 'need'. A person earning $100,000 who is presented with an opportunity for fraud will also factor into the assessment of the risk, his or her need. If one person is debt free, then the utility of a possible $200,000 gain will be different for this person than for a second person who is heavily in debt, for the simple reason that the gain will have greater utility for the indebted person despite earning an identical salary. In other words, it may be more valuable to consider potential fraudsters' 'net wealth' in considering how they will react to opportunity, rather than simply the narrower question of salary level.

Pedneault's third element of the fraud triangle, and the one most relevant to creativity, is the issue of 'rationalisation'. 'Once opportunity and financial need are present in any one individual, the last component commonly found is the ability to rationalize the embezzlement' (p. 55). The vital link to creativity is then provided by Gino and Ariely's finding (2012) that 'a creative personality and a creative mindset promote individuals' ability to justify their behaviour, which, in turn, leads to unethical behaviour' (p. 445).

If creativity enhances an individual's opportunity to identify and exploit an opportunity for fraud, and if creativity strengthens the individual's ability to rationalise such dishonesty, then, in the presence of a financial need, is the creative individual better placed to commit fraud?

Prevention: catching them if we can

Two broad avenues for changing the practice of law-enforcement emerge from this discussion. An analysis of fraud and the Product through the lens of creativity highlights the multifaceted nature of what the fraudster must consider in committing the act. The act of fraud combines opportunity, concealment, and source, and each of these benefits from the application of the characteristics of a creative product. The resourceful criminal uses, for example, *novelty* to identify a diverse range of assets that can be considered as the target of fraud. The most important implication for the practice of law-enforcement is that organisations – both the potential victims of fraud and those organisations attempting to detect and prevent fraud – must adopt a similar creative mindset. To prevent fraud you must first know what it is that is a potential target. Similarly, organisations must understand how characteristics of creativity impact on concealment. They must be open to novelty in the method of concealment, and sensitive to how the organisation itself may unwittingly facilitate this concealment. Organisations must also recognise the value of creativity in relation to the source of fraud. Even when law-enforcement has closed certain avenues, resourceful criminals will continue to look for novel sources – if security measures, for example, rule out the internal employee as a potential source, then who else could act as a proxy for the purposes of committing fraud? Who else has access to assets, or is in a position that is considered above suspicion?

The three *structural* elements of fraud – opportunity, concealment, and source – each relies on novelty, elegance, and genesis to enhance its effectiveness. Resourceful criminals know this, even if only subconsciously, and are relentless in their efforts to develop new products as older schemes are detected and shut down. Indeed, the resourceful criminal can be conceptualised as an agile, flexible businessperson, constantly alert to new opportunities, quick to respond to gaps in the market, able to engage in rapid development cycles, able to move on to the next opportunity when the competition catches up.

The characteristics of the creative *Person* also suggest avenues for productive and proactive law-enforcement. Certain characteristics of the creative person – risk taking, motivation, inhibition – also play strong roles in relation to fraud. We suggested in Chapter 7 that creative people may, indeed, be *vulnerable* to crime. Using this knowledge, organisations are in a position to modify the way that risk is assessed. A more differentiated approach to assessing risk in relation to individual staff could include a consideration of their vulnerability to fraud. Analysing job roles in an organisation could include not just the fact that, for example, 'this role involves handling large sums of money' (and is therefore one that includes the potential for fraud), but might also include identifying what sort of employee might be vulnerable to fraud in that job role. In other words, it means changing the focus of risk assessment in relation to roles from simply analysing the role, to analysing the role and the kind of person who might fill it. Such an approach need not involve refusing to hire creative people – throwing out the baby with the bath water – but could involve special security measures at crucial nodes, as explained in greater detail in Chapter 9 (e.g., pp. 196–199).

Organisations seeking to detect and prevent resourceful crime – in particular fraud – must recognise the role that creativity plays for the criminal. They must then draw on the same fundamental concepts of creative *Products* – novelty, effectiveness, elegance, and genesis – and similar *Personal* qualities – openness and flexibility, for example – to respond effectively.

CHAPTER NINE

Terrorism
A case study

Terrorism is a special case of resourceful crime. It involves products that have the deliberate intention of inflicting death, suffering, and fear on non-combatant populations, very often without any tangible personal gain for the perpetrator. It differs from 'simple' crime, where personal profit is usually paramount. Despite their malevolence, whether we like it or not, terrorists are genuinely creative. As demonstrated most strikingly in the 9/11 atrocity, they sometimes generate highly effective novelty and sometimes this can be of long-lasting effectiveness and applicable in a variety of settings. Terrorists' products must be surprising (novel) and also effective; otherwise law-enforcers would take appropriate precautions or nobody would notice them. Thus, the terrorist Product involves 'functional' creativity. Terrorists operate outside the framework of conventional values and morals while they frequently commit violent crimes in the name of value systems that condemn violence. The harm the terrorists inflict often extends to the perpetrators themselves (e.g., suicide bombers). Thus, the dimension of Person may be of special significance. There is some evidence that terrorist activities are more acceptable in collectivist societies, while they seem to be fostered by the existence of a charismatic leader, i.e., terrorism may depend on a special kind of Press. Functioning outside universally accepted values while claiming to espouse those values involves *cognitive dissonance*,[1] which can be dealt with through special Processes like 'reframing' of terrorist actions – the victims are proclaimed to be guilty, so that the perpetrators' guilt feeling is assuaged.

---

[1] Cognitive dissonance is experienced when a person simultaneously holds two conflicting views or behaves in ways that are mutually contradictory. This state is unpleasant to experience. According to Festinger, Riecken, and Schachter (1956), people dislike the experience of cognitive dissonance and engage in 'dissonance reduction' in one of three ways: (a) they change one of the discordant behaviours or views to make it consistent with the other, (b) they dismiss one of the discordant factors as unimportant, or (c) they focus on information that seems to make the discordant factor concordant. A fourth variant seems to be to blind oneself to the dissonance through rationalisations or even lying.

It was undoubtedly a cold, damp, and dark winter's evening in Paris, on 14 January 1858, as Felice Orsini, the Italian revolutionary and leader of the secretive Carbonari, and three confederates lurked in the shadows along the Rue Le Peletier, waiting for the carriage of his target to pass. Their intention was to assassinate Napoleon III, emperor of the Second French Empire. No stranger to action, Orsini's dissatisfaction with the political situation in his native Italy, and his innate urge to bring about change had led to his imprisonment in the 1840s after he was implicated in revolutionary plots. Orsini did not lack in confidence and was a natural risk-taker. After he was released from prison he distinguished himself leading a company of Romagnols in the First War of Italian Independence (1848–9), where his resourcefulness and courage were put to good use. If successful, Orsini would strike a major blow in support of Italian independence and avenge his own misfortune following the fall of the Second Roman Republic and his support for the Mazzinian Party.

A bold and confident innovator, skilled at recognising opportunities for action, Orsini was, at the time of the attack, somewhat of a celebrity. The account of his opportunistic escape from a prison in Mantua, in 1854, by cutting through bars with a small hacksaw and using an improvised rope to reach the ground 30 metres below his cell, coupled with his clever disguise as a peasant, had all the hallmarks of a flexible, creative problem-solver, willing to break rules in the service of his undoubtedly self-centred aims. The death of his intended victim, Napoleon III of France, on that winter's night would, he believed, further the cause of Italian independence by removing a focus of anti-liberal sentiment in Europe, lead to a popular uprising in France, and provide Italian revolutionaries with the excuse they needed to move against that country's leadership.

Orsini went to Paris in 1857 to begin his preparations, completely confident in his own ability to succeed. This was to be no spontaneous, ill-conceived act of violence, but a meticulous, planned assassination. No room here for sentiment or morals, Orsini would devise an attack that would ensure success, selecting a method, time, and place that would give his quarry's guards no opportunity to intervene. With characteristic ingenuity, Orsini saw that he could design bombs set to explode on impact, by adapting the highly sensitive fulminate of mercury – normally used as an initiator in percussion caps – to a larger scale. Indeed, these are still known today as 'Orsini bombs' and consist of a spherical shell filled with the main explosive and studded with small horns containing fulminate of mercury. The bomb is designed so that at least one of the horns will be crushed on contact with a hard surface, causing the fulminate of mercury to detonate the main explosive. Orsini's bomb design removed the uncertainty of slow-burning, fused weapons. Orsini travelled to England late in 1857, engaging the gunsmith Joseph Taylor to make six copies of his design. Then, leaving nothing to chance, Orsini tested his weapon on at least two different occasions, in Sheffield and in Devonshire, to ensure that it would function as intended and required. Finally, after nearly a year of preparation, and with growing excitement, Orsini was ready to carry out his attack.

As the carriage of Napoleon III and his empress, Eugénie de Montijo, made its way down Rue Le Peletier, taking the couple to see a performance of Rossini's *William Tell*, Orsini and his confederates struck. They were undeterred by a large, mounted escort and many civilians. Three of his highly sensitive bombs were thrown in quick succession, all aimed at the imperial carriage. The first landed in front of the carriage, spraying shrapnel among the emperor's accompanying horsemen and wounding many. The second bomb landed closer, seriously wounding the animals drawing the emperor's carriage and smashing the glass of the carriage itself. The third and final bomb detonated under the emperor's carriage and, although it seriously wounded a policeman rushing to protect the imperial couple, the emperor and empress themselves were saved by the stout construction of the carriage and remained unhurt. Though unsuccessful in its primary aim of assassinating the emperor, the attack nevertheless killed 8 and wounded more than 140, and received widespread publicity both in Europe and North America. Orsini, engrossed in the attack, was himself wounded in the head, but kept his nerve and was able to avoid immediate capture and return to his home where he was arrested the following day by police.

Far from damaging the emperor's status as the French leader, the attack actually increased Napoleon's popularity and did nothing to further Orsini's aims. There was no uprising in France, and no change in Italy. Undaunted, and recognising the need to change tack, Orsini made one, final, attempt to achieve his aims more peacefully, but perhaps no less creatively. Writing from his prison cell, shortly before his execution by guillotine in March 1858, Orsini pleaded with Napoleon III to support the cause of Italian independence.[2] Orsini went to his death undeterred in his aim of bringing about political change in Italy. Flexible and pragmatic

---

[2] One of Orsini's co-conspirators, Carlo di Rudio, later Charles DeRudio, had his sentence commuted to life imprisonment on Devil's Island, from which he escaped. He subsequently made his way to the United States, where he became an officer in the US 7th Cavalry and was a survivor of the Battle of the Little Bighorn in 1876.

to the end, he also wrote an open letter to the youth of Italy condemning political assassination!

Creativity and terrorism

As the case of Felice Orsini illustrates, terrorism – i.e., the use of violence to create fear in order to further religious, political, or ideological goals, and deliberately targeting or disregarding the safety of non-combatants – often involves the application of cunning and ingenuity, the development of new methods or techniques, and the generation of surprising results, and thus can be seen as a particular case of what we have defined as *resourceful* crime (See Introduction, p. 3). It is thus intimately bound up with creativity, despite the fact that, unlike other forms of resourceful crime, it frequently involves little or no direct personal gain for the perpetrator. As Benjamin and Simon (2002, p. 400) remind us about terrorists: 'They are genuinely creative, and their ingenuity and desire to inflict massive casualties will continue to drive them.'

We see clear evidence of this in the terrorist acts that occurred on 9/11. When judged against the framework of the 6Ps of creativity (Chapter 3, pp. 61–71) it is abundantly clear – as it is with Felice Orsini – that the 9/11 terrorists exhibited all the qualities of *Person* that are commonly associated with creativity (see Chapter 7, Table 7.1), whether directed towards good or bad ends. They demonstrated, for example, dissatisfaction with the status quo, an urge to take action, openness, ingenuity, and moral disengagement. Both Orsini and the 9/11 terrorists were resourceful, willing to break norms, resilient, risk-takers, confident in their ability to succeed, and highly motivated.

The qualities of creativity that make the solution to any problem (the Product) more robust – novelty, effectiveness, elegance, and genesis (see Table 3.1) – are just as valuable in the domain of terrorism as they are in engineering, art, or business. Whether judging Orsini's novel hand-grenades or the 9/11 terrorists' reconceptualisation of commercial airliners as flying bombs, it is clear that 'successful' terrorists generate highly effective novelty that, in addition, is frequently also highly *elegant* – i.e., it is typically skilfully executed, complete, and well worked out – and *generic* – i.e., transferable and applicable in a variety of other settings. Indeed, it is almost axiomatic that terrorist Products are both novel and effective (i.e., creative) – if they were not, then they would be detected and prevented. Thus, successful terrorist Products are successful precisely *because* they are creative. It is for this reason that we need to understand how creativity operates in this domain.

The special case of terrorism, however, adds further dimensions to the role of creativity that may not be apparent in other forms of resourceful crime such as fraud. We see these in other aspects of the Person, Press, and Process. Unlike the domain of fraud, terrorists frequently operate in a framework of values and morals that is qualitatively far removed from that of the fraudster. The most obvious example of this can be seen in the case of suicide bombers. It is hard to imagine cases of fraud in which the perpetrators set out with the goal of ruining themselves in the course of their crime. The whole point of fraud is to achieve personal gain. Suicide bombers, by contrast, set out to destroy not only the victims, but also themselves. This suggests that the dimension *Person* plays a particular and unique role in terrorism that differs somewhat from other forms of resourceful crime. Similarly, terrorism is frequently dependent on a special kind of 'environment' or *Press* – one in which, for example, a charismatic leader may play an especially strong role. Associated with these is also the necessity of particularly strong *Processes* – for example, those that make it possible for terrorists to justify their actions in the face of what may be strong cognitive dissonance.

We will examine these issues further in this chapter, using both Orsini and 9/11 as examples, with the aim of identifying the particular features of terrorism as a form of resourceful (creative) crime, and as a means of identifying practical actions to prevent or impede it. As we conduct this analysis of terrorism, we must guard against the danger, highlighted in Chapter 5 (p. 112), that is posed by a tendency to see high levels of creativity only in actions that are perceived, at worst, as morally ambiguous. In other words, the tendency to associate creativity only with good things, and to have a *blind spot* in relation to recognising creativity in negative outcomes risks limiting people's ability to recognise the creativity inherent in terrorism. The danger is that we assume that terrorism and terrorists cannot possibly be creative, and therefore fail to approach the design of counter-measures in the most appropriate way. As we have stated elsewhere, creativity has, unequivocally, a dark side that is manifest, with chilling clarity, in terrorism.

Runco (2010, p. 15) argued that 'creativity does not have a dark side' conceding, however, that 'creative products and efforts can be malevolent' but qualifying this with 'that [malevolence] is apparent in their impact and is not an inherent quality of creativity nor a requisite trait in the creative personality'. For a long time, creativity has been heralded as a positive quality of individuals, and a beneficial characteristic of products, so it is natural for people to reason, 'how can creativity be bad, if I am creative and I am good?' Throughout this book, however, we have drawn attention to aspects of the dark side of creativity (Cropley et al., 2010), not simply out of curiosity, but because we believe that a more complete understanding of creativity can only be achieved if we recognise the variety of forms and shades of grey that exist in this discipline. If these forms include the application of creativity to resourceful crime, then it is a fallacy to argue, as Runco (2010, p. 15) does, that 'discussing the dark side of creativity … could keep someone from encouraging creativity because of the fear that it will lead to … malevolence'. This modern form of the mediaeval prohibition against 'speaking of the devil' lest 'he doth appear' serves only to limit our understanding of creativity and limit progress in the development of counter-measures that can be applied in domains like terrorism and fraud.

Once we recognise that creativity is not restricted to good products, or good people, or fostered only by good environments, and that a process can be implemented with the deliberate aim of generating a bad outcome, then we are open to the application of creativity in crime and, most importantly, open to ways to inform and change the practice of law-enforcement to combat malevolent creativity. To refuse to see creativity in crime, whether in the Person, the Product, the Process, or the Press, is to constrain law-enforcement unnecessarily. Acknowledging creativity in the context of crime – whether terrorism or fraud – allows us first to analyse where it adds value to the criminal enterprise, and second, to take steps to prevent and mitigate its effects.

Who *are the terrorists?*

Our purpose in this section is *not* to attempt to identify or analyse in any detail where terrorists come from, or to profile them in any demographic or cultural sense. We are *not* concerned with identifying, for example, that Islamic suicide bombers are usually male, typically come from middle-class backgrounds and are reasonably well educated. Rather, we seek to highlight those characteristics and traits that tie terrorists – as examples of resourceful criminals – both to other kinds of resourceful criminals (e.g., fraudsters), and to creativity in general. At the same time, we are also concerned with highlighting any unique aspects of terrorists, again in relation to creativity, that shed light on avenues for law-enforcement and preventive measures.

The two cases presented show that success in terrorism is, at the very least, strongly correlated with personal characteristics linked to creativity, if not directly caused by them. For this reason, although functioning outside a conventional *values* framework that condemns violence, and indeed often developing solutions that are inconsistent with the value systems they claim to support, terrorists nevertheless exhibit and draw on the same personal traits that are seen to add value to benevolent creativity. As Table 7.1 in Chapter 7 illustrates, whether creativity is benevolent or malevolent, these *personal traits* include high levels of sensation seeking, openness, ingenuity, resourcefulness and opportunism, self-confidence, norm-breaking, and resilience, as well as low levels of inhibition and conformity. Creativity in both cases is *motivated* by high levels of dissatisfaction, rebelliousness, risk and adventure seeking. Creative people, whether designing a new consumer product or devising a new way to hijack an airliner, are typified by their confidence, excitement, and passion.

Nonetheless, some traits which appear to be common to all creative people (such as empathy) may be lower than normal in resourceful criminals, and especially terrorists. The challenge that we face when considering the profile that differentiates a 'good' creative – for example, an artist or design engineer – from a terrorist is how to use this knowledge in a way that does not throw the baby out with the bathwater. We will return to this in a later section when we consider the implications for law-enforcement and prevention.

The terrorist Product

No single, legal definition of terrorism exists, although there is widespread consensus on what it involves. Earlier in this chapter we defined it by combining 'the use of violence to create fear' with a variety of underlying goals (religious, political, ideological), and highlighted the deliberate targeting or disregard for the safety of non-combatants. In a discussion of creativity and terrorism (crime) our primary focus is to understand the *Product* that sits at the core of terrorism – the things terrorists do – so that we can examine it through the lens of creativity, and, in particular, define the characteristics of creative products. Therefore it is most instructive to think of the terrorist product as the 'act of terrorism', i.e., the hijacking, the bombing, the assassination. We suggested earlier in this chapter that the same characteristics of creativity that are valued in a benevolent product – novelty, effectiveness, elegance, and genesis – are also of value in a malevolent product such as a terrorist act.

Novelty

The literature of creativity research (see, for example, Sternberg and Lubart, 1999, or Cropley and Cropley, 2005) has established that the first two – novelty and effectiveness (also characterised as 'appropriateness', 'usefulness', or 'relevance') – are the core of creativity. It is not hard to see why novelty and effectiveness are so important. Cropley, Kaufman, and Cropley (2008, p. 107) highlighted the importance of novelty in a (benevolent) business context: 'The more creative [novel] a product, the less likely it is that competitors will have anticipated it. It is self-evident that a business entering a market with a product that has never been seen before will, at least initially, have no competition.' This is further reinforced by Yang and El-Haik (2003), writing in the domain of new product development and 'quality'. They said that 'companies that are the first to introduce new products ... usually capture the largest share of the market' (p. 173). They further emphasise that 'Wrestling market share away from a viable competitor is more difficult than it is for the first producer into a market' (p. 173). In other words, novelty and effectiveness have considerable value in a competitive environment.

Both the example of Orsini and the case of 9/11 were contingent on achieving the same kind of surprise. It is self-evident that an act of terrorism that is highly novel (original and surprising) is unlikely to have been anticipated by law-enforcers. It follows that if it has not been anticipated, it is unlikely that any counter-measures exist to prevent it. Like a business, the terrorist who 'enters a market' with a novel product is likely, at least for a short time, to 'have no competition'. Although Orsini failed to kill his intended victim, this was not through lack of novelty. His form of attack was clearly not anticipated and did, indeed, take the emperor and his entourage by surprise. There were no effective counter-measures in place, and the attack failed only because Orsini's bombs were not sufficiently powerful (Yang and El-Haik would say that the product lacked *quality* but not novelty). Had the bombs been more effective, it is highly likely that the emperor would have been killed.

By the same token, the very fact that the terrorists on 9/11 were able to seize control of four aircraft (in spite of a more sophisticated level of security when compared to Orsini) and fly three of them into their intended targets is clear evidence that they achieved a high level of surprise. Whatever counter-measures were in place clearly failed to anticipate this novel form of terrorist act, allowing the terrorists, at least for a short period, to operate without any effective competition. At this point, readers may be anticipating one inherent weakness that reveals itself in the 9/11 example, and that sheds important light on the role of creativity in resourceful crime. This relates to the role that effectiveness plays in characterising creativity, and this will be addressed shortly.

Effectiveness

It is clear that novelty on its own is not enough for creativity (see Chapter 3, p. 53). Neither Orsini nor the 9/11 terrorists can be said to have succeeded simply because they took their opponents by surprise, as important as that is. If surprise alone were sufficient, then it would have been easier for Orsini simply to throw an egg at Napoleon III. It is the combination of novelty *and* effectiveness that must be considered. Indeed, as Cropley and Cropley (2005) argue, there is a definite hierarchy of these characteristics. In a functional sense, the first question, both for benevolent and malevolent products, is 'do they fulfil their purpose?' If a product does not do what it is supposed to do, regardless of how novel it is, it will be judged a failure. Thus effectiveness must be considered alongside novelty in judging the creativity of terrorist products. Orsini's attack, while highly novel, was not entirely effective. He failed to kill Napoleon III and thus, regardless of whatever other casualties he caused, the attack must be regarded as, at best, only *partially* successful. His failure to foment revolution ultimately leading to a change of government in Italy – i.e., his wider purpose – was also not achieved. In Orsini's case, the fault can be traced mainly to the lack of effectiveness of his bombs and not to any lack of novelty.

In the case of the attacks on 9/11, however, we see a slightly different picture. If a virtue can be found in the events on that day, it may lie in the fact that the terrorists attempted to repeat the same act four times in quick succession. This allows us to examine the relationship between novelty and effectiveness, and to draw some conclusions about the way that creativity works. In simple terms, we can track the levels of novelty and effectiveness, and their interaction, over time, and it becomes evident that from the time the first plane was hijacked and crashed into the World Trade Center until the time that the last plane crashed into the Pennsylvania countryside, the novelty of the attacks had declined to a measureable degree. The main factor that changed in this period was that the passengers on UA93 became aware of the fact that other planes had been hijacked and crashed into buildings. We have argued (Cropley, Kaufman, and Cropley 2008, pp. 109–11) that this represented a 'decay' in the novelty of the product that, critically, resulted in a corresponding decay in effectiveness. In simple terms, the fact that the terrorist act was no longer novel (i.e., surprising) for the passengers of UA93 led to a change in their response to that terrorist act. The hijackers no longer enjoyed the advantage of complete surprise, and as a result of their competitors (the passengers) anticipating their product, and reacting with their own 'counter-solution', the terrorists were faced with some competition. That the plane crashed in the countryside and not on what is thought to have been its intended target is evidence enough that the terrorists did not achieve the effectiveness they were seeking.

Not only are novelty and effectiveness prerequisites for creativity, they also interact with each other in ways that can either strengthen or weaken the product. In the case of UA93, the decay of novelty resulting in increased competition led, in effect, to a decay in the effectiveness of the terrorist product. This then suggests that, from the point of view of the resourceful criminal, it is important to preserve the novelty of a product for as long as possible. Doing so serves to prevent the parallel decay of effectiveness. Herein lies a paradox that terrorists face that is perhaps unique to their form of resourceful crime: the effectiveness of a terrorist act is a function of the fear and confusion that it sows and the extent to which people yield to the terrorist demands (its wider, *distal* effects), and the death, damage, and other destruction that it causes (its *proximate* effects). The former depends to a large extent on publicity, which, as we have argued, accelerates the decay of novelty. The latter is maximised, as we have seen, by the maintenance of novelty. The terrorist product must simultaneously attempt to maintain surprise *and* achieve publicity – two characteristics that seem to be mutually incompatible.

Two other characteristics also play a role in 'functional' creativity. *Elegance* – the degree to which a product is skilfully executed, complete, and well worked out – contributes to the overall quality of the product, in particular, reinforcing the effectiveness of the product. As an example we can again consider the 9/11 attacks. It can be argued that a more elegant version of their product would have ensured that the passengers on UA93 were unable to fight back, even if they became aware of the other attacks. This might have been achieved if the terrorists had been able to restrain all the passengers in some way (for example, they could have handcuffed them). Similarly, if the terrorists had collected all cell-phones from the passengers, they might have preserved the novelty, and therefore the effectiveness, of their solution for longer.

Genesis

Genesis – the extent to which the product is transferable and applicable in a variety of other settings – by contrast, may reinforce novelty, offsetting to some degree the decay which occurs as the product becomes well known. *Generic novelty* can be transferred to a new situation to maintain its effectiveness, or it may show how to deal with old situations in a new way. Indeed, 9/11 may itself represent an example of the genesis inherent in the concept of kamikaze attacks used by the Japanese during the Second World War. In fact, the obviousness of the generic application of the novelty involved in the kamikaze attacks raises the question why other groups of terrorists did not employ the 9/11 approach earlier, and also raises the question why people in charge of security apparently did not foresee the possibility of such an attack and adopt appropriate measures. In retrospect, the action the terrorists needed to take is blindingly obvious. The Japanese Air Force had a supply of willing pilots available; the 9/11 terrorists did not. Thus they needed to carry out pilot training. Absurdly, their victims provided this training. The failure to foresee the modus operandi of the 9/11 terrorists is probably an example of the failure of law-enforcers to recognise the creativity of effective malevolent novelty and to be aware of the problem of genesis. Probably no-one recognised the creativity of the kamikaze attacks and conceptualised them as an example of effective novelty that was capable of being successfully repeated if pilots could be obtained.[3]

The generic effect of 9/11 reveals further interesting insights. The attacks undoubtedly suggested ways that the core idea of the attack – using a plane as a flying bomb – might be reapplied in similar ways to other modes of transport. We have all experienced increases in security on other forms of transport, post 9/11, that are a result of the expectation that terrorists might try to repeat the 9/11 modus operandi with trains or ships, for example. A paradox is also evident here. Possibly the greatest effect stemming from the generic nature of the novelty of the 9/11 attacks has been on the reaction of law-enforcement. The attacks drew attention to previously unnoticed problems – for example, the vulnerability of the flight crew in the cockpit – leading to design changes that have significantly upgraded the security of the cockpit on most commercial airliners. In effect, the pilots are now isolated from the passengers by reinforced cockpit doors that have peep-holes, multiple keyed locks, an internal deadbolt, and even a digital code mechanism for entry.

Thus creativity theory suggests that successful terrorists will strive for not just relevant and effective surprise, but also elegant and generic

---

[3] This may also represent another example of the creativity *blind spot*. We have a tendency to associate creativity with good things. Suicide attacks are seen, at least in *Western* cultures, as unacceptably and irrationally wicked. For that reason, we find it hard to associate any level of creativity with them. Yet kamikaze attacks were novel, effective, elegant, and, most importantly, generic – capable of being transferred, with great effect, to new problem domains.

novelty, and the kamikaze example shows how dangerous generic functional creativity generated by evil-doers can be, unless law-enforcers recognise the genesis in malevolent creativity and take steps to block it in the future. Fortunately, the very qualities that increase the quality of the terrorist product also increase its vulnerability to counter-measures. Like creativity in a benevolent, commercial context, creativity in the case of resourceful crime and terrorism is part of a dynamic cycle in which the gains are fleeting and temporary. As one side achieves effective surprise, the other responds to negate this and supersede it, prompting a further cycle of competing effective novelty, which we refer to in Chapter 10 (pp. 204–205) as an 'arms race'.

The terrorist Press

We have already discussed aspects of the Press – the environment in which creativity takes place – that are known to be favourable to creativity. Amabile and Gryskiewicz (1989) identified a number of Press factors that both support and inhibit creativity. There is no reason to suppose that these factors are any different in the case of terrorism or other forms of resourceful crime, despite the fact that terrorists may not operate in an organisation in quite the same sense as Amabile and Gryskiewicz were investigating. Access to appropriate resources, challenging work, a supportive supervisor and a sense of cooperation can all be seen as playing a role, both for Felice Orsini and for the 9/11 terrorists. Equally, it is apparent that time pressure and over-evaluation, two characteristics that inhibit creativity, probably did not play a significant role in constraining either Orsini or the 9/11 terrorists. Orsini, for example, had complete freedom to plan his attack to his own time schedule. He was not subject to any deadline imposed on him, or to any pressure to produce results and show progress. The 9/11 terrorists were well funded, backed by their leadership, reasonably free from interference, and working in a 'collegial' atmosphere.

Leadership

Terrorist groups are 'clandestine and values based' (Price, 2012, p. 17). As a result, members tend to have very similar views on the core issues in their lives. This means that they can easily fuse into emotionally bonded groups of what Atran (2003, p. 1534) called 'fictive kin', who are even prepared to die for what they see as the common good of their 'kin'. This makes the group more cohesive. Terrorist leaders play a special role in this. They have no formal authority over the group and must thus depend on charisma to attract and control its members; people belong because they *believe* in the cause and in the leader, and they are even prepared to die for one or both. The leader becomes a source of irresistible power, who can convince people to 'cross the line', as we have put it earlier (Chapter 7, pp. 149–150). In other words, under the influence of the leader, people may take on extremist views for which they previously had little sympathy or become ready to carry out acts they would previously have rejected. The effect of the leader is thus vital for terrorist groups.

In a clandestine group in which the members face the prospect of sudden death – possibly as a direct result of their own deliberate actions – the leader plays a special role in holding the group together emotionally and ideologically. To do this, the leader has a number of functions, including:

- articulating the values, vision, and mission of the group;
- controlling the flow of information (or even being the *only* source of information);
- being the main source of approval/disapproval and thus controlling rewards and status;
- reframing the victims as evil-doers or necessary sacrifices to the great mission;
- shouldering ultimate responsibility for what happens;
- reducing the anxiety of members of the group;
- reducing guilt.

The effects of isolation on willingness to endorse the views of those who control contact and stimulation have been demonstrated repeatedly in psychological research on brainwashing of prisoners by the Chinese during the Korean War, in cults (Taylor, 2004), and through sensory deprivation (Zubek, 1969). In the case of Orsini, it is his role as the charismatic leader of his three confederates that stands out here as a factor in their attack. In the case of the 9/11 terrorists, the undoubted leadership of Osama bin Laden and the *middle managers* in his terrorist network can be seen as a factor in facilitating the resourceful criminal actions of the terrorists and reinforcing favourable elements of Person (e.g., motivation).

The terrorist Process

The fourth element of the framework for understanding creativity in the context of resourceful crime is the Process. This can be understood in two senses that are relevant to a discussion of creativity and terrorism. First, Process describes those largely cognitive abilities usually characterised as a contrast between divergent thinking and convergent thinking, which are associated with creativity. Like aspects of Person, some of these are common to benevolent and malevolent creativity – for example, the ability to recognise opportunities, an awareness of the problem 'environment', the ability to form remote associates and make unexpected links, the ability to redefine problems, and the ability to recognise and formulate successful solution strategies (see Chapter 7, Table 7.1). Others are dependent on the particular kind of creativity. The ability to deviate from norms may be essentially constructive and therefore associated with benevolent creativity, while destructive deviance is the characteristic of malevolent creativity. Similarly, rule-breaking that focuses on non-statutory rules, for example, breaking social conventions, is an aspect of benevolent creativity, while breaking statutory rules, that is, breaking the law, is the domain of resourceful crime and terrorism.

Coupled with these cognitive abilities, and tied to Gino and Ariely's (2012) findings linking creativity and dishonesty, is the role that 'reframing' (Whittaker, 2007) may play for terrorists. 'Reframing' terrorist acts as, for instance, part of the way 'we' cope with unjust treatment by 'them', or as a symbol of 'our' strength and courage in dealing with 'them', may strengthen a feeling of belonging to an elite group and thus foster solidarity. It may also eliminate guilt feelings by transferring the guilt to the victims, or making mistreatment of others seem reasonable, even heroic.

Because terrorists are operating outside a framework of conventional values and morals, and *know* that they are doing so, it is easy to see that there is a significant level of *cognitive dissonance* associated with, for example, claiming that you are fighting for peace and freedom, while plotting to kill innocent people. Reframing may help to resolve this cognitive dissonance – for example, by proclaiming the victims as guilty or as unavoidable collateral damage, essentially the third way of dealing with dissonance mentioned in footnote (1) above – in order to assuage their own sense of guilt at their actions. If, as Gino and Ariely assert, creative people are better at justifying their unethical behaviour (i.e., at achieving dissonance reduction) we can speculate that this may extend from justifying cheating or stealing, to justifying acts of terrorism through actions such as reframing.

The second sense in which Process can be understood in relation to creativity and terrorism is as the series of steps involved in moving from the identification of a problem, to the implementation of a solution to that problem. In Chapter 4 (pp. 79–87) we introduced a discussion of the stages, or phases, of creativity that highlighted the roles of idea generation and exploitation in creative problem-solving. In the context of resourceful crime, this moves our discussion from one of creativity – the generation of effective novelty – to one of innovation – the *exploitation* of effective novelty. By considering the process involved in moving from idea to act, whether considering Felice Orsini's attempt to assassinate Napoleon III or the 9/11 attacks, we get a better sense of the role that planning, for example, plays in resourceful crime. Both Orsini and the 9/11 terrorists realised that it was not sufficient simply to invent a new kind of grenade or a new way to destroy a building. They understood that their inventions must be tested and evaluated as far as possible (and subject to the need to preserve their novelty or 'surprise value') as part of exploiting their creativity for practical purposes.

Clear evidence of the role of Process is also available from the 7 July 2005 bombings in London. On 20 September 2005, the BBC reported that Scotland Yard detectives had released CCTV footage showing the 7/7 bombers rehearsing their attacks on the London public transport system nine days before the real attacks were carried out. Significantly, for our purposes, Scotland Yard's Deputy Assistant Commissioner, Peter Clarke, 'pointed out that it is "part of a terrorist's methodology" to check timings, lay-out and security precautions' (British Broadcasting Corporation, 2005). While not obviously 'creativity' in the sense of divergent thinking, idea generation, and 'invention', this highly convergent activity – planning, rehearsing, training, and evaluating – is nevertheless a vital part of the process of turning an idea into a successful product, just as it would be for a new musical theatre production, or a new consumer product.

While this might seem to expand the scope of the problem of detecting, preventing, impeding, or mitigating resourceful crime, we argue that it offers additional avenues for law-enforcement. The problem is not simply one of stopping resourceful criminals – terrorists or fraudsters – from being creative. Their success depends on their ability to engage in a process of innovation, and this presents law-enforcement with a range of avenues, across the different phases, and coupled with the 6Ps, through which resourceful crime can be inhibited, blocked, and even prevented. In the final section of this chapter we will consider how our knowledge of when and where creativity occurs can be used to suggest practical implications for law-enforcement.

Implications/counter-measures

While there is value in identifying characteristics and traits that are prevalent among certain kinds of criminals, there can be considerable difficulty in applying this knowledge. Knowing that some 90 per cent of serial killers are males with a tendency to above-average intelligence still leaves us with the fact that some are female, some are males of lower intelligence, and some did *not* wet their beds as teenagers. Injudiciously applied, these statistical correlates hinder law-enforcement as much as help it. Gladwell recounts the case of a Baton Rouge serial killer (Gladwell, 2009, pp. 347–48): the FBI constructed a profile, stating that the killer was white and socially awkward with women. It turned out that Derrick Todd Lee was black and a charming ladies' man. Unless we can use such information in an a priori fashion, to take practical steps to prevent or inhibit resourceful crime, it may be little more, when it is correct, than interesting trivia. In the same way that police cannot arrest all males after a serial killer has struck in the hope of netting the actual killer, we cannot arrest all creative people after a terrorist attack in the hope that we will snare the offender. Equally, if we incarcerated all unskilled labourers who did poorly in school in order to prevent serial murders, while possibly effective, the social and economic costs would be impractical, to say the least. In similar fashion, we could stop encouraging creativity in schools as a means of inhibiting resourceful crime, but the negative consequences would far outweigh any positives.

With respect to resourceful crime, whether fraud or terrorism, the most promising approaches to prevention and inhibition may lie, counterintuitively, not in trying to focus on the traits unique to resourceful crime (such as low empathy), but on those that are *common to all creativity*. However, this must be coupled with knowledge of Press and Process. Cropley (2010) proposed a general approach to tackling *malevolent innovation* that is based on the interaction of phases and dimensions summarised in Chapter 4. In other words, we focus on *normal traits applied in an abnormal way* (perhaps analogous to the method used by William Gordon in Synectics – *making the familiar strange*), rather than abnormal traits applied in a normal or abnormal way.

The constellation of seven phases and six dimensions that are involved in generation of effective novelty was described in Chapter 4 as defining a matrix of forty-two nodes, each node defined by a combination of a P (Personal properties, Personal motivation, Personal feelings, Process, Product, and Press) and a phase (Generation, Illumination,

Implementation, etc.). Table 4.2 showed the special characteristics of each node (e.g., in the node Product/Generation 'one or more candidate solutions are generated', in the node Process/Verification 'the novel configuration is evaluated', or in the node Personal properties/Generation 'tolerance for ambiguity' and 'flexibility' are needed).[4] Table 9.1 uses the same framework of nodes, but lists for each node the particular kind of thinking or motivation, the particular personal properties, and the like that are favourable for innovation in each mode. For instance, whereas according to Table 4.2, in the node Motivation/Implementation 'desire for recognition' and 'hope of reward' are crucial, Table 9.1 shows that this node requires reactive motivation. Thus, where Table 4.2 specifies in a general way what happens in each node, Table 9.1 specifies the actual processes, motives, personal properties, and so on that are *favourable* for innovation.

Rather than using this framework to enhance (benevolent) creativity and innovation – by removing barriers – the same framework can be used as the basis for inhibiting malevolent creativity and innovation – by *inserting* barriers. Because the preventive strategy is specific to the process of malevolent innovation (i.e., *normal traits applied in an abnormal way/setting*), we are not risking imposing barriers to creativity and innovation that are desirable, only to that which we are trying to eliminate.

With forty-two nodes representing many different intersections of Person, Process, Product, and Press with the different stages of creativity and innovation, it is impractical to establish different courses of action to disrupt every possible combination of phase and dimension. Rather than attempting to monitor where terrorists are at any given stage of the innovation process and taking action specific to individual nodes, it makes more sense to try to insert one or more *barriers* across points in the innovation process, in the hope that these will prove difficult, if not impossible, for malevolent innovators to cross. Table 9.1 highlights the phases and dimensions of the malevolent innovation process and illustrates the concepts of phase **barriers** to malevolent innovation. The barriers are marked by the vertical bold lines between Preparation and Activation, between Generation and Illumination, and between Verification and Implementation.

An approach to identifying where these barriers should be placed is to examine each dimension and decide which pole of the dimension is more open to disruption (either by inhibition of the favourable condition or

---

[4] In fact, Table 4.2 lists only thirty-five of the forty-two nodes as, for the sake of brevity, it omits the dimension of Personal feelings.

Table 9.1 *The malevolent innovation phases and dimensions with potential phase barriers*

Dimension	Phase Poles	Invention					Exploitation	
		Preparation: Knowledge, problem recognition	Activation: Problem definition, refinement	Generation: Many candidate solutions generated	Illumination: A few promising solutions	Verification: A single optimal solution is identified	Implementation: A working prototype	Validation: A successful 'product' shows its worth
Process	Convergent vs Divergent	Convergent	Divergent	Divergent	Convergent	Convergent	Mixed	Convergent
Motivation	Reactive vs Proactive	Mixed	Proactive	Proactive	Proactive	Mixed	Reactive	Reactive
Personal Properties	Adaptive vs Innovative	Adaptive	Innovative	Innovative	Innovative	Adaptive	Adaptive	Adaptive
Feelings	Conserving vs Generative	Conserving	Generative	Generative	Generative	Conserving	Conserving	Conserving
Product	Routine vs Creative	Routine	Creative	Creative	Creative	Routine	Routine	Routine
Press	Constraints oriented vs Freedom oriented	Freedom oriented	Freedom oriented	Freedom oriented	Constraints oriented	Constraints oriented	Constraints oriented	Constraints oriented

encouragement of the unfavourable condition). For example, is it easier to disrupt convergent thinking, or divergent thinking in our situation, where we have only indirect control over what the malevolent innovators do? Once we establish which pole of each dimension is the most susceptible to disruption, we can then match this to the ideal constellations in Table 9.1 to find the phase or phases most likely to be affected by barrier(s) to malevolent innovation.

The approach to disrupting malevolent innovation presents some interesting challenges. In the same way that most of the literature on creativity has an assumed benevolent focus, the literature has also focused on ways to help people enhance their ability to think divergently, be suitably motivated, etc. We are now looking at ways to do the opposite: to inhibit, for example, people's ability to think divergently – we are interested in what might be called 'anti-creativity'. The discussion is complicated by the fact that we lack direct control over the subjects of interest. Is it possible to foster a particular kind of thinking, or a particular motivation, or certain feelings, or indeed a particular organisational climate, indirectly? Can we remotely manipulate how terrorists think in order to make them less effective innovators?

General principles for disrupting malevolent innovation

The model of innovation summarised in Table 9.1 suggests two fundamental approaches to disrupting malevolent innovation:

- phase blocks
- dimension blocks

The first approach, already touched on, seeks to identify ways of disrupting the flow of the malevolent innovation process from one phase to the next (i.e., it is based on the columns of Table 9.1 – Preparation, Activation, Generation, Illumination, Verification, Implementation, and Validation). The second seeks to identify social-psychological dimensions that are most amenable to disruption (i.e., the rows of Table 9.1 – thinking processes, motivation, feelings, and the like).

Blocking phases

It is clear that the further we proceed along the path of innovation, the closer we get to a working product. Terrorists take advantage of the first phase, Preparation, by developing required skills and collecting intelligence about their intended target, much in the manner of the 9/11 terrorists. The Preparation phase therefore seems to offer potential for nipping malevolent innovation in the bud. At the same time, we must assume that Preparation manifests itself to varying degrees. Even if we limit the malevolent innovators' opportunities for Preparation, they can still proceed, albeit less well equipped for malevolent innovation. The Preparation phase therefore seems to offer potential primarily in terms of weakening, but not blocking, malevolent innovation. The Verification phase seems to offer the next opportunity for blocking the malevolent innovator. We know that terrorists frequently conduct trials of their intended method of attack. The bombers who attacked London in July 2005 rehearsed their attacks in a form of verification intended to confirm that their 'solution' was indeed the single best method of attack (see the discussion on p. 195). How do we block this verification phase and thus disrupt the malevolent innovator? The final phase that offers an opportunity to block the malevolent innovator is the Implementation phase. Involving wider communication of the product, this phase requires the malevolent innovator to broaden the base of those involved, with the risk that 'competitors' (for instance, counter-terrorism agencies) will learn of it before it can fully be exploited. How can this Implementation phase be disrupted?

These three phases offer scope for blocking the malevolent innovation process because they require interaction between the innovators and the wider world. Preparation requires that malevolent innovators immerse themselves in the environment they are targeting. Verification requires that the malevolent innovator rehearse the malevolent product in a realistic setting. Implementation requires that malevolent innovators 'advertise' their product. To block malevolent innovation in these phases requires strategies that limit the ability of malevolent innovators, in this case terrorists, to immerse themselves in the target environment. The concept of phase blocks tells us *when*, in the process, to apply strategies for disrupting malevolent innovation. The question of *how* to disrupt malevolent innovation – whether inhibiting the favourable, or encouraging the unfavourable – is addressed by considering dimension blocks.

Blocking dimensions

Blocking 'dimensions' (see Table 9.1) focuses on the disruption of process, motivation, feelings, and the like. If we start by looking at the dimensions of the three phases identified above, one fact stands out. The phases of Preparation, Verification and Implementation have nearly identical favourable dimensions. This suggests that an approach based on the following strategies would have potential to block the three key phases identified in the previous section, when combined with other generic phase-blocking strategies described there:

- Disrupting convergent thinking: convergent thinking is favourable to innovation in the three phases of concern. Of the two strategies – inhibiting the favourable and encouraging the unfavourable – it seems to make most sense to try to inhibit the terrorists' ability to think convergently.
- Inhibiting reactive motivation: in the three phases of interest, mixed or reactive motivation is facilitatory. Therefore, the most promising line of attack is to attempt to inhibit reactive motivation in order to disrupt malevolent innovation. This might be achieved, for example, by inter-fering with the ability of terrorists, or other criminals, to collaborate and cooperate with each other.
- Inhibiting adaptive personal properties: in the three phases of interest, adaptive personal properties favour innovation. Therefore to disrupt malevolent innovation we must seek to interfere with the elimination of ambiguity, the development of consensus among terrorists.
- Inhibiting conserving feelings, such as anxiety in the face of uncertainty, or encouraging unfavourable, generative feelings such as excitement or unrealistic optimism.
- Inhibiting the creation of routine, concrete products: in the three phases of interest, the facilitatory focus is on relevant, correct, and effec-tive products. Inhibiting this might involve, for example, restricting the opportunities for terrorists to test their products, as the July 2005 London bombers were able to do.
- Encouraging a low-demand environmental Press: in the three target phases, a high-demand Press is facilitatory. Encouraging the opposite, unfavourable, low-demand Press might involve removing sources of pressure and encouraging non-conformity, etc.

For each dimension, the task of blocking malevolent innovation may be achieved either by inhibiting the favourable, or encouraging the unfavour-able, or possibly a combination of both. Regardless of the approach, there are challenges that remain to be addressed. If, for example, we wish to dis-rupt favourable thinking in the Verification phase (favourable in this case is convergent thinking), it seems intuitively unwise to actively encourage terrorists to improve their ability to think divergently. The dilemma is that some of our strategies, while blocking one phase or dimension, could actually improve the malevolent innovator's capability in a different phase. The conservative approach is therefore probably to focus on inhibiting the favourable, rather than encouraging the unfavourable – however, this is clearly an area where further research is required. Whichever approach is adopted, key questions also remain to be answered – how exactly can a dimension be inhibited, especially where direct control and influence may be limited?

CHAPTER TEN

Practical implications and counter-measures

Criminals and law-enforcers can be regarded as opponents, although they do not compete on a level playing field. Law-enforcers are expected to display conservative Personal properties and conform to societal expectations of proper Process, whereas resourceful criminals may even be admired if they do not do this. Law-enforcers must be careful that creative defensive measures do not cross the line and become illegality. Possibly because of this, law-enforcement organisations are inclined to be inflexible and offer little incentive for or support of law-enforcers' creativity. This suggests the need for public education, appropriate training of police, and for diagnosis of the points at which police organisation particularly obstructs creative police behaviour. Possible creative tactics for looking at crime include adopting the point of view of the opposition ('thinking thief') and redefining the problem.

As we pointed out in the Introduction, crime is now one of the world's largest domains of economic activity, while millions of people suffer the financial, social, and personal effects of fraud, terrorism, drug and people trafficking, organised crime, and the like, offences that are often conducted with considerable creativity. Thus, the obvious question to be asked at this point is: 'What can we do about it?' Gamman and Raein (2010, p. 163) quoted Einstein's dictum that problems cannot be solved using the kind of thinking that caused them in the first place, and various writers (e.g., Committee on Science and Technology for Countering Terrorism, 2002; Wilks and Zimbelman, 2004) have called for *novel* approaches to opposing crime. In this chapter we will use the analysis of crime and creativity we have developed in earlier chapters as the basis for some ideas on how to go about opposing creative crime in a creative way. It will not be possible here to outline specific detailed and concrete measures (i.e., to compile a *tactical* handbook). However, some of the *strategic* implications of applying ideas from creativity to law-breaking can be outlined. We would then hope to see these ideas serve as the starting point for the further development of novel approaches to countering malevolent creativity.

Perpetrators vs law-enforcers

The law-abiding society is interested in preserving both the individual and the common good, so there is a clash of goals between perpetrators and the larger society, and especially its professional law-enforcement agencies. The mainstream makes serious efforts to interfere with the work of law-breakers, and Hilton (2010) pointed out that perpetrator and law-enforcer can thus be seen as *competitors*. Cropley (2005) went so far as to suggest that the competition between them can be compared in some ways to the competition between rival companies trying to develop new products and put the opposition out of business. The creativity of resourceful criminals can be regarded as a process of generation of effective novelty in the face of competition from a rival (i.e., law-enforcers) while law-enforcers must counter the creativity of their competition by preventing it in the first place, disrupting it, or reducing its value to perpetrators to the point where they do not bother.

The law-enforcement–law-breaking arms race

If law-enforcers simply respond defensively to perpetrators' creativity a cycle may be set in motion in which one side generates effective novelty, the other reacts to the novelty, the first side generates new effective novelty, the other reacts again with new measures, and so on in a vicious cycle of novelty generation, response, reaction, new response, new reaction, etc. Hilton and Henderson (2008, p. 178) called this an 'arms race'. A simple example of the arms race is to be seen in Aitken, Moore, Higgs, Kelsall, and Kerger's (2002) report on a crackdown on the street drug scene in Melbourne, Australia. The crackdown involved a deliberate focus on incoming traffic and increased police presence. The crackdown initially achieved its objective, but sellers rapidly adapted to the new conditions by changing their behaviour. This led to displacement of the drug scene to nearby metropolitan areas, discouragement of safe injecting practices, and increased violence and fraud, which in turn had to be countered by police through new measures, and so on. The way to break this sequence of events is for law-enforcers to generate elegant and generic effective novelty in developing defensive measures, thus interrupting the escalation. However, as we will show in the next section, there are major hindrances to this.

The uneven playing field

Unfortunately, the playing field is not level. Law-enforcers are constantly in the public eye: their behaviour is subject to criticism from lawyers and civil rights groups, is scrutinised closely by the media, is the subject of high expectations from the public, and is largely responsible to politicians, for whom getting re-elected is a major issue. All these groups have expectations of how law-enforcers should do their jobs. Thus, any unexpected strategy or tactic is likely to be subject to intense scrutiny, debate, and criticism from some quarters. Of course, it may well be appropriate and advantageous for some aspects of law-enforcement to insist on sticking to the established way of doing things, as this is seen as guaranteeing fairness, avoiding police corruption, and the like, but the fact is that criminals do not experience such pressure to play the game according to tightly limiting rules. The creativity of law-enforcers is restricted by constraints that law-breakers can ignore, with the result that at the organisational level law-enforcers and law-breakers operate under two different sets of environmental 'Press' conditions.

To draw upon an analogy with design, for example, in an engineering context, law-enforcers are forced to search for their solutions in a constrained design space. The requirement to operate within the law, according to tightly limiting rules, excludes many possible solutions. Criminals, on the other hand, have at their disposal the broadest possible design space, as removing the fundamental constraint of 'legality' opens up the range of possible solutions enormously. In simple terms, where in a specific situation law-enforcers might be restricted to choosing from, let us say, ten alternatives, criminals might be able to choose from a thousand. If only a small proportion of possible solutions are highly effective, then it is no surprise that law-enforcers have a much more difficult task.

Creative criminals can use this difference to enhance the effectiveness of their operations, and law-enforcers must learn to adapt in order to deal with the inequity effectively. This suggests the need for *training* of law-enforcers and law-enforcement managers that will help them deal with this state of affairs. We are not referring here to training in correct police procedures, but in how to implement effectively novel approaches within the rules of the game. Of particular importance here is not just learning how to generate ideas – for instance, through brainstorming or similar idea-getting techniques – but learning how to recognise the real problem or how to see the problem in a new way (see, for instance, the discussions of thinking thief or applying the methods of systems engineering discussed below (pp. 219–223)), or how to evaluate the novelty and effectiveness of ideas, for instance, by applying the criteria of functional creativity outlined in Chapter 3 (pp. 216–222) and the Creative Solution Diagnosis Scale assessment tool. In other words, learning to apply a much broader understanding of creative problem-solving to strategic and tactical planning for law-enforcement and to squeeze more value out of the basic process of problem-solving.

Police vulnerability

We have already referred to creative people's *vulnerability* and the danger of 'crossing the line' (pp. 149–150). Law-enforcers also face the problem of avoiding their own creativity becoming dark or at least as being perceived that way by those who scrutinise their work,[1] whereas criminals have no such limitations on the scope of their actions. Western cultures generally are not prepared to compromise fundamental values such as freedom of movement, freedom of information, the presumption of innocence and trial by jury, the right of assembly, and the right to privacy, especially in business and financial issues. Public opinion in the West still protests against and opposes any attempt to compromise these values in order to prevent law-breaking, even in the case of the most obvious guilt. Examples include objections to activities such as searching people and property without due cause, pre-emptive investigations, profiling, and preventive arrest, and incarceration without charges. Besemer's (2006, p. 171) dictum applies: 'Consumers don't like too many surprises.'

The idea that creativity deliberately aimed at 'harming' perpetrators (i.e., creativity that is malevolent relative to criminals but benevolent relative to the greater good) is acceptable under certain circumstances opens up a yawning pit for law-enforcers. In discussing police misconduct, Wolfe and Piquero (2011) pointed out that many police officers place great weight on the 'noble cause' (p. 333) argument to justify behaviours that may be adjudged reprehensible or corrupt by the public, the press, politicians, or internal discipline departments. Clearly, theoreticians and social philosophers understand social good rather differently from officers on the beat. Here, too, Wolfe and Piquero identified *inadequate training* as one area that, in our terms (although this was not the main thrust of Wolfe and Piquero's discussion), leaves officers vulnerable to crossing the line

---

[1] The danger of police officers being perceived as having crossed the line is particularly acute because public expectations of them are so demanding.

between admirable creativity and crime. This vulnerability is greater than that of, for instance, artists, since artists are not sworn to stay on the right side of the line and are even expected to cross it in the name of their art, or may even claim to have done so in order to enhance their mystique. Such training would need to show officers how to generate effective novelty in their work (a) without crossing the line whose parameters are sketched out in Table 7.1 (p. 150) and (b) remaining within the dimensions of the left-hand column of Table 7.2 (p. 158).

Person and Press in law-enforcement

Law-enforcement can be examined from the point of view of the law-enforcers themselves ('police personality'), or from the point of view of the organisational aspects of law-enforcement ('police organisation'). Police personality corresponds to the dimension of Person, which we have taken as one of the building blocks of our analysis throughout the entire book, while police organisation is related to Press.

Personal properties of law-enforcers

In an overview of relevant research, Twersky-Glasner (2005) pointed out that the stereotype of the police personality includes traits like authoritarianism, conservatism (in the sense of resistance to change and clinging to conventional views), and dogmatism. Such traits are almost the polar opposite of the personal properties that creativity research has shown to be favourable for creativity (see for instance Table 3.2, p. 69). In fact, however, the research reviewed by Twersky-Glasner (2005) casts considerable doubt on the accuracy of this stereotype as a true summary of the underlying personality structure of police officers. Nonetheless, aspects of the *organisation* or *institutionalisation* of law-enforcement (i.e., the organisational Press that law-enforcers are subjected to) seem likely to support, activate, or encourage the expression of uncreative or even anti-creative personal properties. For instance, law-enforcers are rightly expected to stand for good order and stability, keep their emotions and behaviour under control, and differentiate clearly and strictly between right and wrong. Thus, although the day-to-day *tactical* activities of police officers on the beat constantly involve the solution of problems, and require risk taking, ingenuity, and flexibility, as Twersky-Glasner (2005) suggested, there is little room at institutional level for making unusual associations or seeing things in a new way, tolerating ambiguity, or being unconventional in the *strategic* principles underlying their work.

This situation is exacerbated by the fact that as the representatives of the 'good guys' police officers are not only responsible for enforcing the law but are also expected to embody its best features such as fairness, respect for the law, and correctness of conduct. If they try to generate novelty aimed at 'getting bad guys off the street' (Caldero and Crank, 2004, p. 29) they risk finding themselves walking the fine line between positive creativity and illegality outlined in Chapter 7 in a particularly sensitive area, especially in situations where public sentiment is close to being on the side of the criminals or where, at the least, people feel ambivalent about the blameworthiness of the crime involved. Indeed, although the idea of applying creativity to frustrate perpetrators (i.e., malevolent creativity seeking to promote a greater good) is acceptable under certain circumstances, it raises issues such as entrapment.

One measure which could be adopted here is a programme of public education. Issues such as creative crime and its almost attractive quality in some cases could be thematised, along with the tendency to see something admirable in such crime. The whole area of *relative* benefit needs to become the subject of public discussion and a distinction made between intrapersonal, interpersonal, and extrapersonal benefit, so that, for instance, the public would better understand that criminals' creativity is benevolent only in the intrapersonal sense (from the point of view of the perpetrator) and is no doubt admirable if you share the perpetrator's perspective (and only then), but negative in the interpersonal and extrapersonal sense. In a similar way, police creativity is malevolent with regard to criminals but benevolent relative to the community as a whole, and is thus admirable. Such public education need not have a school-like quality: the government of Singapore attempted to involve the public by publishing and widely distributing a document entitled 'A Fight Against Terror: Singapore's National Security Strategy'. This was the result of a deliberate decision by the government to involve the public in its efforts to combat terrorism, the public being seen as a resource for opposing crime, not as a block to such efforts which should, if anything, be kept in the dark.

Institutional Press

A problem with law-enforcement agencies involves the way they do business and make leadership decisions. Their traditional management style makes them slow to adapt and change. As French and Stewart (2001) pointed out, law-enforcement still largely uses bureaucratic models with power concentrated at the top and little tolerance of mistakes by those who rock the boat, whereas those who support the time-hallowed way are rewarded. In their unwillingness to change their ways, the institutions suffer from a kind of 'institutional sclerosis' (Florida, 2002), which empowers those who, for the kind of reason just outlined, resist change.

Thus, law-enforcers not infrequently work within a sclerotic organisational structure involving a hierarchical authority and career structure largely based on keeping your nose clean, financial control by government or other regulators, scrutiny by civil rights organisations or watchful media, and the need to observe political correctness. In such organisations, workers are discouraged from seeing the known in a new way, linking ideas that are usually kept separate, redefining problems, or adopting unexpected tactics. Personal characteristics and motives such as openness, unconventionality, or risk taking may be strongly discouraged by a work environment that offers limited freedom to make decisions, has low tolerance of error, and offers little protection to people who generate novelty that goes astray. By contrast, although crime also has its institutional aspects, creative perpetrators are not subject to the same massive institutional constraints as law-enforcers.

As in all organisations, in law-enforcement, novelty is only tolerated within certain limits, no matter how effective, elegant, and generic it is (essentially, the novelty must not rock the boat). Changing this is difficult. In the words of Niccolo Machiavelli (1532/2010, pp. 26–7):

> there is nothing more difficult to bring to hand, more perilous to conduct or more uncertain in its success, than to take the lead in the introduction of a new order of things because the innovator has for enemies all those who have done well under the old conditions and lukewarm defenders in those who may do well under the new.

As Joseph D. McNamara, Chief of Police, Kansas City, Missouri, writing directly about police work put it: 'The toppling of traditions brings forth uneasiness inherent in the process of great change' (Kelling, Pate, Dieckman, and Brown, 1974, p. viii). Those at the top have reached their positions by functioning within the existing system, and, as Jasper (2010) pointed out, changes to the system present great danger to them: old knowledge and skills may become irrelevant, and managers and experienced colleagues may be confronted by the possibility that what they have been advocating and doing for much of their working life may have been wrong, with consequent threats to self-image, pride in their work, and the like. The Kelling et al. report, for instance, showed that a programme involving massive increases in police presence on the streets of Kansas City had no effect on either crime rates or citizens' perception of the threat of crime. As these authors pointed out, this finding runs counter to 150 years of police lore, and contradicts what police recruits in a wide variety of jurisdictions are taught from almost the first day. As a result, there is strong resistance to accepting or acting upon such a finding.

Reluctance to abandon well-established procedures that are running reasonably well has a psychological basis: personnel are familiar with procedures, they may have delivered substantial benefits in the past, may have brought praise and aroused admiration, and are perhaps part of the individual's public persona. Jasper explains the situation in terms of risk avoidance, referring to 'the perils of unknown factors' (p. 93). It is also understandable in terms of theories of self, of dissonance theory, of psychological openness (or lack of it), of learning theory (a behaviour that has repeatedly been positively reinforced in the past will be repeated), or of Mednick's (1962) hierarchy of associations (responses to a stimulus are arranged in a hierarchy of likelihood of being activated, associations frequently made in the past being high in the hierarchy and those made infrequently, low).

Diagnosing an organisation

These remarks may create the impression that police organisation must of necessity block generation of effective novelty because it involves insuperable constraints. However, as various writers have pointed out, it is constraints that make creativity creative (for a summary, see Sternberg and Kaufman, 2010). If there were no constraints there would be no relevance and effectiveness, elegance, or genesis, since a solution would not have to be relevant to anything or effective for anything, while there would be no criteria of elegance and anything could be transferred to anything else. In fact, creativity would be mere generation of variability or, as we have called it earlier in this book, quasi-creativity or pseudo-creativity. For instance, a plan could be made to solve the problem of atmospheric pollution by eliminating fossil-fuel power stations. The problem of the resulting lack of electricity could be 'solved' by finding a technologically advanced civilisation living on a planet orbiting a distant star and persuading them to send us electricity by beaming it through space to a receiver located in the centre of Australia, thus eliminating the need for earthlings to burn coal, oil, or gas. If it were not for the constraints such as the fact that we know of no such civilisation, have no means of contacting them, and have no technology for building the receiver, this solution would be very creative.

On the other hand, too many constraints can rule out creativity, just as Henry Ford's diktat, 'it can be any colour you like as long as it's black', eliminated any novelty in the painting of Model T Fords. There is a danger that police organisation may be too set in its ways. What is needed is an intermediate level of constraint (neither too much nor too little): a system that has its constraints, to be sure, but that continues to be capable of changing. From the point of view of the organisation, creativity requires overcoming hurdles that are present across the 6Ps and seven phases outlined in Chapter 3. Police organisation is unlikely to be overthrown overnight, and, indeed, this may not be desirable. What is needed is for law-enforcers to be able to navigate successfully through this maze of constraints. This is only possible when individuals and organisations have a map that identifies what the specific obstacles are and when and where they are likely to occur.

Cropley and Cropley (2010, 2011) proposed a system for doing precisely this. This system is based on the forty-two nodes defined by the 6Ps and the seven phases of creativity already discussed in detail (see, for instance, Chapter 4, pp. 90–92, Chapter 9, pp. 196–199). It identifies 'nodes' at which highly specific action can be taken to promote or block creativity in an organisation. Each node involves the point of conjunction of one of the Ps and one of the phases: for example, Process in the phase of Generation or Personal motivation in the phase of Implementation. As pointed out in Chapter 9, change in an organisation in order to facilitate creativity need not be across the board, but can focus on the specific nodes where there are blockages. In terms of police procedure, fostering creativity is not a matter of reorganising the entire system, but of identifying the particular nodes where constraints are blocking creativity, showing how they are doing this, and taking appropriate remedial action. In effect, it is the mirror image of phase *blocking* and dimension *blocking* discussed in Chapter 9 (see pp. 199–202).

Crucial states or processes in each node were listed in Table 9.1 (see p. 198). For instance, divergent thinking is the crucial process in the node Process/Activation, while proactive motivation is the key motivational state in the node Personal motivation/Illumination.[2] In the Press/

---

[2] These crucial states have already been listed in Table 9.1, in the context of creativity *blocks*. They are presented here in a slightly different way in accordance with their application to diagnose an organisation.

Illumination node, managerial pressure should be oriented towards giving officers their head (freedom oriented), whereas in the node Press/Implementation, management behaviour must of necessity be in accordance with the real-world constraints under which law-enforcers operate (constraints oriented).

For the sake of ease of understanding and use, the processes and states listed in the individual nodes in Table 9.1 are stated as dichotomies: divergent thinking vs convergent thinking, proactive motivation vs reactive motivation, innovative personality vs adaptive personality, generative feelings vs conserving feelings, routine product vs radical product, and freedom-oriented vs constraints-oriented management style. These dichotomies were worked out on the basis of relevant research and theory in the area of creativity and are summarised in, for instance, Cropley and Cropley (2009). The particular poles of the dichotomies listed in Table 9.1 as favourable for innovation in a particular node are largely based on intuition; they were not derived directly from empirical research on organisations.

The apparent unequivocal mapping of a single pole of Process, Personal properties, Product, and the like onto a particular phase may seem to involve an over-simplification. For instance, Haner's (2005) meta-analysis showed that, in fact, a single phase may involve both poles of a dichotomised dimension. He gave the example of *Reaction*, which involves mainly convergent thinking, although finding a novel method for evaluating a product could require divergent thinking, too. Nonetheless, he pointed out that convergent thinking is 'prevalent' in this phase, and called it its 'main characteristic' (p. 289). We adopt a similar position, and speak here of Processes, Personal properties, Products, and the like that are of 'core importance' in the sense of being the dominant, even if not exclusive, requirement in a particular phase.

The Innovation Phase Assessment Instrument

Cropley and Cropley (2010, 2011) developed an instrument for 'diagnosing' an organisation in terms of the forty-two nodes, the *Innovation Phase Assessment Instrument* (IPAI). Cropley, Cropley, Chiera, and Kaufman (in press) showed that the scale really does measure forty-two empirically separate factors which correspond closely to the theoretical structure outlined in Table 9.1 (p. 198). The scale is also highly reliable. Using this scale it is possible to make a diagnosis that, let us say, a particular organisation's employees are willing to innovate and that management are moderately ready to encourage innovation, but that staff do not know how to generate novelty. Such a diagnosis leads directly to suggestions for remediation, in this case, training in problem definition, idea generation, and recognition of solutions. Examples of items from the scale are shown in Table 10.1.

Case study

Table 10.2 shows fictitious data for the analysis of a non-existent police department. These data have been invented simply as a demonstration of the kind of data that the IPAI yields, and are intended purely for illustrative purposes. The node scores shown in the body of the table are the mean scores for each node based on the responses of a group of fictitious police officers working in the non-existent police department. Each column in the table is summed to give a mean score for each phase, and each row is summed to give a mean score for each dimension.

These data indicate that the organisation has a low overall score (77.9/168). In simple terms, it is, on balance, an organisation that is unfavourable to innovation. In relative terms, it is strongest in the phase of Implementation, and weakest in the phases of Cognition and Validation. This means that the department is good at implementing novel procedures when they are decided upon. However, it is poor at developing its own novel ideas and resistant to outside assessment. Again in relative terms, the strongest dimension in the organisation is Motivation, and the weakest is Press. Officers are interested in novel procedures, but receive inadequate support from management. This low level of support may explain why they do not produce much novelty themselves (low score for Cognition) and are wary of external feedback about their work (low score for Validation): officers are motivated to innovate, but they are not encouraged to develop and test novel ideas, even though they would like to do so.

These scores can be further differentiated by examining individual nodes. In the present example, however, this analysis would become tedious, as there are so many nodes with low scores: for instance most nodes in the phase of Preparation are low, but the exceptions (Process and Personal properties) indicate that officers can come up with ideas and are capable of doing so, but that they receive little support (Press = 1.2) and, not surprisingly, are thus poorly motivated (Motivation = 1.3) and feel negative about idea generation (Feelings = 1.2) with resultant low level of production of novelty (Product = 1.1).

Table 10.1 *Examples of items for the stages of Preparation, Generation, and Validation*

Phase	Human factor	Sample item ('In this organisation …')	'Correct' answer
Preparation	Process	Before a new project in undertaken, staff focus exclusively on their own jobs	False
	Motivation	Staff will work hard for the satisfaction of doing a good job	True
	Personality	Staff are satisfied with the way things are done	False
	Feelings	Staff value change positively	True
	Product	Challenges to old perspectives rarely emerge	False
	Press	We have clearly defined staff roles	False
Generation	Process	Staff often link unrelated disciplines	True
	Motivation	Staff enjoy the challenge of contradictory ideas	True
	Personality	Staff are anxious about making mistakes	False
	Feelings	Staff feel overwhelmed by too many ideas	False
	Product	Staff produce lots of ideas	True
	Press	Staff are encouraged to find solutions quickly	False
Validation	Process	Staff protect the ideas they produce from external scrutiny	False
	Motivation	Staff feel a need for feedback from the external world	True
	Personality	Staff are open to criticism from outsiders	True
	Feelings	Staff feel under attack when others judge their work	False
	Product	Products are not released unless we are very confident that they will succeed	False
	Press	Wild ideas are supported if they solve the problem	True

Table 10.2 *Organisational profile using the IPAI*[a]

Phase[b]/Dimension[c]	Preparation	Activation	Cognition	Illumination	Verification	Implementation	Validation	Total
Process	3.1	2.1	1.4	2.1	3.1	2.3	1.8	**15.9**
Personal motivation	1.3	3.2	1.3	3.3	3.4	3.2	0.8	**16.5**
Personal properties	2.6	1.8	2.0	1.4	1.5	3.1	2.0	**14.4**
Personal feelings	1.2	2.4	1.0	2.1	2.8	2.7	0.5	**12.7**
Product	1.1	1.6	1.8	2.7	0.5	2.4	0.5	**10.6**
Press	1.2	0.0	1.3	1.2	1.2	2.9	0.0	**7.8**
Total	**10.5**	**11.1**	**8.8**	**12.8**	**12.5**	**16.6**	**5.6**	**77.9**

[a] Each individual node can have a score ranging from 0 (non-ideal) to 4 (ideal).

[b] Each individual phase (Preparation, Implementation, etc.) can have a score ranging from 0 (non-ideal) to 24 (ideal). This is the sum of the scores across the six dimensions in that phase.

[c] Each individual dimension (Process, Motivation, etc.) can have a score ranging from 0 (non-ideal) to 28 (ideal). This is the sum of the scores across the seven phases for that dimension.

On the basis of these data, specific recommendations could be made to the organisation. Recommendations could be based around action in relation to whole phases, whole dimensions or individual nodes, and could be tailored to the goals and aspirations of the organisation. For example, this organisation has indicated that it has limited resources to devote to remedial action, and therefore wishes to focus remedial action on a limited number of very specific areas. On that basis, the recommendation for this organisation could be to target the weaknesses in the Cognition phase (specifically to train staff in processes for idea generation, such as brainstorming, and, to take steps to engender a more freedom-oriented environment during the Cognition phase, e.g., by defining tasks loosely, by overtly rewarding novelty, and by giving staff sufficient time to generate ideas). We can then speculate that if these remedial actions were effective, we would observe an improvement in the scores for the Cognition/Process and Cognition/Press nodes, and that this would strengthen both the score for the Cognition phase and the organisation's overall IPAI score.

Operational strategies for creatively opposing crime

One way of applying creativity in opposing crime is to develop novel and unexpected – but, it is to be hoped, effective – broad or strategic approaches to law-enforcement, even within the personal and institutional constraints already discussed above. We will present two examples in this section. Our purpose is not to advocate adoption of these measures in the exact form described here, but to offer them as examples of novel procedures or as possible stimulation for the development of new approaches.

Thinking thief

Although he was writing in the context of design, and indeed, 'design against crime', Hilton (e.g., Hilton, 2010; Hilton and Henderson, 2008) supported the competition approach to understanding interactions between perpetrators and law-enforcers, whom he specifically labelled competitors. However, he proposed a novel approach to opposing crime: looking at it not from the perspective of the victims or law-enforcers, but from that of their opposition (i.e., the perpetrators). Ekblom (1997, p. 250) called this 'thinking thief'. It is necessary in order to oppose the work of the 'adaptive criminal' (1997, p. 249). Hilton then proposed a method for thinking thief in a systematic and goal-directed way, which he called the 'cyclic countering of competitive creativity' or '4Cs' approach.

Presented in a schematic way and assuming that the opposing sides are law-enforcers, on the one hand, and perpetrators on the other, the procedure involves the following steps:

1. Interviews are conducted with known offenders in a particular area of focus such as burglars, scam artists, or terrorists.
2. Using ethnographic methods to analyse the interviews (see the discussion in Chapter 2, pp. 38–40), a picture is built up of the typical *persona* of such perpetrators: their motivation, ways of identifying targets, ways of reacting to impediments to their actions, reaction to changed conditions, way of assessing whether a particular situation is worth the trouble, etc.
3. One or a group of law-enforcers assumes the perpetrator's persona; in role play they try to 'get into their characters' (Hilton and Henderson, 2008, p. 183).
4. Law-enforcers outline crime prevention proposals to the personas, who attack the proposals and work out ways through which the proposed preventive measures could be circumvented or even used as the inspiration for a new approach to offending. The reactions are those of the persona the role player(s) have 'become', not their reactions as, let us say, police officers.
5. The procedure is referred to as 'cyclic' because it can be repeated in the cyclical arms race already described as the personas adapt to law-enforcement measures and seek to subvert them, or as, for instance, new technology, social developments, changes in police operating procedures, or even legal rulings produce new background conditions.

Hilton and Henderson's (2008) discussion suggests that the procedure enables the perpetrators' opponents (in their case, designers, but in ours, law-enforcers) to break the corset of their own way of operating and the set ways of thinking (i.e., Process) about crime imposed by the customs and conventions of their profession. In this way the procedure provides 'counter perspectives' that enable law-enforcers to understand perpetrators' beliefs, attitudes, experiences, and motives better and grasp how perpetrators see and think about opportunities. This provides ideas on preventive measures and possibly suggests ways of reducing the value of the offences to the perpetrators, perhaps below the threshold at which the offence becomes more trouble than it is worth. In Hilton and Henderson's research, the particular value of the procedure lay in the personas' creativity in (a) working out how to subvert new counter-measures proposed by the law-enforcers, and (b) identifying new opportunities for criminal action offered by the counter-measures themselves. The researchers specifically identified creative thinking processes in these reactions of the personas.

Hilton and Henderson (2008) pointed out that the personas were able in some cases to 'think ahead' of real-life perpetrators. For instance, press reports of new technology or changed legal interpretations could immediately be incorporated into the thinking of the personas, who could work out new opportunities for crime arising from these developments *prior to the actual appearance of the new criminal methods in the real world*, and communicate these insights to law-enforcers in advance. This made it possible to stifle new criminal procedures in the cradle by producing a decay function so steep as to make the crime completely ineffective or even dangerous for perpetrators. They also made the interesting point that the personas' thinking as criminals could break the cycle involved in the 'arms race' between perpetrators and law-enforcers. The 4Cs approach also offers an example of a situation where it would be advantageous to keep measures worked out secret. Having, as it were, 'read the criminals' minds' by anticipating how they might react to preventive measures, it would be foolish to then publicise this fact, thus warning law-breakers which measures to avoid.

Red teaming

Fishbein and Treverton (2004) pointed out that 'organizations need to institutionalize sustained, collaborative efforts by analysts to question their judgements and underlying assumptions, employing both critical and *creative* modes of thought' (emphasis added). Hilton's 4Cs approach can be seen as a way of systematising such efforts. In this, it is one member of a family of techniques designed to help analysts broaden their approach to conflicts with competitors by, for instance, anticipating competitors' actions and avoiding surprise or, as we would put it, nullifying the novelty of a competitor's moves or cancelling out their effectiveness. Although not directly based on Hilton's (2010) work, the procedure known as 'red teaming' (see http://redteamjournal.com/about/red-teaming-and-alternative-analysis/) operates on similar principles: viewing a problem from the adversary's perspective and working out the adversary's possible strategies or tactics. This requires Processes such as divergent thinking, Personal properties such as openness and flexibility, Personal motivation such as risk taking, and an environmental Press that is open to the unexpected and can tolerate errors, all properties related to creativity (see Table 4.2,

p. 88). According to the website just cited, red teaming has been applied increasingly to issues of security in recent years, although the practice is also suitable for much broader application, for instance, in business or the military, where it could be applied in order to analyse possible courses of action from a competitor's point of view.

Problem-finding – a systems engineering approach

Hari (2010) outlined an approach based on the *Integrated Customer Driven Method* (ICDM) for generating effectively novel counter-measures. Instead of treating the combating of malevolent creativity – in this case, terrorism, but his approach is capable of being applied more generally – as an exercise in creative problem-*solving*, Hari treated it as an exercise in problem-*finding*. He looked at this from the point of view of systems engineering and focused on the 'functional' characteristics of creative solutions, especially engineering solutions: effectiveness, novelty, elegance, and genesis (Cropley and Cropley, 2005). From the systems engineering point of view, the problem-finding approach involves examining the nature of the problem and especially asking whether the right problem is being addressed. This resembles the distinction in systems engineering between verification and validation. Verification asks: 'are we solving the problem right?'[3] whereas validation asks: 'are we solving the right problem?' A problem-finding approach makes it possible to see combating crime in a new light. The following example from Tibi (2003) demonstrates this process.[4] Although it refers specifically to combating terrorism, its essence is transferable to other forms of creative crime, that is, the approach possesses genesis, in particular, seminality.

Is the problem of terrorists hijacking passenger aircraft really one of preventing them from getting guns onto the aircraft? Or is the real problem negating the danger posed by a terrorist once he or she has succeeded in getting a gun onto an aircraft? The former definition of the problem focuses attention on seeking solutions on things like metal detectors and security screening, which occur in the airport environment, are rooted to a particular point in the check-in process and a particular spot in the terminal, are extremely inflexible, and are heavily dependent on

---

[3] With apologies for the incorrect grammar.

[4] We are not advocating the Tibi approach, which many readers would no doubt regard as unethical, dangerous, suicidal, or even hare-brained. Our interest is in the example of the complete change of focus (from events on the ground to events in the air and from technological to human-focused solutions) involved in re-defining the problem.

technological measures such as metal detectors, and as a result, are also susceptible to technology-based counter-measures such as guns made not of metal (easily detectable), but of plastic (difficult to detect). The redefinition focuses attention on events *inside* the aircraft. It could lead to a redefinition of the problem as being not how to pile up ever-changing defensive measures within the airport (in the course of the arms race), but of how best to make use of the substantial resources available within the aircraft, especially the passengers; UA93 showed that even without any preparation of any kind and in a situation where they were confronted with a procedure so novel as to be previously unheard of, the passengers were capable of assessing the situation and organising themselves quickly and effectively, despite the tragic consequences of their actions. Looking at the passengers this way suggests solutions such as arming them with non-lethal, dart-firing guns. Among other things, this involves seeing the familiar element of passengers in a new way by perceiving them as part of the resources available for developing a solution (overcoming the terrorists) rather than as a major component of the problem (helpless and passive victims needing to be protected).

Both approaches are directed at solving the underlying problem of hijacking, yet they generate radically different solutions, some of which (like metal detectors) have already experienced very substantial decay of novelty and are not 100 per cent effective, in any case, so that they are easy for terrorists to counteract. The metal detector also gives potential terrorists ample opportunity to study their competitors and devise their own creative ways of subtracting value from (nullifying) their competitors' efforts. Enlisting the passengers, by contrast, offers the opportunity of giving free rein to their capacity for thinking up brand new novel solutions on the spot, which will not have experienced any decay. As Hari (2010) pointed out, in many situations (such as in a terrorist hijacking) the need to find a rapid solution is simply too acute to be left to a sluggish bureaucratic procedure that may eventually admit that a preventive measure has become ineffective through decay, and the development of new technologies to combat the new situation.

Hari (2010, p. 334) described the ICDM as a systematic way of rapidly generating constantly changing novel problem definitions in a process of 'continuous creativity' (p. 334). This is based on team meetings and creativity-fostering techniques such as brainstorming or TRIZ (Theory of Inventive Problem Solving) in a process of 'agile' systems engineering. In a project in which the principles of agile systems engineering were applied to developing solutions to terrorist activities by means of creative problem-finding, it was found that the solutions suggested exhibited a high degree of novelty and promise of effectiveness, and a high level of elegance, but low levels of genesis. Low genesis means that the solutions proposed were often highly specific procedures that applied only to a particular situation. However, this has the advantage of dealing with the problem that genesis is a two-edged sword: by being transferable, law-enforcers' generic creativity suggests new approaches not only to law-enforcers but to perpetrators, too. Where a particular solution will not be re-used this is of no consequence. Provided that the generation of effective novelty is agile enough (i.e., that it involves continuous creativity), lack of genesis can even be seen as an advantage.

A relatively simple example of a tactical measure involving application of the strategy of problem redefinition as a systematic approach to developing defensive measures against crime is seen in recent shifting of the focus of actions against child pornography away from *supply* to *demand*, that is, from catching the makers of pornography to deterring users. Production and distribution of sexually explicit materials involving minors are difficult to detect and prevent through conventional means. In the United States, however, federal laws prohibit not only the supply but also the *receipt* through the mail of sexually explicit materials involving minors. As a result, law-enforcement officials have begun to redefine the problem as being not how to block *distribution* of child pornography but how to block *receipt* of such material. Whereas tracking back to the source of material (i.e., trying to solve the problem of distribution) is almost impossible, tracking recipients is simple, since these people have to identify themselves and at least their virtual location in order to take delivery. Some police forces are now using sting operations to apprehend purchasers of child pornography. In these operations, agents may offer non-existent pornography for sale and solicit orders, or pretend to be users themselves and trap genuine users with whom they make contact. However, such stings raise serious concerns about entrapment, as there is substantial public distaste for police officers departing from the conventional role of reacting to crime rather than, as some observers would say, provoking it in the first place.

In the Philippines, Cebu City police also redefined the problem in order to prevent crime. The field of crime involved was illegal fishing by blowing up fish with dynamite, collecting the floating dead fish in a boat, and bringing the illegal catch ashore where it could profitably be sold. The problem was proving who was the illegal fisher, because when police intercepted a boat loaded with illegally caught fish no-one on board the boat would claim ownership of the cargo (understandably). The police then redefined the problem as not being that of catching offenders (i.e., the phase of Validation), but of making boats unavailable to would-be criminals or perhaps making boat hire too expensive (i.e., preventing the Implementation phase). Philippines law permits impounding of material evidence of a crime. The boat loaded with illegally caught fish was crucial such evidence, without which there would be no evidence that a crime had been committed. Consequently, boats caught with an illegal fish catch were simply held while the ownership of their illegal cargo was investigated, which might take years. In the meantime, the boat would no longer be available for illegal fishing and owners of boats not impounded might well demand such high hire fees, in view of the danger of losing the use of their boat, that the illegal fishing would no longer be financially worthwhile and the criminals would cease operations of their own free will (in a manner of speaking).

In Fargo, North Dakota, in 2007, police had the problem of how to catch people against whom there were outstanding arrest warrants but whom they were unable to locate in order to execute the warrants. They redefined the problem from how police could go to the criminals to how to get the criminals to come to the police. Rock musician and reality TV star Ozzy Osbourne was due to perform in Fargo and the police sent out invitations to a non-existent Ozzy Osbourne meet-and-greet party – which they claimed would precede the genuine concert – to the last-known addresses of a large number of wanted persons. No fewer than forty such people turned up and were arrested.

The child pornography example and the Ozzie Osbourne sting provide good examples of situations where secrecy was vital. Without secrecy, the decay of effectiveness of such measures would be so rapid as to make the measures useless. In the case of the Cebu city approach to illegal fishing, on the other hand, rapid decay of novelty would be highly favourable as, if anything, public knowledge of the tactic of impounding fishing boats would inhibit decay of effectiveness. Even when there is no question of entrapment, police stings often arouse considerable public criticism, as they somehow do not seem to be right, despite the fact that the motivation of the police is undoubtedly benevolent relative to the general good (although malevolent in relation to the criminals), and principally aimed at extrapersonal benefit, criteria we have proposed as defining 'good' application of malevolent creativity.[5]

---

[5] In fact, an indignant Osbourne sharply criticised the Police Department involved.

Public unease in this case can be contrasted with the admiration for the criminal con men depicted in the 1973 movie *The Sting*, in which a young con man teams up with a master of their craft to cheat a criminal banker out of a fortune. Although it must be admitted that the victim in the movie was a mobster, Generation and Implementation of effective novelty seems to be almost admirable in criminals but reprehensible in law-enforcers; a focus on intrapersonal benefit for the perpetrators seems to be acceptable in the malevolent creativity of con artists, whereas there is unease about the interpersonal malevolence but extrapersonal benevolence seen in the creativity of law-enforcers. These considerations suggest public education involving thematising the whole issue of approval of criminal creativity but uneasiness about police creativity. It also suggests police training in the way activities such as police stings are presented to the public by police spokespersons or senior officers.

Closing remarks

Our purpose in this book has been to show that some crime (what we call 'resourceful' or 'creative' crime) can be looked at in something other than a bureaucratic way. We have done this by applying concepts from psychological creativity research to the Perpetrators (Person), the Processes, the Personal properties, motives, and feelings, the Products, and the environment in which crime occurs (Press). We have shown that people regarded as criminals and those regarded as positively creative contributors to society have many common characteristics in all these domains. Because creativity is so highly valued in our society, there is even grudging admiration of some criminal behaviour, or else refusal to accept that crime can be creative.

Both of these states of affairs have negative consequences for law-enforcers, the former by arousing public resistance to appropriate measures, the latter by limiting law-enforcers' counter-measures to tit-for-tat reactions in a kind of arms race with law-breakers, and in the latter part of the book we have made some suggestions for action. However, we have not tried to provide a comprehensive practical catalogue of operational procedures for police to implement in order to oppose crime more effectively, that is, we have not attempted to write a cookbook of recipes for creative police work. Indeed, there would be something absurd about doing that, since the core of creativity is generating novelty, and a list of pre-digested solutions would run completely counter to this principle.

Rather, our intention is to persuade those involved in law-enforcement as researchers, theorists, social commentators, policy makers, or on-the-street practitioners to see creative crime differently and to think about novel approaches to opposing it. Where we have given concrete examples of novel practices, this has not been in the hope that precisely these practices will be adopted, but that the examples will make clearer what we are proposing, and encourage law-enforcers to generate their own effective novelty.

Bibliography

Agnew, R. (1999). A general strain theory of community differences in crime rates. *Journal of Research in Crime and Delinquency*, 36: 123–55.

(2011). *Toward a unified criminology: integrating assumptions about crime, people and society*. New York University Press.

Aitken, C., Moore, D., Higgs, P., Kelsall J., and Kerger, M. (2002). The impact of a police crackdown on a street drug scene: evidence from the street. *International Journal of Drug Policy*, 13: 189–98.

Akinola, M., and Mendes, W. B. (2008). The dark side of creativity: biological vulnerability and negative emotion lead to greater artistic creativity. *Personality and Social Psychology Bulletin*. Downloaded from http://wendyberrymendes. com/cms/uploads/Akinola2008-percent20Thepercent20dark%20side%20of. pdf on 26 January 2011.

Albert, R. S. (1990). Identity, experience and career choice among the exceptionally gifted and talented. In M.A. Runco (ed). *Theories of creativity* (pp. 13–34). Newbury Park, CA: Sage.

Aluja, A., and Garcia, L. (2005). Sensation seeking, sexual curiosity and testosterone in inmates. *Neuropsychobiology*, 51: 28–33.

Amabile, T. M. (1983). *The social psychology of creativity*. New York: Springer.

Amabile, T. M., and Gryskiewicz, N. D. (1989). The creative environment scales: Work Environment Inventory. *Creativity Research Journal*, 2: 231–54.

Amabile, T. M., Goldfarb, P., and Brackfield, S. C. (1990). Social influences on creativity: evaluation, coaction, surveillance. *Creativity Research Journal*, 3: 6–21.

Andreasen, N. C. (1987). Creativity and mental illness: prevalence rates in writers and their first degree relatives. *American Journal of Psychiatry*, 144: 1288–92.

Andrews, D. A., and Bonta, J. (2010). Rehabilitating criminal justice policy and practice. *Psychology, Public Policy, and Law*, 16: 39–55.

Andrews, D. A., Bonta, J., and Wormith, J. S. (2006). The recent past and near future of risk/need assessment. *Crime and Delinquency*, 52: 7–27.

Atran, S. (2003). Genesis of suicide terrorism. *Science*, 299: 1534–39.

Australian Competition and Consumer Commission (2012). *Targeting scams: report of the ACCC on scam activity 2011*. Canberra, ACT: Commonwealth of Australia.

Averill, J. R., and Nunley, E. P. (2010). Neurosis: the dark side of emotional creativity. In D. H. Cropley, A. J. Cropley, J. C. Kaufman, and M. A. Runco (eds.), *The dark side of creativity* (pp. 255–76). Cambridge University Press.

Baas, M., De Dreu, C. K. W., and Nijstad, B. A. (2008). A meta-analysis of 25 years of mood–creativity research: hedonic tone, activation, or regulatory focus? *Psychological Bulletin*, 134: 779–806.

Bacon, Francis (1909 [1627]). *Essays, civil and moral and the new Atlantis*. New York: Collier.

Baer, J. (1998). The case for domain specificity of creativity. *Creativity Research Journal*, 11: 173–78.

(2011). Domains of creativity. In M. A. Runco and S. R. Pritzker (eds.), *Encyclopedia of creativity*, Vol. II (pp. 404–408). San Diego, CA: Academic Press.

Bailin, S. (1988). *Achieving extraordinary ends: an essay on creativity*. Dordrecht: Kluwer.

Barron, F. X. (1955). The disposition towards originality. *Journal of Abnormal and Social Psychology*, 51: 478–85.

(1969). *Creative person and creative process*. New York: Holt, Rinehart and Winston.

(1972). *Artists in the making*. New York: Seminar Press.

Barroso, J.-M. (2009). Message to the European Commission Conference 'Can creativity be measured?' Brussels, May 2009.

Bartol, C., and Bartol, A. (2010). *Criminal behavior: a psychosocial approach*, 9th edn. Englewood Cliffs, NJ: Prentice Hall.

Batey, M., and Furnham, A. (2006). Creativity, intelligence and personality: a critical review of the scattered literature. *Genetic, Social, and General Psychology Monographs*, 132: 355–429.

Baucus, M. S., Norton, W. I., Jr, Baucus, D. A., and Human, S. E. (2008). Fostering creativity and innovation without encouraging unethical behavior. *Journal of Organizational Behavior and Human Decision Processes*, 72: 117–35.

Benjamin, D., and Simon, S. (2002). *The age of sacred terror*. New York: Random House.

Bernstein, P. L. (1996). *Against the gods: the remarkable story of risk*. New York: John Wiley and Sons.

Besemer, S. P. (2006). *Creating products in the Age of Design: how to improve your new product ideas!* Stillwater, OK: New Forums Press.

Besemer, S. P., and O'Quin, K. (1999). Confirming the creative product three-factor analysis matrix model in an American sample. *Creativity Research Journal*, 12: 287–96.

Bledow, R., Frese, M., Anderson, N., Erez, M., and Farr, J. (2009). A dialectic perspective on innovation: conflicting demands, multiple pathways, and ambidexterity. *Industrial and Organizational Psychology*, 2: 305–37.

Boba, R. L. (2005). *Crime analysis and crime mapping*. Thousand Oaks, CA: Sage.

Bodankin, M., and Tziner, A. (2009). Constructive deviance, destructive deviance and personality: how do they interrelate? *Amfiteatru Economic Journal*, 11: 549–64.

Boden, M. A. (2004). *The creative mind: myths and mechanisms*, 2nd edn. London: Routledge.

Boyer, P. (1985). *By the bomb's early light: American thought and culture at the dawn of the atomic age*. New York: Pantheon.

Breetzke, G. D. (2006). Geographical information systems (GIS) and policing in South Africa: a review. *Policing: An International Journal of Policing Strategies and Management*, 29: 723–40.

Brisman, A. (2010). 'Creative crime' and the phytological analogy. *Crime, Media and Culture*, 6: 205–25.

British Broadcasting Corporation (BBC) (2005). http://news.bbc.co.uk/2/hi/uk_news/4263176.stm, accessed 26 June 2012.

Brophy, D. R. (1998). Understanding, measuring and enhancing individual creative problem solving efforts. *Creativity Research Journal*, 11: 123–50.

Brower, R., and Stahl, J. M. (2011). Crime and creativity. In M. A. Runco and S. R. Pritzker (eds.), *Encyclopedia of creativity*, 2nd edn (pp. 318–22). San Diego, CA: Academic Press.

Brown, R. T. (1989). Creativity: what are we to measure? In J. A. Glover, R. R. Ronning, and C. R. Reynolds (eds.), *Handbook of creativity, perspectives on individual differences* (pp. 3–32). New York: Plenum.

Bruner, J. S. (1962). The conditions of creativity. In H. Gruber, G. Terrell, and M. Wertheimer (eds.), *Contemporary approaches to cognition* (pp. 1–30). New York: Atherton.

Bryson, B. (2004). *A short history of everything*. London: Black Swan.

Burkhardt, H. (1985). *Gleichheitswahn parteienwahn* [Obsession with equality]. Tübingen, Germany: Hohenrain.

Buss, D. M. (1991). Evolutionary personality psychology. *Annual Review of Psychology*, 45: 459–91.

Byers, S. N. (2007). *Introduction to forensic anthropology*. Boston, MA: Allyn and Bacon.

Cadbury, D. (2004). *Seven wonders of the industrial world*. London: Harper Perennial.

Caldero, M. A., and Crank, J. P. (2004). *Police ethics: the corruption of noble cause*. Cincinnati, OH: Anderson.

Cameron, J. (2002). *The artist's way: a spiritual path to higher creativity*, 2nd edn. New York: Jeremy P. Tarcher/Putnam.

Canadian Intellectual Property Office (2007). What can you patent? Retrieved from http://strategis.gc.ca/sc_mrksv/cipo/patents/pat_gd_protect-e.html#sec2 on 20 November 2007.

Cattell, J., Glascock, J., and Washburn, M. F. (1918). Experiments on a possible test of aesthetic judgment of pictures. *American Journal of Psychology*, 29: 333–36.

Chan, D. W. (2011). Confucianism. In M. A. Runco and S. R. Pritzker (eds.), *Encyclopedia of creativity* (pp. 246–252). San Diego, CA: Academic Press.

Christensen, C. M. (1997). *The innovator's dilemma: when new technologies cause great firms to fail.* Boston, MA: Harvard Business School Press.

Cohen, A. K. (1955). *Delinquent boys: the culture of the gang.* Glencoe, IL: The Free Press.

Cohen, L. M., and Ambrose, D. (1999). Adaptation and creativity. In M. A. Runco and S. Pritzker (eds.), *Encyclopedia of creativity* (pp. 9–22). San Diego, CA: Academic Press.

Coleman, T. G. (2008). Managing strategic knowledge in policing: do police leaders have sufficient knowledge about organizational performance to make informed strategic decisions? *Police Practice and Research*, 9: 307–22.

Collins, M. A., and Amabile, T. M. (1998). Motivation and creativity. In R. J. Sternberg (ed.). *Handbook of creativity* (pp. 297–312). Cambridge University Press.

Colvin, S. S., and Meyer, I. F. (1906). Imaginative elements in the written work of schoolchildren. *Pedagogical Seminar*, 13: 91.

Comer, M. J. (1977). *Corporate fraud.* London: McGraw Hill.

Committee on Science and Technology for Countering Terrorism (2002). *Making the nation safe: the role of science and technology in countering terrorism.* Washington, DC: National Research Council/National Academy of Science.

Commonwealth of Australia (2008). *Report of the Australia 2020 Summit Creative Australia.* Canberra: Department of Prime Minister and Cabinet.

Cooper, A., Rossmo, D. K., Schmitz, P., and Byleveld, P. (2000). Using GIS and visual aerial photography to assist in the conviction of a serial killer. *Paper presented at the Fourth Annual International Mapping Research Conference,* San Diego, CA.

Craft, A., Gardner, H., and Claxton, G. (eds.) (2008). *Creativity, wisdom and trusteeship: exploring the role of education.* Thousand Oaks, CA: Corwin Press.

Crang, M., and Cook, I. (2007). *Doing ethnographies.* London: Sage.

Cropley, A. J. (1967). *Creativity.* London: Longmans.

  (1990). Creativity and mental health in everyday life. *Creativity Research Journal*, 3: 167–78.

  (1995). Creative performance in older adults. In W. Bos and R. Lehmann (eds.), *Reflections on educational achievement. Papers in Honour of T. Neville Postlethwaite* (pp. 75–87). Münster, Germany: Waxmann.

  (1997). Creativity: a bundle of paradoxes. *Gifted and Talented International*, 12: 8–14.

  (2001). *Creativity in education and learning.* London: Kogan Page.

  (2009). Teachers' antipathy to creative students: some implications for teacher training. *Baltic Journal of Psychology*, 10: 86–93.

  (2010). Creativity in the classroom: the dark side. In D. H. Cropley, A. J. Cropley, J. C. Kaufman, and M. A. Runco (eds.), *The dark side of creativity* (pp. 297–315). Cambridge University Press.

  (2012). Creativity and education: some Australian perspectives. *International Journal of Creativity and Problem Solving*, 22(1): 9–25.

Cropley, A. J., and Cropley, D. H. (2009). *Fostering creativity: a diagnostic approach for higher education and organizations.* Cresskill, NJ: Hampton Press.
    (2010). The innovative institutional environment: theoretical insights from psychology. *Baltic Journal of Psychology*, 11: 73–87.
Cropley, A. J., and Davis, J. C. (1976). Psychological factors in juvenile delinquency. *Canadian Journal of Behavioural Science*, 8: 68–77.
Cropley, A. J., and Sikand, J. S. (1973). Creativity and schizophrenia. *Journal of Consulting and Clinical Psychology*, 40: 462–68.
Cropley, D. H. (2005). Eleven principles of creativity and terrorism, *Science, Engineering & Technology Summit on Counter-Terrorism Technology*, 4th Homeland Security Summit and Homeland Exposition, Canberra, Australia.
    (2010). Malevolent innovation: opposing the dark side of creativity. In D. H. Cropley, A. J. Cropley, J. C. Kaufman, and M. A. Runco (eds.), *The dark side of creativity* (pp. 339–59). Cambridge University Press.
Cropley, D. H., and Cropley, A. J. (2000). Fostering creativity in engineering undergraduates. *High Ability Studies*, 11: 207–19.
    (2005). Engineering creativity: a systems concept of functional creativity. In J. C. Kaufman and J. Baer (eds.), *Faces of the muse: how people think, work and act creatively in diverse domains* (pp. 169–85). Hillsdale, NJ: Lawrence Erlbaum.
    (2008). Elements of a universal aesthetic of creativity. *Psychology of Aesthetics, Creativity and the Arts*, 3: 155–61.
    (2010a). Recognizing and fostering creativity in design education. *International Journal of Technology and Design Education*, 20: 345–58.
    (2010b). Functional creativity: 'products' and the generation of effective novelty. In R. J. Sternberg and J. C. Kaufman (eds.), *The Cambridge handbook of creativity* (pp. 301–17). New York: Cambridge University Press.
    (2011). Understanding value innovation in organizations: a psychological framework. *International Journal of Creativity and Problem Solving*, 21(1): 17–36.
    (2012). A psychological taxonomy of organizational innovation: resolving the paradoxes. *Creativity Research Journal*, 24: 229–40.
Cropley, D. H., and Kaufman, J. C. (2012). Measuring functional creativity: empirical validation of the Creative Solution Diagnosis Scale. *Journal of Creative Behavior*, 46: 119–37.
Cropley, D. H., Kaufman, J. C., and Cropley, A. J. (2008). Malevolent creativity. *Creativity Research Journal*, 20: 105–15.
    (2011). Measuring creativity for innovation management. *Journal of Technology Management and Innovation*, 6(3): 13–30.
Cropley, D. H., Cropley, A. J., Kaufman, J. C., and Runco, M. A. (eds.) (2010). *The dark side of creativity.* Cambridge University Press.
Csikszentmihalyi, M. (1988). Society, culture and person: a system view of creativity. In R. J. Sternberg (ed.), *The nature of creativity* (pp. 325–39). Cambridge University Press.

(1996). *Creativity: flow and the psychology of discovery and invention.* New York: Harper Collins.

(1999). Implications of a systems perspective for the study of creativity. In R. J. Sternberg (ed.), *Handbook of creativity* (pp. 313–35). Cambridge University Press.

(2006). Foreword: developing creativity. In N. Jackson, M. Oliver, M. Shaw, and J. Wisdom (eds.), *Developing creativity in higher education: an imaginative curriculum* (pp. xviii–xx). London: Routledge.

Dacey, J., and Lennon, K. (1998). *Understanding creativity: the interplay of biological, psychological, and social factors.* San Francisco, CA: Jossey-Bass.

Dasgupta, S. (2004). Is creativity a Darwinian process? *Creativity Research Journal,* 16: 403–14.

Davis, M. A. (2009). Understanding the relationship between mood and creativity: a meta-analysis. *Organizational Behavior and Human Decision Processes,* 108: 25–38.

Descartes, R. (1991 [1644]). *Principles of philosophy* (trans. V. R. Miller and R. P. Miller). Boston, MA: Kluwer.

De Grave, K. (1995). *Swindler, spy, rebel: the confidence woman in nineteenth-century America.* Columbia, MO: University of Missouri Press.

Dillon, T. A., Lee, R. K., and Matheson, D. (2005). Value innovation: passport to wealth creation. *Research-Technology Management,* 50: 22–36.

Dunne, T., and Raby, F. (2001). *Design noir: the secret life of electronic objects.* Basel: August/Birkhauser.

Economist Technology Quarterly (2002). Thanksgiving for innovation (pp. 13–14).

Eisenberg, J. (2005). *Creativity in sport.* Toronto: Chestnut Publishing.

Eisenberger, R., and Rhoades, L. (2001). Incremental effects of reward on creativity. *Journal of Personality and Social Psychology,* 81: 728–41.

Eisenman, R. (1991). *From crime to creativity: psychological and social factors in deviance.* Dubuque, IA: Kendall/Hunt.

(2008). Malevolent creativity in criminals. *Creativity Research Journal,* 20: 116–19.

(2010). Creativity and crime: how criminals use creativity to succeed. In D. H. Cropley, A. J. Cropley, J. C. Kaufman, and M. A. Runco (eds.), *The dark side of creativity* (pp. 204–17). Cambridge University Press.

Ekblom, P. (1997). Gearing up against crime: a dynamic framework to help designers keep up with the adaptive criminal in a changing world. *International Journal of Risk Security and Crime Prevention,* 2: 249–65.

Ekblom, P., and Tilley, N. (2000). Going equipped: Criminology, situational crime prevention and the resourceful offender. *British Journal of Criminology,* 40: 376–98.

English, J., and Jones, C. (2003). Creativity and innovation in education: the Tasmanian experience. *16th Annual Conference of Small Enterprise Association of Australia and New Zealand,* 28 September–1 October 2003.

Ewing, R. (2011). The arts and Australian education: realising potential. *Australian Education Review, No 58.* Melbourne: ACER.

Eysenck, H. J. (1995). *Genius: the natural history of creativity*. Cambridge University Press.

(1997). Creativity and personality. In M. A. Runco (ed.), *The creativity research handbook* (Vol. 1, pp. 41–66). Cresskill, NJ: Hampton Press.

Facaoaru, C. (1985). *Kreativität in wissenschaft und technik* [Creativity in science and technology]. Bern: Huber.

Felson, M. (2002). *Crime and everyday life*, 3rd edn. Thousand Oaks, CA: Sage.

Festinger, L., Riecken, H., and Schachter, S. (1956). *When prophecy fails*. University of Minnesota Press.

Fishbein, W., and Treverton, G. (2004). Rethinking 'alternative analysis' to address transnational threats. *Occasional Papers, Vol. 3, No. 2*. Washington, DC: Sherman Kent Center for Intelligence Analysis.

Florida, R. (2002). *The rise of the creative class and how it's transforming work, life, community and everyday life*. New York: Basic Books.

Florida, R., and Goodnight, J. (2005). Managing for creativity. *Harvard Business Review*, 83(7): 124–31.

Formosa, S. (2010). Maltese criminological landscapes: a spatio-temporal case where physical and social worlds meet. In E. Buhmann, M. Pietch, and E. Kretzler (eds.), *Digital landscape architecture 2010* (pp. 150–57). Heidelberg: Wichmann.

French, B., and Stewart, J. (2001). Organizational development in law enforcement environment. *FBI Law Enforcement Bulletin*, 14–19.

Fromm, E. (1990). *Greatness and limitations of Freud's thought*. New York: New American Library.

Gabora, L. (2002). The beer can theory of creativity. In P. Bently and D. Corne (eds.), *Creative evolutionary systems* (pp. 147–58). Amsterdam: Elsevier.

Gabora, L., and Holmes, N. (2010). Dangling on a tassel on the fabric of socially constructed reality: reflections on the creative writing process. In D. H. Cropley, A. J. Cropley, J. C. Kaufman, and M. A. Runco (eds.), *The dark side of creativity* (pp. 277–96). Cambridge University Press.

Galton, F. (1869). *Hereditary genius*. London: Macmillan.

Gamman, L., and Raein, M. (2010). Reviewing the art of crime: what, if anything do criminals and artists/designers have in common? In D. H. Cropley, A. J. Cropley, J. C. Kaufman, and M. A. Runco (eds.), *The dark side of creativity* (pp. 155–76). Cambridge University Press.

Gammel, I. (1946). *The twilight of painting*. New York: Putnam's Sons.

Gascón, L. D., and Kaufman, J. C. (2010). Both sides of the coin? Personality, deviance and creative behavior. In D. H. Cropley, A. J. Cropley, J. C. Kaufman, and M. A. Runco (eds.), *The dark side of creativity* (pp. 235–54). Cambridge University Press.

Ghiselin, B. (1955). *The creative process*. New York: Bantam Books.

Gino, F., and Ariely, D. (2012). The dark side of creativity: original thinkers can be more dishonest. *Journal of Personality and Social Psychology*, 102: 445–59.

Gladwell, M. (2008). *Outliers: the story of success*. New York: Little, Brown and Company.

(2009). *What the dog saw and other adventures*. London: Allen Lane.

Goncalo, J. A., Vincent, L. C., and Audia, P. G. (2010). Early creativity as a constraint on future achievement. In D. H. Cropley, A. J. Cropley, J. C. Kaufman, and M. A. Runco (eds.), *The dark side of creativity* (pp. 114–33). Cambridge University Press.

Gottfredson, M., and Hirschi, T. (1990). *A general theory of crime*. Stanford University Press.

Gottschalk, P., and Gudmundsen, Y. S. (2009). An empirical study of intelligence strategy implementation. *International Journal of Police Science and Management*, 12: 55–68.

Grayling, A. C. (2003). *What is good? The search for the best way to live*. London: Phoenix.

Gruber, H. E. (1993). Creativity in the moral domain: ought implies can implies create. *Creativity Research Journal*, 6: 3–15.

Gruber, H. E., and Davis, S. N. (1988). Inching our way up Mount Olympus: the evolving systems approach to creative thinking. In R. J. Sternberg (ed.). *The nature of creativity: contemporary psychological perspectives* (pp. 243–70). Cambridge University Press.

Grudin, R. (1990). *The grace of great things: creativity and innovation*. New York: Ticknor and Fields.

Guilford, J. P. (1950). Creativity. *American Psychologist*, 5: 444–54.

Gupta, A. K., Smith, K. G., and Shalley, C. E. (2006). The interplay between exploration and exploitation. *Academy of Management Journal*, 49: 693–706.

Hadamard, J. (1945). *Psychology of invention in the mathematical field*. New York: Dover Publications.

Haner, U.-E. (2005). Spaces for creativity and innovation in two established organizations. *Creativity and Innovation Management*, 14: 288–98.

Hare, R. D. (2006). Psychopathy: a clinical and forensic overview. *Psychiatric Clinics of North America*, 29: 709–24.

Hare, R. D., and Neumann, C. N. (2006). The PCL-R Assessment of Psychopathy: development, structural properties, and new directions. In C. Patrick (ed.), *Handbook of psychopathy* (pp. 58–88). New York: Guilford.

Hari, A. (2010). A systems engineering approach to counterterrorism. In D. H. Cropley, A. J. Cropley, J. C. Kaufman, and M. A. Runco (eds.), *The dark side of creativity* (pp. 329–38). Cambridge University Press.

Harris, M. (2006). *Cultural anthropology*. Boston, MA: Allyn and Bacon.

Haseman, B. C., and Jaaniste, L. O. (2008). The arts and Australia's national innovation system (1994–2008). *CHASS Occasional Paper*, 7: 7–39.

Hausman, C. R. (1984). *A discourse on novelty and creation*. Albany, NY: State University of New York Press.

Hayward, K., and Young, J. (2004). Cultural criminology: some notes on the script. *Theoretical Criminology*, 8: 259–73.

Hecht, D. K. (2010). Imagining the bomb. In D. H. Cropley, A. J. Cropley, J. C. Kaufman, and M. A. Runco (eds.), *The dark side of creativity* (pp. 72–90). Cambridge University Press.

Helson, R. (1983). Creative mathematicians. In R. S. Albert (ed.), *Genius and eminence: the social psychology of creativity and exceptional achievement* (pp. 311–30). Elmsford, NY: Pergamon.

(1996). In search of the creative personality. *Creativity Research Journal,* 9: 295–306.

(1999). A longitudinal study of creative personality in women. *Creativity Research Journal,* 12: 89–102.

Hennessey, B. A., and Amabile, T. (1999). Consensual assessment. In M. A. Runco and S. R. Pritzker (eds.), *Encyclopedia of creativity* (pp. 347–59). San Diego, CA: Academic Press.

Henning, B. G. (2005). *The ethics of creativity: beauty, morality, and nature in a processive cosmos.* University of Pittsburgh Press.

Herrmann, W. (1987). *Auswirkungen verschiedener Fussballtrainingsstile auf Leistungsmotivation* [Effects of different football coaching styles on motivation]. Unpublished Master's thesis, University of Hamburg.

Hilton, K. (2010). Boundless creativity. In D. H. Cropley, A. J. Cropley, J. C. Kaufman, and M. A. Runco (eds.), *The dark side of creativity* (pp. 134–54). Cambridge University Press.

Hilton, K., and Henderson, K. (2008). Developing criminal personas for designers. *Papers from the British Criminological Society Conference,* 8: 175–86.

Hollin, C. R. (1989). *Psychology and crime: an introduction to criminological psychology.* London: Routledge.

Howe, C., McWilliam, D., and Cross, G. (2005). Chance favours only the prepared mind: incubation and the delayed effects of peer collaboration. *British Journal of Psychology,* 96: 67–93.

Hudson, L. (1968). *Frames of mind.* London: Methuen.

Hull, D. L., Tessner, P. D., and Diamond, A. M. (1978). Planck's principle. *Science,* 202: 717–23.

Huxley, L. (1901). *Life and letters of Thomas Henry Huxley,* Vol II. New York: Appleton.

James, K., and Taylor, A. (2010). Positive creativity and negative creativity (and unintended consequences). In D. H. Cropley, A. J. Cropley, J. C. Kaufman, and M. A. Runco (eds.), *The dark side of creativity* (pp. 33–56). Cambridge University Press.

James, K., Clark, K., and Cropanzano, R. (1999). Positive and negative creativity in groups, institutions and organizations: A model and theoretical extension. *Creativity Research Journal,* 12: 211–26.

Jamison, K. R. (1993). *Touched with fire: depressive illness and the artistic temperament.* New York: Free Press.

Jasper, J. M. (2004). A strategic approach to collective action: looking for agency in social movement choices. *Mobilization,* 9: 1–116.

(2010). The innovation dilemma: some risks of creativity in strategic agency. In D. H. Cropley, A. J. Cropley, J. C. Kaufman, and M. A. Runco (eds.), *The dark side of creativity* (pp. 91–113). Cambridge University Press.

Johnson, J. A. (1983). Criminality, creativity, and craziness: structural similarities in three types of nonconformity. In W. S. Laufer and J. M. Day (eds.),

Personality theory, moral development, and criminal behaviour (pp. 81–105). Lexington, MA: D. C. Heath.

Julius, A. (2002). *Transgressions: the offences of art.* London: Thames and Hudson.

Kampylis, P. G. (2010). Fostering creative thinking: the role of primary teachers. *Jyväskälä Studies in Education,* Whole No. 115.

Kampylis, P. G., and Valtanen, J. (2010). Redefining creativity: analyzing definitions, collocations, and consequences. *Journal of Creative Behavior,* 44: 191–214.

Kanazawa, S. (2003). Why productivity fades with age: the crime–genius connection. *Journal of Research in Personality,* 37: 257–72.

Kasof, J., Chen, C., Himsel, A., and Greenberger, E. (2007). Values and creativity. *Creativity Research Journal,* 19: 105–22.

Katyal, N. K. (2002). Architecture as crime control. *Yale Law Journal,* 111: 1039–1139.

Kaufman, G. (2003). Expanding the mood-creativity equation. *Creativity Research Journal,* 15: 131–35.

Kaufman, J. C., and Baer, J. (2012). Beyond new and appropriate: who decides what is creative? *Creativity Research Journal,* 24: 83–91.

Kaufman, J. C., and Beghetto, R. A. (2009). Beyond big and little: the Four C Model of Creativity. *Review of General Psychology,* 13: 1–12.

Kaufman, J. C., Cropley, D. H., Chiera, B. A., and White, A. E. (submitted). Is Hannibal Lecter creative? How we evaluate the creativity of different levels of malevolence.

Kaufman, J. C., Baer, J., Cropley, D. H., Reiter-Palmon, R., and Nienhauser, S. (in press). Furious activity vs. understanding: how much expertise is needed to evaluate creative work? *Psychology of Aesthetics, Creativity and the Arts.*

Kay, S. (1996). The development of a personal aesthetic in creative accomplishments. *Journal of Aesthetic Education,* 30: 111–14.

Kelling, G. L., Pate, A., Dieckman, D., and Brown, C. E. (1974). *The Kansas City Preventive Patrol Experiment.* Washington, DC: The Police Foundation.

Kim, W. C., and Mauborgne, R. (2004). Value innovation: the strategic logic of high growth. *Harvard Business Review,* 82: 172–80.

Kipper, D., Green, D., and Prorak, A. (2010). The relationship among spontaneity, impulsivity, and creativity. *Journal of Creativity in Mental Health,* 5: 39–53.

Kirton, M. (1989). *Adaptors and innovators: styles of creativity and problem solving.* London: Routledge.

Kitchen T. (2007). Effective crime prevention strategies and engagement with planning process in Bradford, England. Downloaded from www.unhabitat. org/grhs/2007 on 23 April 2011.

Koberg, D., and Bagnall, J. (1991). *The universal traveler: a soft systems guide to creativity, problem solving and the process of reaching goals.* Menlo Park, CA: Crisp Publications.

Kozbelt, A. R., and Meredith, D. (2011). Lifespan melodic originality trajectories in classical composers: a hierarchical linear modeling approach. *International Journal of Creativity and Problem Solving,* 21(2): 63–79.

Kozbelt, A. R., Beghetto, R. A., and Runco, M. A. (2010). Theories of creativity. In R. J. Sternberg and J. C. Kaufman (eds.), *The Cambridge handbook of creativity* (pp. 20–47). New York: Cambridge University Press.

KPMG (2010). Fraud and Misconduct Survey 2010: Australia and New Zealand. www.kpmg.com/AU/en/IssuesAndInsights/ArticlesPublications/Fraud-Survey/Pages/Fraud-Survey-2010.aspx, accessed 29 May 2012.

(2011). Fraud barometer: December 2011 readings. www.kpmg.com/au/en/issuesandinsights/articlespublications/fraud-barometer/pages/default.aspx, accessed 5 June 2012.

Krohn, M. D., Lizotte, A. J., and Hall, G. P. (eds.) (2009). *Handbook on crime and deviance*. Heidelberg: Springer.

Kuszewski, A. M. (2009). The genetics of creativity: a serendipitous assemblage of madness. *METODO Working Papers*, No. 58. New York: METODO Social Sciences Institute.

Landenberger, N. A., and Lipsey, M. (2005). The positive effects of cognitive-behavioral programs for offenders: a meta-analysis of factors associated with effective treatment. *Journal of Experimental Criminology*, 1: 451–76.

Lemert, E. M., Lemert. C. C., and Winter, M. (2000). *Crime and deviance: essays and innovations of Edwin M. Lemert*. Lanham, MD: Rowman and Littlefield.

Lewis, T. (2005). Creativity: a framework for the design/problem solving discourse in technology education. *Journal of Technology Education*, 17: 35–52.

Licate, D. A. (2010). *Innovations and organizational change in Ohio Police Departments*. Unpublished doctoral dissertation, Kent State University, Kent, OH.

Longshore, D., Turner, S., and Stein, J. (1996). Self-control in a criminal sample: an examination of construct validity. *Criminology*, 34(2): 209–28.

Lombroso. C. (1889). *The man of genius*. London: W. Scott.

Ludwig, A. M. (1998). Method and madness in the arts and sciences. *Creativity Research Journal*, 11: 93–101.

Lynam, D., and Miller, J. (2004). Personality pathways to impulsive behaviour and their relations to deviance: results from three samples. *Journal of Quantitative Criminology*, 20: 319–41.

Lynn, R. (1971). *An introduction to the study of personality*. London: Macmillan.

Machiavelli, N. (1532/2010). *The prince* (trans. W. K. Marriott). Shelbyville. KY: Wasteland Classics.

MacKay, C. (1852) *Memoirs of extraordinary popular delusions and the madness of crowds*, 2nd edn. Library of Economics and Liberty. Retrieved 25 June 2012 from www.econlib.org/library/Mackay/macEx2.html.

MacKinnon, D. W. (1978). *In search of human effectiveness: identifying and developing creativity*. Buffalo, NY: Creative Education Foundation.

Mainemelis, C. (2010). Stealing fire: creative deviance in the evolution of new ideas. *Academy of Management Review*, 35: 558–78.

Manning, P. K. (2001). Technology's ways: information technology, crime analysis, and the rationalization of policing. *Criminal Justice: The International Journal of Policy and Practice*, 1: 83–103.

Martin, J. N. (1997). *Systems engineering guidebook: a process for developing systems and products*. Boca Raton, FL: CRC Press.

Martin, M. W. (2006). Moral creativity. *International Journal of Applied Philosophy*, 20(1): 55–66.

Martindale, C. (1989). Personality, situation, and creativity. In J. A. Glover, R. R. Ronning, and C. R. Reynolds (eds.), *Handbook of creativity* (pp. 211–28). New York: Plenum.

Martinsen, O. (2011). The creative personality: a synthesis and development of the Creative Person Profile. *Creativity Research Journal*, 23: 185–202.

Marzbali, M. H., Abdullah, A., Razak, N. A., and Tilaki, M. J. M. (2011). A review of the effectiveness of crime prevention by design approaches to sustainable development. *Journal of Sustainable Development*, 4: 160–72.

Maslow, A. H. (1973). Creativity in self-actualizing people. In A. Rothenberg and C. R. Hausman (eds.), *The creative question* (pp. 86–92). Durham, NC: Duke University Press.

May, R. (1976). *The courage to create*. New York: Bantam.

Mazar, N., Amir, D., and Ariely, D. (2008). The dishonesty of honest people: a theory of self-concept maintenance. *Journal of Marketing Research*, 45: 633–44.

McCann, M. (2005). International perspectives on giftedness: experimental and cultural observations of IQ and creativity with implications for policy and curriculum design. *International Education Journal*, 6: 125–133.

McIntyre, K. C., and McIntyre, E. (2007). Rethinking creativity and approaches to teaching. *The International Journal of the Book*, 4(1):, 15 22.

McIntyre, P. (2006). Creative practice as research: 'testing out' the systems model of creativity through practitioner based enquiry. In R. Velila (ed.), *Speculation and innovation: applying practice led research in the creative industries* (pp. 201–225). Brisbane: Queensland University of Technology.

McLaren, R. B. (1993). The dark side of creativity. *Creativity Research Journal*, 6: 137–144.

McMullan, W. E. (1978). Creative individuals: paradoxical personages. *Journal of Creative Behavior*, 10: 265–275.

McWilliam, E., and Dawson, S. (2008). Teaching for creativity: towards sustainable and replicable pedagogical practice. *Higher Education*, 56: 633–43.

McWilliam, E., Dawson, S., and Tan, J. P.-L. (2011). Less elusive, more explicit. In P. Thomson and J. Sefton-Green (eds.), *Researching creative learning: methods and issues* (pp. 113–25). London: Routledge.

Mednick, S. A. (1962). The associative basis of creativity. *Psychological Review*, 69: 220–32.

Merton, R. K. (1938). Social structure and anomie. *American Sociological Review*, 3: 672–82.

Mill, J. (1829). *Analysis of the phenomena of the human mind.* New York: A. M. Kelley.

Miller, A. I. (1992). Scientific creativity: a comparative study of Henri Poincaré and Albert Einstein. *Creativity Research Journal,* 5: 385–418.

Miller, R. V. (2011). *Miller's Australian competition and consumer law annotated,* 33rd edn. Sydney: Thomson Reuters.

Millward, L. J., and Freeman, H. (2002). Role expectations as constraints to innovation: the case of female managers. *Creativity Research Journal,* 14: 93–109.

Morgan, D. N. (1953). Creativity today. *Journal of Aesthetics,* 12: 1–24.

Moustakis, C. E. (1977). *Creative life.* New York: Van Nostrand.

Mumford, M. D., and Moertl, P. (2003). Cases of social innovation: lessons from two innovations in the 20th century. *Creativity Research Journal,* 13: 261–6.

Nebel, C. (1988). *The dark side of creativity: Blocks, unfinished works and the urge to destroy.* New York: Whitston Publishing Company.

Necka, E. (1986). On the nature of creative talent. In A. J. Cropley, K. K. Urban, H. Wagner, and W. H. Wieczerkowski (eds.). *Giftedness: a continuing worldwide challenge* (pp. 131–40). New York: Trillium.

Nichols, J. G. (1972). Creativity in the person who will never produce anything original and useful: the concept of creativity as a normally distributed trait. *American Psychologist,* 27: 717–27.

Nickerson, R. S. (1998). Confirmation bias: a ubiquitous phenomenon in many guises. *Review of General Psychology,* 2: 175–220.

Nietzsche, F. (1968). *The will to power.* New York: Vintage.

Nobel Foundation (1967). *Nobel lectures, Physics 1901–1921.* Amsterdam: Elsevier.

O'Brien, A., and Donelan, K. (eds.) (2008). *The arts and youth at risk: global and local challenges.* Newcastle upon Tyne, UK: Cambridge Scholars Publishing.

O'Brien, K. (2011). *Pilot Pen creativity report.* Bankstown, NSW: Pilot Pen.

O'Connor, J. J., and Robertson, E. F. (2003). Jules Henri Poincaré. Retrieved from http://www-history.mcs.st-andrews.ac.uk/Mathematicians/Poincare.html in July, 2006.

Oral, G. (2006). Creativity of Turkish prospective teachers. *Creativity Research Journal,* 18: 65–73.

Osborn, A. F. (1953). *Applied imagination.* New York: Scribner's.

Parnell, P. C. (2003). Introduction: crime's power. In P. C. Parnell and S. C. Kane (eds.), *Crime's power* (pp. 1–32). New York: Palgrave Macmillan.

Patrick, C. (1935). Creative thought in poets. *Archives of Psychology,* 26: 1–74.

(1937). Creative thought in artists. *Journal of Psychology,* 4: 35–73.

(1938). Scientific thought. *Journal of Psychology,* 5: 55–83.

Pedneault, S. (2009). *Fraud 101: techniques and strategies for understanding fraud,* 3rd edn. Hoboken, NJ: John Wiley and Sons.

Perkins, D. N. (1981). *The mind's best work.* Cambridge, MA: Harvard University Press.

Peterson, H. (ed.) (1954). *A treasury of the world's great speeches.* Danbury, CT: Grolier.

Peterson, M. (2005). *Intelligence-led policing: the new intelligence architecture.* Washington, DC: US Department of Justice, Office of Justice Programs.

Pirelli, G., Gottdiener, W. H., and Zapf, P. A. (2011). A meta-analytic review of competency to stand trial research. *Psychology, Public Policy and Law*, 17: 1–53.

Pilzer, P. Z. (1994). *Unlimited Wealth*, 2nd edn. New York: Crown.

Planck, M. (1948). *Wissenschaftliche Selbstbiographie. mit einem Bildnis und der von Max von Laue gehaltenen Traueransprache* [Usually referred to in English as 'Scientific autobiography and other papers']. Leipzig, Germany: Johann Ambrosius Barth.

Plucker, J. A. (1998). Beware of simple conclusions: the case for content generality of creativity. *Creativity Research Journal*, 11: 179–82.

Poincaré, H. (1913). Mathematical creation. In H. Poincaré (ed.), *The foundation of science*. New York: Science Press.

Price, B. C. (2012). Targeting top terrorists. *International Security*, 36(4): 9–46.

PricewaterhouseCoopers (2011). Cyber crime: protecting against the growing threat. *Global economic crime survey*. November 2011. www.pwc.com/crimesurvey.

Prindle, E. J. (1906). The art of imagining. *Transactions of the American Institute for Engineering Education*, 25: 519–47.

Ramsland, K. (2010). *The forensic psychology of criminal minds*. New York: Berkley Boulevard.

Ratcliffe, J. H. (2008). *Intelligence-led policing*. Cullompton, Devon: Willan.

Rechtin, E., and Maier, M. (2000). *The art of systems architecting*. Boca Raton, FL: CRC Press.

Reuter, M., Roth, S., Holve, K., and Hennig, J. (2006). Identification of a first candidate gene for creativity: A pilot study. *Brain Research*, 1069: 190–7.

Reyerson, K. L. (1982). Commercial fraud in the middle ages: the case of the dissembling pepperer. *Journal of Medieval History*, 8: 63–72.

Rhodes, M. (1961). An analysis of creativity. *Phi Delta Kappan*, 42: 305–10.

Richards, R., Kinney, D. K., Benet, M., and Merzel, A. P. (1988). Assessing everyday creativity: characteristics of the Lifetime Creativity Scales and validation with three large samples. *Journal of Personality and Social Psychology*, 54(3): 476–85.

Rickards, T. J. (1993). Creativity from a business school perspective: past, present and future. In S. G. Isaksen, M. C. Murdock, R. L. Firestien, and D. J. Treffinger (eds.), *Nurturing and developing creativity: the emergence of a discipline* (pp. 155–176). Norwood, NJ: Ablex.

(1999). Brainstorming. In M. A. Runco and S. R. Pritzker (eds.), *Encyclopedia of creativity*, Vol. 1 (pp. 219–227). San Diego, CA: Academic Press.

Roberts, M., and Erickson, W. (2010). *Housing and designing out crime*. (Downloaded from www.westminster.gov.uk/workspace/assets/publications/Designing-Out-Crime-1280245316.pdf on 24 April 2011.)

Rogers, C. R. (1954). Towards a theory of creativity. *ETC: A Review of General Semantics*, 11: 249–260.

Rorty, R. (1979). *Philosophy and the mirror of nature.* Princeton University Press.

Rossman, J. (1931). *The psychology of the inventor: a study of the patentee.* Washington, DC: Inventors' Publishing Co.

Rothenberg, A. (1983). Psychopathology and creative cognition: a comparison of hospitalised patients, Nobel laureates and controls. *Archives of General Psychiatry,* 40: 937–942.

Rothman, A. (1982). Genius and biographers: the fictionalization of Evariste Galois. *American Mathematical Monthly,* 89(2): 84–106.

Royce, J. (1898). The psychology of invention. *Psychological Review,* 5(2): 113–134.

Ruggiero, V. (2010). *Organized crime: between the formal and the informal economy.* Santiago, Chile: Global Symposium on Security Transformation. Downloaded from www.securitytransformation.org/gc_publications.php on 20 May 2011.

Runco, M. A. (2010). Creativity has no dark side. In D. H. Cropley, A. J. Cropley, J. C. Kaufman, and M. A. Runco (eds), *The dark side of creativity* (pp. 15–32). Cambridge University Press.

Runco, M. A., and Nemiro, J. (2003). Creativity in the moral domain: integration and implications. *Creativity Research Journal,* 15: 91–105.

Salcedo-Albarán, E., Kuszewski, A., de Leon-Beltran, I., and Garay, L. J. (2009). *Rule-breaking from illegality: a trans-disciplinary inquiry.* Working Paper No 63, (31 December 2009). Downloaded from http://papers.ssrn.com/sol3/papers.cfm?abstract_id=1528842 on 5 February 2013

Sampson, R. J., and Wilson, W. J. (1995). Toward a theory of race, crime and urban inequality. In J. Hagan and R. Peterson (eds.), *Crime and inequality* (pp. 37–54). Stanford University Press.

Sawyer, R. K., John-Steiner, V., Moran, S., Sternberg, R. J., Feldman, D. H., Nakamura, J., and Csikszentmihalyi, M. (2003). *Creativity and development.* Oxford University Press.

Scheppele, K. L. (2004). Constitutional ethnography: an introduction. *Law and Society Review,* 38: 389–406.

Schmid, T. (2012). An interdisciplinary vision for creativity and creative problem solving: a health science perspective in regional Australia. *International Journal of Creativity and Problem Solving,* 22(1): 77–96.

Schneier, B. (2000). *Secrets and lies: digital security in a networked world.* New York: Wiley.

Schuldberg, D. (2000–2001). Six sub-clinical spectrum traits in normal creativity. *Creativity Research Journal,* 13: 5–16.

Scott, T. E. (1999). Knowledge. In M. A. Runco and S. R. Pritzker (eds.), *Encyclopedia of creativity,* Vol. II (pp. 119–129). San Diego, CA: Academic Press.

Semmer, E. (1870). Resultate der Injektion von Pilzsporen und Pilzhefen in's Bluth der Thiere [Effects of injecting fungus spores into the blood of animals]. *Virchows Archiv,* 50: 158–60.

Shaw, M. P. (1989). The Eureka process: a structure for the creative experience in science and engineering. *Creativity Research Journal,* 2: 286–98.

Shepard, J. M. (2006). *Sociology*, updated 9th edn. Belmont, CA: Wadsworth.

Silvia, P. J., Kaufman, J. C., Reiter-Palmon, R., and Wigert, B. (2011). Cantankerous creativity: honesty–humility, agreeableness, and the HEXACO structure of creative achievement. *Personality and Individual Differences*, 51: 687–89.

Simon, H. (1990). Interview. *Carnegie-Mellon University Magazine*, Autumn.

Simonton, D. K. (1988). *Scientific genius: a psychology of science*. New York: Cambridge University Press.

(2007). The creative process in Picasso's Guernica sketches: monotonic improvements versus nonmonotonic variants. *Creativity Research Journal*, 19: 329–44.

(2009). Varieties of (scientific) creativity: a hierarchical model of disposition, development, and achievement. *Perspectives on Psychological Science*, 4: 441–52.

(2010). So you want to become a creative genius? You must be crazy! In D. H. Cropley, A. J. Cropley, J. C. Kaufman, and M. A. Runco (eds.), *The dark side of creativity* (pp. 218–34). Cambridge University Press.

Singer, J. K. (2010). Creativity in confinement. In D. H. Cropley, A. J. Cropley, J. C. Kaufman, and M. A. Runco (eds.), *The dark side of creativity* (pp. 177–203). Cambridge University Press.

Slater, B. H. (2006). 'Aesthetics' Retrieved from www.iep.utm.edu/a/aestheti.htm#H2 on 30 July 2007.

Stein, M. I. (1953). Creativity and culture. *Journal of Psychology*, 36: 311–322.

Sternberg, R. J. (1985). *Beyond IQ: a triarchic theory of human intelligence*. New York: Cambridge University Press.

(2010). The dark side of creativity and how to combat it. In D. H. Cropley, A. J. Cropley, J. C. Kaufman, and M. A. Runco (eds.), *The dark side of creativity* (pp. 316–28). Cambridge University Press.

Sternberg, R. J., and Davidson, J. E. (1999). Intuition. In M. A. Runco and S. R. Pritzker (eds.), *Encyclopedia of creativity*, Vol. II (pp. 57–69). San Diego, CA: Academic Press.

Sternberg, R. J., and Kaufman, J. C. (2010). Constraints on creativity. In J. C. Kaufman and R. S. Sternberg (eds.), *Cambridge handbook of creativity* (pp. 467–82). New York: Cambridge University Press.

Sternberg, R. J., and Lubart, T. I. (1995). *Defying the crowd: cultivating creativity in a culture of conformity*. New York: Free Press.

(1999). The concept of creativity: concepts and paradigms. In R. J. Sternberg (ed.), *Handbook of creativity* (pp. 3–15). Cambridge University Press.

Sternberg, R. J., Kaufman, J. C., and Pretz, J. E. (2002). *The creativity conundrum: a propulsion model of kinds of creative contributions*. New York: Psychology Press.

Taylor, I. A. (1975). An emerging view of creative actions. In I. A. Taylor and J. W. Getzels (eds.), *Perspectives in creativity* (pp. 297–325). Chicago, IL: Aldine.

Taylor, K. E. (2004). *Brainwashing: the science of thought control*. Oxford University Press.

Taylor, S. E. (1989). *Positive illusion and well-being: creative self-deception and the healthy mind.* New York: Basic Books.

Taylor, S. E., and Brown, J. D. (1988). Illusion and well-being: a social psychological perspective on mental health. *Psychological Bulletin*, 103: 193–210.

TenHouten, W. D. (1999). Handwriting and creativity. In M. A. Runco and S. R. Pritzker (eds.), *Encyclopedia of creativity* (Vol. 1, pp. 799–805). San Diego, CA: Academic Press.

Tibi, D. Y. (2003). *Autoimmune concept for dealing with the problem of airplane hijacking.* Paper presented at the Technologies, Systems, and Architecture for Transnational Defense Conference, AeroSense, SPIE, Orlando, Florida, April.

Tiger, L. (1979). *Optimism: the biology of hope.* New York: Simon and Shuster.

Tiger, L., and Fox, R. (1971). *The imperial animal.* New York: Holt, Rinehart and Winston.

Tobler, W. (1970). A computer movie simulating urban growth in the Detroit region. *Economic Geography*, 46: 234–40.

Torrance, E. P. (1965). *The Minnesota studies of creative thinking: widening horizons in creativity.* New York: Wiley.

Toynbee, A. (1962). Has America neglected its creative minority? *California Monographs*, 72: 7–10.

Treffinger, D. J., Sortore, M. R., and Cross, J. A. (1993). Programs and strategies for nurturing creativity. In K. Heller, F. J. Mönks, and A. H. Passow (eds.), *International handbook for research on giftedness and talent* (pp. 555–67). Oxford: Pergamon.

Trivers, R. (1985). *Social evolution.* Menlo Park, CA: Benjamin/Cummings.

Trivers R. (2011). *The folly of fools: the logic of deceit and self-deception in human life.* New York: Basic Books.

Twersky-Glasner, A. (2005). Police personality: what is it and why are they like that? *Journal of Police and Criminal Psychology*, 20: 56–67.

Unsworth, K. L. (2001). Unpacking creativity. *Academy of Management Review*, 26: 286–97.

Walberg, H. J., and Stariha, W. E. (1992). Productive human capital: learning, creativity and eminence. *Creativity Research Journal*, 5: 23–340.

Walczyk, J. J., Runco, M. A., Tripp, S. M., and Smith, C. E. (2008). The creativity of lying: divergent thinking and ideational correlates of the resolution of social dilemmas. *Creativity Research Journal*, 20: 328–42.

Wallas, G. (1926). *The art of thought.* New York: Harcourt Brace.

Ward, T. B., and Kolomyts, J. (2010). Cognition and creativity. In R. J. Sternberg and J. C. Kaufman (eds.), *The Cambridge handbook of creativity* (pp. 93–112). New York: Cambridge University Press.

West, M. A. (2002). Sparkling fountains or stagnant ponds: an integrative model of creativity and innovation implementation in work groups. *Applied Psychology: An International Review*, 51: 355–424.

Whittaker, D. J. (ed.) (2007). *The terrorism reader.* London: Routledge.

Wikipedia (2012). Enron: http://en.wikipedia.org/wiki/Enron, accessed 26 June 2012.

Wilks, T. J., and Zimbelman, M. F. (2004). Using games theory and strategic reasoning concepts to prevent and prevent and detect fraud. *Accounting Horizons*, 18(3): 173–84.

Williams, A. P., Ostwald, M. J., and Askland, H. H. (2011). The relationship between creativity and design and its implications for design education. *Design Principles and Practices: An International Journal*, 5: 57–72.

Wilson, C. (1984). *A criminal history of mankind*. London: Granada.

Winner, E., and Hetland, L. (2000). The arts and academic achievement: what the evidence shows. *Journal of Aesthetic Education*, 34: 3–4.

Wolfe, S. E., and Piquero, A. R. (2011). Organizational justice and police misconduct. *Criminal Justice and Behavior*, 38: 332–53.

Wolff, M., and Asche, H. (2009). Towards geospatial analysis of crime scenes: a 3D crime mapping approach. In M. Sester, L. Bernard, and V. Paelke (eds.), *Advances in GIScience* (pp. 429–48). Berlin: Springer.

Woodman, R. W., Sawyer, J. E., and Griffin, R. W. (1993). Toward a theory of organizational creativity. *Academy of Management Review*, 18: 293–321.

Yang, K., and El-Haik, B. (2003). *Design for Six Sigma: a roadmap for product development*. New York: McGraw-Hill.

Zaitseva, M. N. (2010). Subjugating the creative mind: the Soviet biological weapons program and the role of the state. In D. H. Cropley, A. J. Cropley, J. C. Kaufman, and M. A. Runco (eds.), *The dark side of creativity* (pp. 57–71). Cambridge University Press.

Zubek, J. (ed.) (1969). *Sensory deprivation: fifteen years of research*. New York: Appleton Century Crofts.

Zuo, L. (1998). Creativity and the aesthetic sense. *Creativity Research Journal*, 11: 309–13.

Index

Lightning Source UK Ltd.
Milton Keynes UK
UKOW06f1001050816

280033UK00009B/258/P